SPORT GOVERNANCE
IN THE
GLOBAL COMMUNITY

James E. Thoma, Ph.D.
Mount Union College, USA

and

Laurence Chalip, Ph.D.
Griffith University, Australia

Fitness Information Technology, Inc.
P.O. Box 4425, University Avenue
Morgantown, WV 26504 USA

Library of Congress Card Catalog Number: 95-83191

ISBN 1-885693-03-6

Copyeditor: Sandra R. Woods
Cover Design: Micheal Smyth
Production Editor: Eric J. Buchanan
Printed by: BookCrafters

Printed in the United States of America
10 9 8 7 6 5 4 3 2 1

Fitness Information Technology, Inc.
P.O. Box 4425, University Avenue
Morgantown, WV 26504 USA
(800) 477-4348
(304) 599-3482 (phone/fax)
E-MAIL: FIT@ACCESS.MOUNTAIN.NET

SPORT MANAGEMENT LIBRARY

The **SPORT MANAGEMENT LIBRARY** is an integrative textbook series targeted toward undergraduate students. The titles included in the Library are reflective of the content areas prescribed by the NASPE/NASSM curriculum standards for undergraduate sport management programs.

FORTHCOMING TITLES IN THE SPORT MANAGEMENT LIBRARY

ABOUT THE AUTHORS

James Thoma is a professor of Sport Management and Chairman of the Department of Physical Education, Health Sports Medicine, and Sport Management at Mount Union College in Alliance, Ohio, USA. He has worked internationally in sport as an administrator, athletics/track and field coach, and teacher in Malaysia, Brunei Darussalam, and Saudi Arabia. He was the national teams coordinator for The Athletics Congress/USA and worked as an administrator with the 1980 United States Olympic track and field team. His coaching duties included the Brunei national team at the 1985 Southeast Asian Games in Bangkok and 1986 Asian athletics championships in Jakarta. He has held a faculty position at the United States Sports Academy after being a secondary school mathematics teacher and coaching athletics at The Ohio State University and Otterbein College, Ohio. He has been secretary of the North American Society for Sport Management and is currently on its international committee.

Laurence Chalip is a Senior Lecturer with the Faculty of Business and Hotel Management at Griffith University's Gold Coast Campus in Queensland, Australia. He has worked in New Zealand, Korea, Australia and the USA in sport as an administrator, coach, and researcher. He was a member of the International Anthropology Project at the Los Angeles Olympic Games, and an executive member of the Seoul Organizing Committee for Olympic Cultural Performance and Research. He has held faculty positions at the University of Chicago, the University of Waikato, and the University of Maryland, where he remains an adjunct member of the graduate faculty. He twice served as a lecturer for the International Olympic Academy in Greece.

TABLE OF CONTENTS

FOREWORD————————————————

One of the most important social phenomena to have developed during the 20th century is sport. The truth of this today is unquestionable, and with every day that passes, sport expands further into all sectors. On the eve of the third millennium, sport has achieved total universality. This is no surprise, as sport has confirmed itself as a means of education, source of health and improved quality of life, an element of recreation and leisure occupation, first-rate entertainment, factor of social communication, etc.

This growing spread and development of sport throughout the world is reflected in a complex, extensive and highly distinct structure and organization, which varies greatly according to the objectives pursued and the countries in which it is developing.

The International Olympic Committee, the International Sports Federations and Associations and the National Olympic Committees form the basis of the present sporting structures, but we must not forget that the sports policy of each country has a considerable influence on this whole, particularly internally, but also on an external level according to the international importance of the country in question.

Sports events on a world-wide scale, especially the Olympic Games and some World Championships, require an ever-greater temporary organizational framework of increasing complexity and professionalism, with highly-trained staff.

All this is combined with the contribution of the traditional and loyal volunteer following, without which the development of world sport would not be possible.

Performing a global analysis of this structure is a truly difficult task, because of its widespread, complex and interdisciplinary nature. For that reason, the book *Sport Governance in the Global Community* is of particular importance, as, on the basis of extensive investigation and data compilation, it presents the facts in a straightforward and clear manner. This text will therefore be a tremendous asset to all those interested in exploring the magnificent reality of sport that we experience.

We are living in a golden age of sport, and all the signs indicate that the future will be even better. This exciting reality deserves to be studied and explained; and this book is a major contribution to that exploration.

H.E. Mr. Juan Antonio Samaranch
President of the International Olympic Committee

PREFACE

The National Association for Sport and Physical Education - North American Society for Sport Management Sport Management Program Standards designated Sport Governance as an essential cognitive area that must be learned in order for administrators to be competent in the sport world. The editorial committee for this book series wisely delineated knowledge of international sport governance as needed. Thus, the idea for this book germinated.

As the authors of *Sport Governance in the Global Community*, we were presented with a number of problems. First, no book on global sport governance had been written. There was no mold, no document to improve upon, no other angle that could be explored. Therefore, we created a text that we felt would explain a wide spectrum of issues -- all related and critical to understanding sport governance across country borders. To that end this book was written as a "What is out there" that must be understood, not a "How to manage" throughout the world of international sport.

Second, this is a foundation book. As previously stated, there was some feeling that this book could be an international management book. It is not. We felt that long before a manager deals with the everyday tasks as an international or global manager, one must understand the parameters within which the managerial tasks are taking place. Once these parameters (organizations with their interrelated functions, decision-making rationale) have been learned, then specific functions, such as cultural awareness training, marketing, public relations, personnel, and finance, could be expanded upon.

Third, how best to explain a topic of which, as we learned in our research, some administrators of international sport and most sport management professors had little understanding? We chose to address the issues both from theoretical and practical viewpoints, depending on the topic. For example, the topic of policy analysis was written from a theoretical and methodological base that provides the manager a foundation for specific action. Alternately, a number of chapters were written so the reader would know specifically what happens within the global community, for example, event bidding and hosting, national teams.

Fourth, a major question was the method used to convey what is happening within the international sport world that follows the rules to the letter and what happens through the rules but is shaped by the politics and personalities involved. This is a problem as the practical rules are often adaptations within accepted norms of the written rules. Reference is made to this in chapter 6 on bidding, chapter 7 on hosting, and chapter 10 on politics and boycotts.

During our sport lives, we have both worked in various capacities in the international sport world. We know the written rules and regulations. However, we also know that as with any managerial work, the personalities of the administrators and officials, dictated by the external and internal parameters of the sport or activity, create variations of the rules. We chose to limit this text to the rules and facts as prescribed in the numerous constitutions, bylaws, and working manuals of the international sport organizations. This text does not deal with innuendo, gossip, in-fighting, or political expediency. It would be impossible to know every private conversation and reason for a rule creation or change. As stated, this text deals with the "what is" that is in print and verifiable. Often anecdotes and examples are used but only to illustrate a salient point.

Fifth, we expect this book to be read by both native and nonnative speakers of English. Therefore, care was taken to use words that would be understood by the readership. At times this proves difficult as presenting university-level material in English leaves a possibility that the material may not be fully understood by the nonnative English speakers. This is a problem of which we are keenly aware. We have tried to address it.

Sixth, it is recognized that some of the material and examples presented may be dated by the time this book is published. We have no control over this. However, this fact alone serves to emphasize the dynamic nature of international sport today, especially professional sport. This constant change also serves to punctuate the need for present and future sport managers to understand the foundations of international sport. In addition, from this book it is expected that the reader will develop a keen eye for international issues that often-times are covered in the sport pages of a favorite newspaper.

Seventh, we have deliberately limited most event and bidding text to multisport events, such as the Olympic Games, the Pan American Games. This was done for two reasons. First, since each international federation sponsors many events, it would be beyond this book's scope to discuss even a small proportion of their events. Second, it was felt that if multisport events were presented, individual sports could be seen to be a proportion of a larger event. This should not be taken to be an insult to any sport or event; we are each proud of our backgrounds in individual sports.

Eighth, understanding national culture is the most important aspect that a person dealing internationally must appreciate and comprehend. We do not specifically deal with cultural awareness in this text. However, it is an ever-present factor for the international manager. The reader must always understand that whatever business successes one has internationally happens within the context of a nation's culture. Thus, this book is a supplement to, not a substitute for, training and cultural sensitivity.

Ninth, the phrase "international sport governance" may mean different things to different people. This book deals with matters of sport governance or sport administration that cross national boundaries. It is particularly concerned with the ways in which sport is organized and managed internationally. Nevertheless, international sport governance often includes a distinctly local element. For example, international sport events are typically managed locally by the host city or country. However, the process of bidding for these events is international, and the production of such events requires extensive liaison with international sport organizations. Thus, the bidding for and management of international sport events are discussed.

International sport governance of this kind can be distinguished from matters that implicate international sport, but that are strictly local or national. For example, when the United States Olympic Committee (USOC) chose to boycott the 1980 Summer Olympic Games in Moscow, Anita DeFrantz (who was then a member of the rowing team) and 25 other plaintiffs sued in DeFrantz v. United States Olympic Committee [492 F.Supp. 1181 (U.S. District Court. District of Columbia 1980)]. In the suit, the plaintiffs sought to compel the USOC to send a team to the Olympics in Moscow. Although the Olympics are an international event, the suit against the USOC was strictly a domestic United

States affair. Thus, the legal arguments and the court decision (against the plaintiffs) are not matters of international sport governance. Issues of this kind, which are fundamentally local, are beyond the scope of this book.

Organization of this text has been designed to couple availability of knowledge with the readers' critical thought processes. Each chapter is organized into four sections:

1. There is a capsule summary at the beginning of each chapter. This briefly delineates what will be discussed.
2. The body of the chapter is next. Some chapters will by the nature of the subject require a more theoretical background before application is presented. Other chapters move more quickly into the applied world as this was deemed the most effective means to convey and illustrate the information.
3. Following the body of the chapter is the concluding summary. This section places the entire chapter in perspective.
4. The last part of the each chapter, excluding chapters 1 and 12, contains four sections that challenge the reader to critically analyze what has been presented. Most of the questions are open-ended. It is imperative that careful thought be given to the problems presented in order for the reader to fully grasp their significance. The Ethical Debate section provides an opportunity for exploration of the ethical nature of international sport -- an area of growing concern to the working professional.

For the professor these four sections allow for both individual, group, and class activity. Some of the scenarios require the student to research the topic; library resources and personal communication will be required. If students are required to think critically, they will be able to grasp more completely how sport is governed globally.

The appendices conclude the book. Appendix A offers greater detail for those interested in multisport international competitions. Examination of this information provides further information into the components of these events. Appendix B can serve as a resource for those seeking additional information on global sport organizations.

We would like to acknowledge those people who have assisted in the development of this book:

To the athletes, coaches, administrators, and students with whom we have shared the stimulation of sport;

To John J. MacAloon, Kaye Meyer, Ollan Cassell, Thomas P. Rosandich, and John Dutson, who nurtured our growth in the world of international sport;

To Mari Tollakson, Jim and Bev Montrella, Mamie Rallins, Chris Green, Mireira Lizandra, Neil Nadkarni, June Baughman, Jackie Simcic, Bob Garland, and Cheryl Paine for their valuable research assistance;

To the personnel at the United States Olympic Committee, Sport Canada, the Atlanta Committee for the Olympic Games, and the many international and national federations and sport organizations that contributed valuable research material;

To Cara McEldowney, Camille Santoro, and Patricia Rhea for their graphics expertise;

To Mount Union College and the University of Maryland for the services each provided;

To Albert Applin, Ted Fay, Mireia Lizandra, and Sandra Woods for their critical and helpful critique of this manuscript;

To Andrew Ostrow and Fitness Information Technology, Inc. for having the foresight to create the Sport Management Library;

To Janet Parks and the Editorial Board of Gordon Olafson, Brenda Pitts, and David Stotlar for their helpful suggestions, encouragement, and tolerance;

To Waliah Poto, Jean Dalesandro, and Judy Thoma for the many hours of typing (JT could have not survived without you); and

To our families, who both encouraged and tolerated our work to complete this book.

James Thoma, Laurence Chalip

CHAPTER ONE ──────────

INTRODUCTION

The athletes and officials assemble for the march into the stadium. Each team carries its banner as it parades in front of the grandstand while being recognized by the assembled dignitaries. As the teams take their places on the infield, first an athlete and then an official takes the oath to perform in an honest manner. The athletes and officials march out and the games begin!

Does this scenario seem familiar? Probably. But this was not the Olympic Games. This was a scene from a school track meet in Kota Kinabalu, Malaysia, on the northwest coast of Borneo! Sport has linked the global community.

In today's newspapers are the stories of professional sports marketing globally, North American professional sports reaching to new continents with franchises, international legal battles over athletes' rights, etc. One can not be a sport fan without realizing that the traditional organization of sport is changing. Even traditional amateur sport, i.e. Olympic sport, is changing as its revenue increases primarily due to television rights and licensing, which both now span the globe.

Many administrators, educators and students have little or no knowledge of the terms of reference into which the sport world has moved. The paradigm has shifted and those whose reference points are fixed by past experience will not have the understanding of this new world of international sport. In order to assist in staying with the shift, this book has been written. From this effort the authors and editors hope that the future sport leaders and administrators will more quickly grasp the environment in which the events will be managed.

Historical Perspective

Sport has long had an international dimension. From 776 B.C. the ancient Olympics were contested between city states. So a case could be made that this book introduces little that is new. And so it may be. However, since 1896 when Baron Pierre de Coubertin initiated a rebirth of the Olympics, modern technology has assisted the Olympic Movement to spread to nearly 200 countries.

This technology (see Chapter 12) has helped create mass markets such that sporting events transcend the narrow scope of sport into the vast world of entertainment. One does not have to live in an urban area to appreciate international sport as the beaming of television waves through satellites; mass communication and expeditious travel allow global corporations to reach even into the remotest villages of Borneo. In these villages watching the World Cup of soccer is a must and an American National Basketball Association game can be seen weekly. Thus, any village with a television, a satellite receiver and an electric generator can watch sports from many countries.

Many major corporations have realized that marketing through sport is a cost effective way to reach their target markets, e.g., Coca Cola sponsors soccer's World Cup; Nike and Reebok are but a few of the shoe and apparel companies creating international stars of athletes; Nestle promotes it chocolate drink, Milo, by being omnipresent at sporting events in Southeast Asia. It is, therefore, no coincidence that these and other companies have pumped money into sports, which has allowed sport to grow globally.

It is because of this expansion that an understanding of the vast dimensions of international sport is required. More and more people will be seeking administrative positions in a sport world where knowledge and appreciation of cultures and the manner in which "others" perform is required.

Justification

The authors contend that most people do not fully appreciate the amount of information needed by an individual in order for that person to have a minimum understanding of sport in the global arena. This information is really only one part of a sport administrator's general knowledge that would include finance, marketing, public relations, communications, legal issues, decision making and human resources management. The inclusion of sport governance beyond the administrative boundaries of one's country has now become important to the understanding of the total realm of sport management.

In like respect, the knowledge of international governance is but a part of the person's international competency requirements. Robert Hanvey (1976) further delineated areas in which global education is important:

1. Perspective consciousness - appreciation of the world's differences
2. State of planet awareness - the understanding of global issues
3. Cross-cultural awareness - knowledge of the ways in which people may be similar or different from others
4. Systemic awareness - the understanding of the orderly way in which international organizations conduct their affairs
5. Options for participation - through international knowledge and understanding, administrators (in our case) will be able to address methods to proceed with their business.

In addition to this listing, one could add political awareness for the understanding of national and international politics with the appropriate protocol.

Although we, as the authors of this book, recommend that every person in sport management understand how sport is governed throughout the world, we fully realize that not every sport manager will be a global manager. John J. MacAloon (1992) presented three criteria he uses to define an international sport manager:

...over a period of five years:

1. Derive the majority of their professional activity and income from sport,
2. and the majority of that from international sport,
3. and the majority of that from labor outside of, or commissioned by outsiders to, their native countries.

Surely, few (MacAloon estimates fewer than 2,000 in 1992) administrators fit this definition. However, this in no way lessens the need to understand the sport world's global village any more than saying that the teaching of mathematics is of little use since so few people become engineers and scientists. If one is to work in the world of sport, one must understand that its dimensions are far greater than a college in the United States, a province in Canada or a country in Africa.

Scope of the Global Community

The contents of this text have been designed as a foundation of knowledge for the administrator, professor and student with respect to international sport. The topics have been selected to survey and, therefore, acquaint the reader with that aspect of sport that either supports or directs programs that cross country borders.

Risk analysis is discussed in Chapter 2. From this discussion, the administrator gains a macroscopic view from which international decisions can be based.

Chapters 3 covers the Olympic Movement. The Olympic sports form a basis for Olympism - the global movement that is not known by many and understood by fewer. This material then presents the organizational framework within which traditional, non-professional sport is organized.

The next two chapters, 4 and 5, are closely linked. Chapter 4 begins by discussing sport's relationship with culture. From the understanding of culture's importance to sport, the diffusion of sport will be examined for its implications for international development. Chapter 5 then looks at internal country mechanisms that deal with international sport. The United States and Canadian governance models form the dichotomy - private and public funding - which serve to illustrate the primary methods in which governance is accomplished within a country.

Chapters 6 and 7 form a pair dealing with the same general topic - the international event. First, the bid process is explained using the International Olympic Committee's procedure since derivatives of this method are used for bidding for non-Olympic events. Once an organization is awarded an international event, there is a long and detailed process in moving from paper plans to running the events to closing the games' organization. Understanding the complexity of these topics is important.

Nearly everyone has seen a country's elite athletes while watching a world championships or an Olympic Games. However, the process by which these athletes are selected to represent their country and the procedure to get them to the event is rarely known. The material in Chapter 8 should enlighten and inform the reader by presenting an explanation of these processes throughout the world.

Chapter 9 explains Sport For All - a worldwide movement. This movement can involve highly skilled athletes, but is primarily focused on mass participation. Knowledge of these worldwide programs will assist in their wider implementation.

A topic that confounds sport administrators is addressed in Chapter 10 - Politics and Boycotts. Because of the high profile that sport has grown to command in many countries, the political ramifications of the administrator's decisions need to be examined. This material used in concert with policy analysis (Chapter 2) will provide greater insight for the sport manager into understanding how and why decisions are made as they are.

One topic that seems to have exploded onto the scene in the mid 1980's is that of professional sport moving across country borders. Although the movement is not new, with mass communications becoming easier and worldwide marketing growing, the information in Chapter 11 assists the reader in knowing what has happened and where it may lead.

Chapter 12 moves forward from the previously presented information. In Chapter 12 the focus shifts to what *may* occur in international sport. Many factors are creating changes that all administrators - sport or otherwise - will need to address in order to have their business or event succeed. This chapter should provide everyone with information that will stimulate his or her imagination and allow for planning due to shifts in technology, philosophy and economics.

In the process of researching and writing this book, a number of caveats became evident. In order to gain a better perspective of the material included herein, it is imperative that the Preface be read. If you have not done so, please read the Preface before proceeding to Chapter 2.

Concluding Summary

This information is a step forward for sport education programs into realms rarely discussed and little understood. However, this material is merely one aspect of what an educational program needs in order to be fully internationalized. Thoma (1991) presented a seven step pyramid for internationalizing a university's sport management curriculum (Figure 1.1). The material in this book fits into level five, just before gaining practical experience. On some occasions, however, students and educators will have international sport experience which will greatly enhance their comprehension of this material.

For the practitioners, this material should assist in your focus of the sport business world's big picture around which your work revolves. Taken as background and as a knowledge base, the manager will be better able to analyze international situations in order to make better decisions.

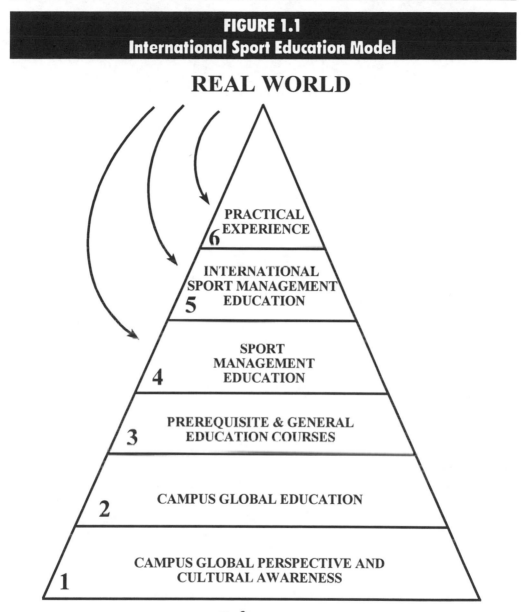

FIGURE 1.1
International Sport Education Model

REAL WORLD

6 PRACTICAL EXPERIENCE

5 INTERNATIONAL SPORT MANAGEMENT EDUCATION

4 SPORT MANAGEMENT EDUCATION

3 PREREQUISITE & GENERAL EDUCATION COURSES

2 CAMPUS GLOBAL EDUCATION

1 CAMPUS GLOBAL PERSPECTIVE AND CULTURAL AWARENESS

References

Hanvey, R. (1976). *An attainable global perspective*. Denver, Colorado: Center for Teaching International Relations.

MacAloon, J.J. (1992). "International Sport Management, Intercultural Relations Theory." Sport Management Theory Conference, New Orleans.

Thoma, J. (1991). "International Sport Management Education: A Model for Crossing Country Borders." North American Society for Sport Management Conference,

CHAPTER TWO————————————————

POLICY ANALYSIS FOR

INTERNATIONAL

SPORT GOVERNANCE

Overview

This chapter examines formal methods that can assist international sport managers to effectively identify and choose among policy alternatives. Three levels of analysis are identified and described: the governmental level, the agency level, and the individual level. The chapter then describes three analytic tools: ideology analysis, political risk analysis, and stakeholder analysis. Uses of each for international sport management problems are described.

Introduction

In order to govern sport, international sport managers require means by which to make effective choices among policy alternatives. Managers need to be able to determine likely outcomes of different choices. Working in international environments imposes significant political constraints as the interests of different nations and competing political systems confront one another. Policy analysis provides tools managers can use to appraise the relative merits and difficulties of policies under consideration.

A variety of definitions has been applied to the term *policy* by different authors. However, most definitions share a common reference to the choices of decision makers for actions to be taken in the future. Dimock, Dimock, and Fox (1983) provide a useful definition: "Policy is deciding at any time or place what objectives and substantive measures should be chosen in order to deal with a particular problem, issue, or innovation" (p. 40).

Policy analysis refers to systematic procedures for evaluating policy alternatives. Quade (1982) describes policy analysis as

> A form of applied research carried out to acquire a deeper understanding
> of sociotechnical issues and to bring about better solutions. Attempting
> to bring modern science and technology to bear on ... problems, policy
> analysis searches for feasible courses of action, generating information

and marshalling evidence of the benefits and other consequences that would follow their adoption and implementation, in order to help the policymaker choose the most advantageous action. (p. 5)

An extensive assortment of techniques for analyzing policy alternatives has been developed over the past four decades (see Patton & Sawicki, 1993, for an overview). Three techniques are particularly useful in international sport management: ideology analysis, political risk analysis, and stakeholder analysis. Each operates at a different level of political analysis. Thus, it is useful to begin our discussion with a brief description of each level and its place in the analysis of international sport policymaking.

Analyzing Political Action

In his classic study of the Cuban missile crisis, Allison (1971) shows that three levels of analysis are required in order to understand policies. Each of the three levels highlights different aspects of national, organizational, or individual behavior. An adequate understanding requires that all three levels be elaborated: (a) a level at which the government is treated as a single entity, (b) a level that analyzes the interactions among the various organizations and agencies that formulate and implement policy, and (c) a level which scrutinizes the political power and actions of key individuals.

At the highest level, the analyst simply treats each government as if it were a rational actor. The analyst asks two questions:

1. What is it that this government is trying to achieve?
2. What means is the government likely to use to attain its ends?

As an illustration, consider the 1988 Summer Olympic Games in Seoul, Korea. Many countries, particularly those with communist governments, did not have diplomatic relations with The Republic of Korea (South Korea) in the early 1980s. The Korean government used activities surrounding the Olympic Games as a means to develop political and economic relations, particularly with countries like Hungary which had communist governments (Riordan, 1990). For example, as part of the Olympic Arts Festival, Korean and Hungarian television embarked on a joint dramatic production. Projects of this kind were encouraged, and even facilitated, by the Korean government. Cultural exchanges and joint projects provided the levers that the Korean government required to establish new political and trading relations. At this level of analysis, we can understand the Korean government's interest in and use of the Olympic Games to attain political and economic ends. We have treated the government as if it were a single entity--as if it were a single person rationally pursuing an identifiable set of objectives.

At the middle level, the analyst examines the various organizations involved in formulating and implementing a policy. The analyst asks two questions:

1. Which organizations or departments are involved?
2. What standard operating procedures are they likely to use?

Let's look again at the 1988 Summer Olympic Games in Seoul. In order to symbolize those Games' themes of harmony and progress, the author of the joint Korean/Hungarian television production sought to have the production staged on the demilitarized zone between North Korea and South Korea. However, that plan required the military organizations responsible for security along that border to be included in planning and implementing the production. The standard operating procedures of the military forces along that border include no provision for performances like the one proposed. Indeed, to the military organizations, the proposal seemed to be a security nightmare. Consequently, the performance took place in Seoul, and not at the border. At this level of analysis, we see how policy planning and implementation are affected by the standard procedures and outlooks of the organizations involved.

At the most elemental level, the analyst scrutinizes key participants in policy development. The analyst asks three questions:

1. Who are the key persons involved?
2. What are their goals and interests?
3. What sources of influence can each bring to bear?

Let's use the 1988 Summer Olympics one more time. The Korean organizers sponsored two separate social science research teams during the Games. In fact, the inclusion of two separate research teams was never part of the organizers' planning. Rather, it was an outgrowth of political maneuvering by key individuals. The Cultural Affairs group of the Seoul Olympic Organizing Committee recruited, funded, and accredited an international team of scholars to evaluate the Seoul Olympics. At the same time, Professor Shin-pyo Kang from the anthropology department at Hanyang University recruited an international team of scholars to study the international cultural impact of the Seoul Olympics. The participation of this second research team was initially opposed by organizers of the evaluation team as an interference. However, Professor Kang obtained support from a leading national newspaper, and directly lobbied Seh-jik Park, president of the Seoul Olympic Organizing Committee. He managed to convince President Park that the second research team would serve to document the international significance of the Seoul Olympics. Consequently, the second team was funded and accredited under the direct authority of the president of the Seoul Olympic Organizing Committee. At this level of analysis, we see how individual initiative and political maneuvering affect project planning and implementation.

The answers to questions posed at each level of analysis help to shape the policy analyst's appraisal of events and alternative courses of action. In the contexts of international sport, three related analytic techniques can prove particularly useful: ideology analysis, political risk analysis, and stakeholder analysis. *Ideology analysis* provides a basis for further description at the rational actor level of analysis. *Political risk analysis* provides a significant tool for elaborating the organizational level of analysis. *Stakeholder analysis* provides techniques by which to enumerate and characterize key individuals involved in policy formulation and implementation. The relationship between each method and its level of analysis is illustrated in Figure 2-1.

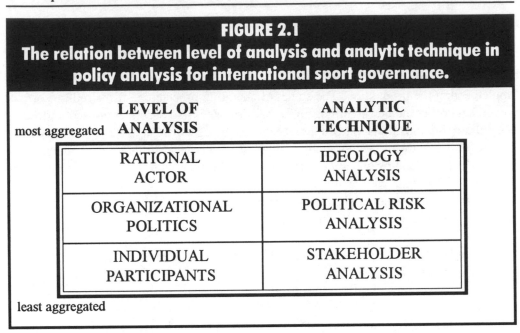

FIGURE 2.1
The relation between level of analysis and analytic technique in policy analysis for international sport governance.

	LEVEL OF ANALYSIS	ANALYTIC TECHNIQUE
most aggregated		
	RATIONAL ACTOR	IDEOLOGY ANALYSIS
	ORGANIZATIONAL POLITICS	POLITICAL RISK ANALYSIS
	INDIVIDUAL PARTICIPANTS	STAKEHOLDER ANALYSIS
least aggregated		

Ideology Analysis

In everyday usage, we are used to thinking about ideologies in terms of their political labels, such as nationalism, fascism, Marxism, and democracy. But ideologies can be more generally understood as specifications of beliefs and purposes. Skidmore (1989) defines *ideology* this way:

> [An ideology] is a reasonably coherent pattern of ideas ... about the purposes of collective life, about the ways to attain social goals, about the relationship between the individual and others, and about how resources are to be developed and distributed. [It] succeeds in simplifying these ideas considerably. [It] provides a program, and incites action. (p.7)

Ideologies are important because they provide cohesion by specifying group purposes and shared views of reality. Organizations with clearly articulated ideologies are able to mobilize member loyalties and actions by asserting that the organization serves a noble social purpose. The organization's ideology helps explain, evaluate, and provide direction by indicating answers to pivotal questions, such as: What are basic human needs? What is it possible for individuals and societies to achieve? What are appropriate social goals?

Because an ideology designates the organization's purposes, it can limit the range of policy options the organization might choose. When choosing among policy alternatives, the debates among policymakers within the organization may revolve around specifications and interpretations of the organization's ideology. Thus, in order to manage effectively, it is useful for the manager to have a strong command of the organization's ideology.

One international sport organization in particular, the International Olympic Committee (IOC), has an explicitly developed ideology, *Olympism*. Because the IOC plays such a significant role in the development and promotion of international sport and because its methods serve as the model for most international sport governance, the next chapter describes IOC governance and ideology in detail. For our purposes now, it is sufficient to note that Olympism contends that the practice of sport promotes optimal human development. Consequently, Olympism advocates the spread of Olympic sports throughout the world.

King (1991) describes the use of ideology analysis to promote Calgary's bid to host the 1988 Winter Olympic Games. As the bid was being formulated, the bid staff read IOC materials describing Olympism, and discussed the interpretation of Olympism with every IOC member, saying: "You are the trustees of the Olympic ideals. Please help us understand what the Games are about" (p. 54). Their resulting analysis of Olympism was built into King's speech to the IOC when the bid was presented. He said:

> There exists a mutual desire to hold the Games in different parts of the world to help spread and strengthen the Olympic movement. I've seen the positive power of Olympism at work in Calgary already. I've seen the way my own children speak with pride about Calgary's Olympic dream... We share the dream of spreading the Olympic movement... (p. 96)

King attributes part of the success of Calgary's bid to the bid team's analysis of Olympism (see, especially, p. 215).

Political Risk Analysis

Political risk analyses are used to evaluate the potential for loss in international business dealings. Political risk analyses are particularly important when planning an international event, such as a world championship, a title boxing match, or an Olympic Games. There are typically several sites to choose among, each with its own advantages and disadvantages. Sites are usually chosen well in advance of the event itself. For example, the Olympic site is chosen 7 years in advance. Political stability is an important factor for event preparation. Domestic strife, revolutions, or coups can cause currency fluctuations, problems in the delivery of required supplies, delays in event preparation, or even cancellation of the event itself. Radical changes in national policies, such as import restrictions or new forms of taxation, can similarly alter the feasibility of hosting an event or completing a sports exchange.

Coplin and O'Leary (1983) identify four key sources of political risk: (a) regime change, (b) political turmoil, (c) government restrictions, and (d) economic policies. Each can affect program development and event feasibility differently.

Regime Change

Changes in regime result in a shift in the political leadership of a country. Even when a change occurs legally, as through elections, there can be alterations in a country's policies that, in turn, affect its sport governance. For example, when the National Party was elected to government in New Zealand in 1975, it took a more lenient stance on sporting contacts with South Africa than had been taken by the Labour Party, which had previously been in power. No action was taken to discourage the New Zealand Rugby Football Union from touring South Africa. That tour became the grounds for a boycott of the Montreal Olympics by the nations of sub-Saharan Africa.

Political risks are magnified when regime changes occur extra-legally, as through assassination, revolution, or military coup. Under these circumstances, businesses, government offices, and/or borders may be closed. Even when public offices remain open, government officials may delay processing key documents or impede business transactions until policies of the new regime are specified. During transitions of these kinds, it could become impossible to host a planned event in that country.

Political Turmoil

Political turmoil refers to such activities as peaceful demonstrations, strikes, riots, terrorism, or war. Political turmoil threatens international sports exchanges and events when participating organizations feel endangered. The increased sense of risk can raise domestic interest rates, which, in turn, increases the cost of the money that must be raised to host an event or execute an exchange. Political turmoil can also redirect a nation's energies away from the routine activities required for administration of international trade, such as trade licensing, currency exchange, and customs operations. Declines in performance of these duties can adversely affect event or exchange feasibility. Finally, political turmoil may provoke a hostile response from potential participants in the event or exchange. For example, the Soviet Union's invasion of Afghanistan led directly to the boycott by the United States and its allies of the Moscow Olympics in 1980.

Government Restrictions

Four types of restrictive government policies can be identified. First, tariffs may be raised. Higher tariffs may substantially increase the cost of importing sports equipment or supplies required for event production. A second form of restriction is official interference in currency transfers. This can result in delays of payments, sometimes causing cash flow problems for overseas suppliers or event organizers. Third, governments can set rules that restrict foreign participation in domestic business activities. Such rules can restrict foreign investment in sports programs or events, or may hamper the use of foreign management expertise. Fourth, import licensing regulations may be changed or strictly enforced in order to restrict the importation of certain goods. For example, in 1956, the Australian government's enforcement of quarantine for horses entering the country made it impossible for the Olympic equestrian events to be held in Melbourne (which was the host city for the 1956 Olympic Games). Consequently, the equestrian events were held in Stockholm, Sweden.

Economic Policies

The economic policies of a country can aggravate inflation or restrict economic activity. Monetary policies that encourage rapid increases in the money supply can cause severe inflation, making event planning and implementation particularly difficult. Conversely, when governments impose austerity measures to correct past errors in economic policy, the economy often suffers from low growth and high unemployment. Under these circumstances, the domestic market for sport, including international sport, may shrink. In January 1995, following the sudden collapse of the Mexican peso, the

International Amateur Athletic Federation (IAAF) publicly expressed its concern that Mexico might be unable to host the 1997 world championships. Mexico did indeed have to forego hosting these championships.

The Political Risk Study

Coplin and O'Leary (1983) specify seven key elements for reports on the political risks associated with a particular country:

1. **Background factors** should be examined. These include the country's geography, its political relations, and social and economic problems. Other matters to be described include the sources of political power, labor relations, the government's disposition toward international business, and key political issues.

2. **Key political individuals, groups, and institutions** should be described. Particular attention should be paid to the ways that each might affect regime changes, political turmoil, government restrictions, and economic policies.

3. The **three regimes most likely to be in power** in the next year and a half should be described. Each is identified and discussed in the order of its likelihood of coming to power.

4. The **nature and magnitude of potential political turmoil** over the next year and a half should be examined. Recent patterns of political turmoil and their effects should be discussed. This discussion is followed by forecasts of potentials for turmoil under each of the regimes identified in preceding section.

5. The study should **forecast the likelihood of changes in government restrictions on international business** over the next year and a half. Particular attention is paid to potential changes in policies affecting taxation, foreign investment, currency exchange, expatriation of capital, and requirements for procuring supplies or labor. These factors are examined for each of the three potential regimes.

6. The **likelihood that the government will significantly change import restrictions** over the next year and half is forecast for each of the three potential regimes. Attention is paid to both tariff and nontariff barriers.

7. The **economic policies** of each of the three potential regimes are forecast. Each forecast includes descriptions of government spending, monetary policies, labor policies, and restrictions on the importation of capital.

Political risk analyses can be developed that are tailored to the needs of the international sport manager. Methods for generating key elements of a country study, including the requisite forecasts, are described in detail by Coplin & O'Leary (1983). However, in many instances the effort of preparing a tailored study can be spared, since serviceable political risk studies are often available from organizations with which the sport manager already has a relationship, such as an international bank. In other cases, substantial portions of the analysis can be obtained from government agencies. For example, the United States government annually updates and publishes analyses of the political and economic situation in countries throughout the world. These analyses are available for sale through the U.S. Government Printing Office and are for sale to the general public (regardless of citizenship).

Example: The Calgary Olympics

In order to get a clearer sense of factors that might go into a political risk analysis, we can look once again at the Calgary Olympics. Although Canada has historically been a relatively stable country politically, the decision to award the bid to Calgary had to be made in the presence of some risk, because the IOC had to award the bid several years in advance of the Winter Olympic Games. The IOC needed to consider factors that might impair Calgary's ability to host those Games successfully. Let's consider examples of each of the seven political risk factors described by Coplin and O'Leary (1983), and how they might have concerned the IOC. The purpose here is not to provide a detailed political risk analysis for Calgary; rather, the objective here is to illustrate the kinds of issues that IOC analysts would have included in their appraisal.

1. Canada's support of the 1980 boycott of the Moscow Olympics was a **background factor** of particular concern (King, 1991, p. 53). The threat of a tit-for-tat boycott of the Olympic Games was a significant IOC concern. Competing bids from Cortina d'Ampezzo, Italy and Falun-Are, Sweden, seemed less likely to prompt such a boycott because these two countries had sent teams to Moscow.

2. Canadian environmental activists were significant **individuals and groups** that could have affected Calgary's ability to host the Games successfully. Environmentalists were concerned that a large international sporting event would have a negative impact on the Banff National Park. Indeed, an earlier bid by Calgary (in 1972) failed, in part, because the organizers failed to take environmentalists' concerns into account (King, 1991, p. 9).

3. The three potential **regimes** in Canada at the time were the Liberal, the Progressive Conservatives, and the New Democratic Party. At the time of the bid, the Liberals were in power nationally, but the Progressive Conservatives were in power in Alberta (Calgary's province). A key concern for the IOC was the degree to which Prime Minister Pierre Trudeau's Liberal government would honor the IOC requirement that all athletes and sports officials have ready access to the Olympic site. Indeed, Trudeau had told the organizers, "You must recognize that in certain matters, even the IOC charter could not prevail over the security of a nation or any other matter of national interest" (quoted in King, 1991, p. 61).

4. Perhaps the biggest threat of **political turmoil** came from advocates of an independent Quebec. Although polls showed that only a minority of Quebec residents favored independence at the time of the bid, advocates of independence had come to power in Quebec several years earlier (in 1976). Were Quebec to become independent, the political and economic stability of Canada would change drastically. In particular, the federal government would probably have been unable to fulfill its promise of Canadian $200 million to support the Games in Calgary (cf. King, 1991, p. 148).

5. Regardless of regime, Canadian policies had consistently been favorable to **international business**. As long as Canada remained a unified nation, there

was scant threat of new policies unfavorable to Calgary's hosting of the Winter Olympics in 1988.

6. Similarly, there was scant threat of new **import restrictions** that might hamper the Games. Further, the fact that the federal government had promised substantial subsidy for the Games suggested that any special needs for the Games would be accommodated.

7. The **economic policies** of the Liberal regime were a matter of some concern. The National Energy Program undermined the economies of western provinces. The new energy source tax drained dollars from the Alberta economy, driving many businesses into bankruptcy. By 1983, 40,000 Calgarians were out of work. Calgary seemed unable to finance the Games unless the federal government delivered its promised subsidy (see King, 1991, p. 123 for a discussion).

Stakeholder Analysis

Stakeholders are individuals or groups who are affected by or who can affect the organization's objectives. Stakeholder analysis is a formal procedure for identifying stakeholders, mapping their potential impact, and deriving strategies appropriate to anticipated stakeholder impact. Stakeholder analysis is therefore proactive. It seeks to prevent stakeholder actions that might be adverse to the organization's goals, while facilitating the exploitation of any opportunities stakeholders might provide. Stakeholder analysis is particularly useful when bidding for or planning an event. For example, in its campaign to win the 1996 Summer Olympic Games, the Atlanta Bid Committee developed an extensive stakeholder analysis. That analysis established the basis for strategies to obtain the support of key community groups and IOC members.

Mendelow (1987) specifies three steps for stakeholder analysis: (a) identifying stakeholders, (b) specifying stakeholder attributes, and (c) developing a stakeholder strategy. Each of these steps is described below.

Identifying Stakeholders

At this stage, it is important to identify specific stakeholders. Generic categories (e.g., employees, suppliers, clients, competitors) may provide useful prompts, but these categories must ultimately be replaced by the names of individuals or groups. One useful technique is to analyze past issues or activities in which the organization has been involved and to identify those persons and groups that were also involved. A related technique is to specify persons and groups that are involved in any issues or projects with which the organization is currently involved. In so doing, it is useful to think through each stage of project planning and implementation, and to identify individuals and groups who might become involved.

The list of stakeholders is then tabulated, and details about each stakeholder (e.g., interests, political contacts, contract renewal date, size, hobbies) are collated. At this stage it can also prove useful to diagram stakeholder interactions with each other. The resulting map can prove useful during subsequent strategic planning.

For example, the Calgary Olympic organizers realized that they needed support from federal, provincial, and city levels of government. They identified key officials at each level, determined their backgrounds and interests, and lobbied each for support (King, 1991).

Specifying Stakeholder Attributes

It is useful to specify three kinds of attributes: orientation, opinion, and power. These attributes point to policies the organization can implement in its interactions with each stakeholder.

Orientation simply refers to the degree to which a stakeholder favors or opposes the organization. The organization will seek to keep favorable stakeholders well informed about its objectives, problems, and achievements. On the other hand, it will be careful to screen information provided to those who oppose the organization.

Each stakeholder's **opinions** about issues facing the organization are listed. The analyst cross-references this information against the degree to which the stakeholder is likely to be active, aware but inactive, or latent when dealing with that issue. The organization will have to develop strategies for dealing with active stakeholders. However, in the case of aware and latent stakeholders, the organization will have the option of merely monitoring the stakeholder or actively seeking to recruit the stakeholder as an ally.

Finally, each stakeholder's sources of **power** are listed. These are important because they suggest the degree to which the stakeholder could affect the organization and because they can suggest bases for effective strategies to address likely effects. At this stage, the analyst considers such elements as the stakeholder's resources, sources of authority, political clout, and access to key decision makers.

For example, the Calgary bid team recognized that all IOC members were expected to vote on the site of the Winter Olympic Games, whether or not their own countries sent athletes to them. Thus, Calgary's analysts paid special attention to IOC members who were not typically lobbied by cities bidding for a Winter Olympic Games. They lobbied those members to obtain their support for Calgary. Calgary was unique in its efforts to lobby IOC members from countries not fielding a team to the Winter Olympics. King (1991, p. 66) attributes Calgary's success at bidding, in part, to this element of his bid team's stakeholder strategy.

Developing A Stakeholder Strategy

Although specific tactics will be developed for each stakeholder, Mendelow (1987) identifies six generic stakeholder strategies. These can be used as tools to assist formulation of specific tactics.

The *big gun strategy* is used with stakeholders who actively favor the organization. In this instance, the organization seeks to improve the stakeholder's ability to influence or control other stakeholders. For example, the organizers of the Calgary bid invited Iona Campagnolo, the federal minister of Fitness and Amateur Sport, to work with them on planning means to finance new facilities (King, 1991).

The *defense strategy* is used with stakeholders who are against the organization but are relatively powerful. Two tactics are possible. The organization may simply choose to mobilize whatever defenses are available. However, the organization could simultaneously seek ways to switch the orientation of these stakeholders. Thus, the Calgary organizers sought to blunt objections from environmentalists by promising not to host the Games in a national park (King, 1991).

The *alliance strategy* is used with stakeholders who are powerful and who actively favor the organization. In this instance, the organization seeks to further the sense of mutual interest by cooperating on matters of shared concern. Here, for example, the Calgary Olympic organizers worked closely with Calgary business leaders who recognized the Games' potential economic benefit to the city. These businessmen could help the organizers develop a network of support, and could lobby key legislators.

The *switch strategy* is used with stakeholders who actively oppose the organization, but who have low power. In this case, the organization tries to locate issues that are of interest to the stakeholder and that the organization can affect. The effort here is to switch the stakeholder to a more favorable orientation by demonstrating common cause. Thus, although some Calgarians initially worried about the impact of an Olympic Games on their city, the organizers mustered support by touting the strong potential economic advantages for a city suffering high unemployment.

The *hold strategy* is commonly applied to latent stakeholder groups. The objective is to preserve the status quo. The stakeholder is monitored, and contingency plans are developed to ensure a pro-organization stance if the stakeholder shifts from latent to aware or active. In the case of Calgary, local- and provincial-level politicians from provinces outside Alberta could be monitored by the Calgary Olympic organizers. Contingency plans could then be put into place to make certain that those politicians would, if they became active, support the federal government's Canadian $200 million subsidy of the Games.

The *build strategy* is used with aware and latent stakeholders who are likely to favor the organization. The objective here is to build stakeholder awareness and interest in order to recruit the stakeholder as an ally. For example, in order to recruit local-level support, the Calgary organizers wanted influential persons in the community to support the Games publicly. One strategy to obtain active support was to lobby clergy and social agencies, stressing the potential economic benefits of the Games--a concern shared jointly by the organizers, clergy, and most social activists.

Concluding Summary

Methods of policy analysis can be used to reduce uncertainties and thereby improve the quality of management decisions. Formal models of analysis can be particularly useful for coping with the political complexities of international sport governance. Three techniques that have been found to be useful in international sport governance are ideology analysis, political risk analysis, and stakeholder analysis.

Ideology analysis helps the manager identify the beliefs and purposes that guide an organization's actions. This technique can prove particularly useful when formulating arguments favoring or opposing policy alternatives. In Olympic sport, for example, policies are commonly debated in terms of their purported consistency (or lack of consistency) with Olympic ideology, Olympism.

Political risk analysis helps the manager specify the nature and degree of risk when doing business with a particular country. This technique is particularly useful when deciding whether to undertake a project in a particular country or when choosing among countries for implementation of a project. For example, the technique should be applied when deciding whether to schedule an event in a particular country or when choosing among potential sites for an event.

Stakeholder analysis helps the manager to identify individuals and groups that could facilitate or hinder attainment of the organization's goals. It also provides tools for formulating strategies to blunt adverse stakeholder impacts, while enabling opportunities stakeholders may provide. Stakeholder analysis is particularly useful during project planning, such as bidding for or preparing to host an event.

Discussion, Analysis, Application, and Debate

Issues For Discussion

1. What do you see as the relative advantages and disadvantages of examining policies at multiple levels of analysis, as Allison recommends?
2. In what ways could you use an analysis of a sport organization's ideology to make yourself more effective when working with that organization?
3. What matters of political risk might be particularly important to you if you were examining the feasibility of hosting an international sports event in another country?
4. If you were to build a computerized database of stakeholder information, what kinds of details might you want to include? Why?

Matter For Analysis

The methods described in this chapter are commonly applied in nonsport branches of diplomacy and international business. However, the methods have not been specifically tailored for application to international sport governance. In what ways does the administration of international sport differ from diplomacy or the management of nonsport businesses? What impact, if any, do those differences have for the practice or application of these policy analytic methods? For example, does the use of these methods in international sport settings affect the kinds of data required, the accessibility of data, the ways the data are analyzed, or the uses made of the analyses?

Applications

1. Identify a large organization that provides sport services (e.g., Special Olympics International, the Boys and Girls Clubs, the NCAA). Examine its mission statement, policy statements, and/or statements of purpose. If possible, interview key admin- istrators. Develop a coherent statement of the organization's official ideology by determining the following: What are the organization's purposes and how do those purposes relate to the organization's descriptions of its place in the world? What human needs and social goals does the organization seek to fulfill? Why? How? In what ways are these objectives reflected in debates during the organization's decision making?

2. Select a country with which you are relatively unfamiliar. Using current library resources, develop a political risk analysis for that country. What implications do you draw for choosing to have international sports events hosted in that country within the next year, 2 years, 5 years, or 10 years? What implications do you draw for international sports exchanges with that country? What does your analysis tell you about selling sporting goods to that country?

3. Choose a current issue in sport policy (e.g., gender equity, drug testing, right-to-play rules). Specify a policy you would like to advocate for that issue. With the help of library resources, determine who the key stakeholders are, what their attributes are, and what strategies would be appropriate to deal with those stakeholders if you were to advance your policy.

Ethical Debate

Stakeholder analysis requires that substantial information about each stakeholder be collected in order to optimize the potential to influence that stakeholder. How ethical is it to collect personal and professional information about people in order to exert influence over them? What limitations, if any, would seem to be appropriate?

References

Allison, G.T. (1971). *Essence of decision: Explaining the Cuban missile crisis*. Boston: Little, Brown.

Coplin, W.D., & O'Leary, M.K. (1983). *Introduction to political risk analysis*. Croton- on-Hudson, NY: Policy Studies Associates.

Dimock, M.E., Dimock, G.O., & Fox, D.M. (1983). *Public administration*. New York: Holt, Rinehart & Winston.

King, F.W. (1991). *It's how you play the game: The inside story of the Calgary Olympics*. Calgary: Script.

Mendelow, A.L. (1987). Stakeholder analysis for strategic planning and implementation. In W.R. King & D.I. Cleland (Eds.), *Strategic planning and management handbook* (pp. 176-191). New York: Van Nostrand Reinhold.

Patton, C.V., & Sawicki, D.S. (1993). *Basic methods of policy analysis and planning* (2nd ed.). Englewood Cliffs, NJ: Prentice Hall.

Quade, E.S. (1982). *Analysis for public decisions* (2nd ed.). New York: Elsevier Scientific.

Riordan, J. (1990). The tiger and the bear: Korean-Soviet relationship in light of the Olympic Games. In B-I. Koh (Ed.), *Toward one world beyond all barriers* (Vol. 1, pp. 331-344). Seoul: Poong Nam.

Skidmore, M.J. (1989). *Ideologies: Politics in action*. San Diego: Harcourt, Brace, Jovanovich.

CHAPTER THREE

THE

OLYMPIC MOVEMENT

Overview

Critical to the understanding of international sport governance is knowledge of the organizations represented within the Olympic Movement. This chapter defines the ideology of the Olympic Movement -- Olympism -- and delineates and defines the Movement's three elements -- the International Olympic Committee, the national Olympic committees, and the international federations. This chapter concludes with the description of IOC regional sport organizations through which the IOC's educational and developmental programs are administered.

Introduction

It is particularly useful for the international sport manager to understand the governance of Olympic sport. There are two reasons: First, Olympic sports continue to expand their role as the world's largest and most significant source of international sport activity (Landry, 1990); second, Olympic forms of governance and event production have become models for international sport administration and event development in non-Olympic contexts (MacAloon, 1987). This chapter examines the ideology of the International Olympic Committee (IOC), describes its governance, and concludes by characterizing the structure of the international sports federations (IFs) and regional sports organizations.

Olympism

The IOC's agenda extends well beyond production of the Summer and Winter Olympic Games. In fact, the IOC sees itself as the steward of an international social movement. Thus, within Olympic circles, one hears reference to "the Olympic Movement." The ideology that specifies the IOC's beliefs and purposes is called "Olympism."

The modern Olympic Movement dates from the founding of the International Olympic Committee on June 23, 1894. Pierre de Coubertin, a French aristocrat, is typically credited as the founder of the modern Olympic Movement. His writings are regarded as the fountainhead of Olympic ideology. Chalip's (1992) analysis of Coubertin's agenda for the Olympic Movement is summarized here.

Coubertin sought educational reform. He was persuaded that mind and body should be educated jointly. For him, the physical exertion required by sports served three educational objectives. First, Coubertin felt that aesthetic appreciation is cultivated by the participant's experience of the body in sport. This was important to Coubertin because he believed that a well-developed sense of aesthetics is a prerequisite to the wise use of knowledge. Second, Coubertin saw international sport as a tool for the establishment of peace and cross-national understanding. For Coubertin, sport was a vehicle via which to stimulate cross-national encounters and learning. Third, he valued the pursuit of excellence. He felt that the pursuit of excellence in sport could teach participants to respect excellence more generally.

For Coubertin, sport obtained its impact via participation, and not as a result of merely spectating. Consequently, he sought the expansion of opportunities for people to participate in sport, including the construction of new facilities and the establishment of new programs. The Olympic Games themselves were intended to stimulate interest in sport and to promote the development of sports activities.

Coubertin's early ideals are still espoused by Olympic leaders. For example, Juan Antonio Samaranch, president of the IOC, said:

> Olympism surpasses sports. It is inseparable from education in its widest and most complete sense. It combines physical activity, art and the spirit and tends toward the formation of the complete [human being]. Thus, it concerns all, whatever our age, our sex, or our performances. It is an "assembler," a unique factor of reconciliation and comprehension... (quoted in Segrave, 1988, p. 159)

As with any ideology, the ideals and requirements of Olympism are a matter for continuing debate and reinterpretation. The contemporary ambitions of Olympism are specified in Fundamental Principles 2 and 3 of the *Olympic Charter* (International Olympic Committee, 1994). (References to the *Olympic Charter* are for the version "In force as from September 24, 1993.") Fundamental Principle 2 states:

> Olympism is a philosophy of life, exalting and combining in a balanced whole the qualities of body, will and mind. Blending sport with culture and education, Olympism seeks to create a way of life based on the joy found in effort, the educational value of good example and respect for universal ethical principles. (International Olympic Committee, 1993, p.10)

Fundamental Principle 3 states:

> The goal of Olympism is to place everywhere sport at the service of the harmonious development of man, with a view to encouraging the establishment of a peaceful society concerned with the preservation of human dignity. (International Olympic Committee, 1993, p.10)

Fundamental Principle 4 establishes the IOC as the custodian of Olympism: "The Olympic Movement, led by the IOC, stems from modern Olympism." (International Olympic Committee, 1993, p.10)

The objectives to be derived for the Olympic Movement are then specified in Fundamental Principle 6:

> The goal of the Olympic Movement is to contribute to building a peaceful and better world by educating youth through sport practiced without discrimination of any kind and in the Olympic spirit, which requires mutual understanding with a spirit of friendship, solidarity and fair-play. (International Olympic Committee, 1993, p.11)

In order to promote Olympism, an International Olympic Academy (IOA) was established in 1961 in Olympia, Greece. The IOA organizes 1 and 2 week educational sessions for sports administrators, journalists, academics, and others who work within the Olympic Movement. Sessions focus on issues of Olympism and the governance of Olympic sports. Each National Olympic Committee (NOC) is also encouraged (but not required) to establish its own National Olympic Academy.

Despite the IOC's constant and explicit reference to Olympism, critics of the Olympic Movement argue that IOC practices are not, in fact, steered by the lofty aims of Olympism. Hoberman (1986) calls the failure of the IOC to live up to its own ideals "the Olympic crisis":

> The Olympic crisis is permanent and is rooted in both the procedure and the core doctrine of the IOC. Since the Games are on a rotational basis, they are exposed to an endless variety of political considerations. Guaranteeing public order is a major task at every Olympiad, and it has become practical to assign Olympic festivals to the most repressive societies. Even relatively liberal societies have succumbed to the temptation to abridge civil liberties on behalf of international sport festivals... The gap between the IOC's pretensions and its performance is too wide to ignore. (pp. 2-3)

Simson and Jennings (1992) go further:

> Olympic sport ... is a secretive, elite domain where the decisions about sport, our sport, are taken behind closed doors, where money is spent on creating a fabulous life style for a tiny circle of officials rather than providing facilities for athletes, where money destined for sport has been siphoned away to offshore bank accounts and where officials preside forever, untroubled by elections. (pp. ix-x)

These critics argue that the Olympic Movement is inherently flawed—that its structure prevents it from living up to its own aspirations. According to the critics, Olympism has become a mere curtain of legitimation for sport practices that are elitist and potentially repressive. Some evidence for this view is provided by Czula, Flanagan, and Nasatir (1976), who found that Olympic athletes often explicitly reject Olympic ideals. A later study (Czula, 1978) found that the structure of experiences provided to athletes in their particular sports affects their attitudes towards Olympism. These findings support the view of critics that the governance of Olympic sport is pivotal. We turn, then, to an examination of the structure of Olympic governance.

Olympic Governance

The International Olympic Committee (IOC) is a nongovernmental, nonprofit organization headquartered in Lausanne, Switzerland. It retains all rights to the Olympic Games and their associated symbols, including the five Olympic rings, the Olympic flag, the Olympic anthem, the Olympic motto ("Citius, Altius, Fortius"), the Olympic flame, and the Olympic torch. When a city is awarded the right to organize an Olympic Games, the IOC grants use of its symbols. In fact, the *Olympic Charter* requires that the Olympic flag be displayed at all Olympic venues, that the Olympic flame burn in the main stadium, and that the Olympic anthem be played during the opening and closing ceremonies.

Olympic symbols are particularly important because they are the stock and trade of the Olympic Movement. As part of its overall mission, which is to develop and protect the Olympic Movement in its respective country, each National Olympic Committee (NOC) is required to protect the Olympic symbols and the designations "Olympic" and "Olympiad." Commercial rights to Olympic symbols are reserved for the IOC. However, NOCs have the right to develop their own emblem and to exploit that emblem commercially in their own country.

The Olympic Games consist of the Games of the Olympiad and the Olympic Winter Games. It is useful to note that the term "Olympiad" has a precise meaning in Olympic governance, but is frequently misused by academics and journalists. The term does not refer to the Games themselves, but rather to the 4 year period following the Games. In effect, the Games celebrate the Olympiad, which begins when the Games are opened. Hence, it is correct to call the summer Olympics "the Games of the Olympiad," but it is incorrect to call them merely "the Olympiad." Further, since the Olympic Winter Games occur in the middle of an Olympiad (being juxtaposed by 2 years from the summer Games), the Olympic Winter Games do not mark the beginning or ending of an Olympiad. Hence, the term Olympiad is not applied to the Olympic Winter Games.

The IOC is governed by its members. Members are chosen by the IOC itself (i.e., the existing members), and not by NOCs or national governments. Members serve until 75 years of age, although they may retire prior to that age. In addition to participation in IOC governance, members are responsible for promoting development of the Olympic Movement in their respective countries. The implication is often misunderstood. IOC members are not representatives of their own nations. Rather, as Rule 20 of the *Olympic Charter* specifies, "Members of the IOC are its representatives in their respective countries and not delegates of their countries within the IOC" (International Olympic Committee, 1993, p.30). In fact, the distinction is amplified further in Rule 20: "Members of the IOC may not accept from governments, organizations, or other legal entities or natural persons, any mandate liable to bind them or interfere with the freedom of their action and vote" (International Olympic Committee, 1993, p.30). (These rules have been the primary source of accusations [e.g., Simson & Jennings, 1992] that the IOC is undemocratic and elitist.)

There is no requirement that every country with a member NOC have an IOC representative. Indeed, many countries do not. However, Rule 20 does stipulate that there can be only one member in each country, unless the country has hosted an Olympic Games; countries that have hosted an Olympic Games may (but are not required to) have two members.

Membership in the Olympic Movement (which is distinct from membership in the IOC) is broadly defined. Rule 3 of the *Olympic Charter* specifies:

> In addition to the IOC, the Olympic Movement includes the International Federations (IFs), the National Olympic Committees (NOCs), the Organizing Committees of the Olympic Games (OCOGs), the national associations, clubs and the persons belonging to them, particularly the athletes. Furthermore, the Olympic Movement includes other organizations and institutions as recognized by the IOC. (International Olympic Committee, 1993, p. 13)

The Olympic Movement has spawned an extensive array of regional Olympic organizations, each officially recognized by the IOC. Regional Olympic organizations include the Association of National Olympic Committees (ANOC), the Association of National Olympic Committees of Africa (ANOCA), the Olympic Council of Asia (OCA), the Pan American Sports Organization (PASO), the European Olympic Committees (EOC), and the Oceania National Olympic Committees (ONOC). The IOC also recognizes associations of IFs, including the Association of Summer Olympic International Federations (ASOIF), the Association of International Winter Sports Federations (AIWF), the Association of IOC Recognized International Sports Federations (ARISF), and the General Association of International Sports Federations (GAISF). These multisport associations provide a venue for sport organizations that share common administrative or regional concerns to discuss matters of policy and, where possible, to formulate shared positions on issues of governance.

In order to facilitate communication among the many organizations of the Olympic Movement, the IOC organizes periodic meetings with the IFs and meetings at least once every 2 years with the NOCs. The agenda is determined by the IOC President. In addition, it organizes an Olympic Congress at least once every 8 years. The Olympic Congress is composed of all organizations recognized by the IOC. The agenda is determined by the IOC Executive Board.

There are three organs for IOC governance: the Session, the Executive Board, and the President. Rule 22 of the *Olympic Charter* specifies that "The Session is the supreme organ of the IOC" (International Olympic Committee, 1993, p.34). The Session adopts, modifies, and interprets the *Olympic Charter*, and elects IOC members. The Session is a general meeting of all members of the IOC (but not the broader membership of the Olympic Movement). The Session is held annually, although additional (extraordinary) Sessions may be called by the President or a third of the members. Decisions of the Session are final, although it may delegate powers to the Executive Board.

The Executive Board consists of the President, four Vice-Presidents, and six additional members elected upon secret ballot by the Session. Terms are at least 4 years. The Board meets when convened by the President or at the request of a majority of its members. The Executive Board is responsible for managing IOC finances, preparing the annual report, submitting the names of persons it recommends for IOC membership, establishing the agenda for IOC Sessions, keeping the records of the IOC, assuring proper organization of the Olympic Games, and appointing the Director General and Secretary General (who oversee the daily business affairs of the IOC).

The IOC elects its President by secret ballot from among its members. The initial term is 8 years. The President may then be reelected for successive 4 year terms. The President presides over all IOC activities, and is responsible for establishing or decommissioning IOC commissions and working groups. The President designates all commission and working group members.

In recent years, increasing volumes of IOC work have been assigned to the commissions, and the number of commissions has tended to proliferate. A review of commission mandates suggests the range of concerns in IOC governance. IOC commissions include Commission for the International Olympic Academy, Eligibility Commission, Athletes Commission, Cultural Commission, Finance Commission, Juridical Commission, Medical Commission, Commission for the Olympic Movement, Joint Mass Media Commission, Press Commission, Radio Commission, Television Commission, Commission for the Program, Olympic Solidarity Commission, and Sport for All Commission.

National Olympic Committees

The NOCs are responsible for development and promotion of the Olympic Movement in their respective countries. They are expected to be independent of their respective national governments and to be responsible directly to the IOC. The IOC's requirements of NOCs are extensive. Those requirements are specified in Rule 31 of the *Olympic Charter*. NOCs are required to

2.1 propagate the fundamental principles of Olympism at national level [including] diffusion of Olympism in the teaching programmes of physical education and sport in schools and university establishments. They see to the creation of institutions which devote themselves to Olympic education. In particular, they concern themselves with the establishment and activities of National Olympic Academies, Olympic Museums and cultural programmes related to the Olympic Movement.

2.2 ensure the observance of the *Olympic Charter* in their countries;

2.3 encourage the development of high performance sport as well as sport for all;

2.4 help in the training of sports administrators by organizing courses and ensure that such courses contribute to the propagation of ... Olympism;

2.5 commit themselves to taking action against any form of discrimination and violence in sport, and against the use of substances and procedures prohibited by the IOC or the IFs. (International Olympic Committee, 1993, pp.46-47)

Membership in the NOC must include the members of the IOC in the NOC's country (if any) and all national federations (NFs) affiliated to the IFs governing sports included in the Olympic program. NOC membership must also include all athletes who have taken part in the Olympic Games. However, the athlete must retire from the NOC no later than the end of the third Olympiad after the last Olympic Games in which he or she competed. Other members (e.g., NFs of other sports, multisport organizations, or representatives of civic authorities) may be included at the NOC's discretion.

NOCs are assigned specific tasks under paragraphs 8.1 and 8.2 of the bylaw to Rules 31 and 32 of the *Olympic Charter*:

8.1 They constitute, organize and lead their respective delegations at the Olympic Games and at the regional, continental or world multi-sports competitions patronized by the IOC....

8.2 They provide for the equipment, transportation and accommodation of the members of their delegations [including insurance]. They are responsible for the behaviour of the members of their delegations. (International Olympic Committee, 1993, pp.52-53)

NOCs are granted specific rights by the IOC. These include (a) the exclusive power to determine representation of their respective countries at all multisport competitions patronized by the IOC, (b) the authority to determine which city in their respective country may apply to organize an Olympic Games, and (c) the right to formulate proposals and give opinions to the IOC.

Olympic Solidarity

NOCs, particularly those in developing countries and the newly independent nations of Eastern Europe, require some assistance in order to fulfill the obligations and tasks they are assigned by the *Olympic Charter*. Olympic Solidarity is assigned the task of providing that assistance. Funded by a share of profits from Olympic television rights fees, its budget has increased substantially in recent years: from US$5 million in 1987 to US$25 million in 1991. By 1992, Olympic Solidarity administered four sport development programs: technical sports courses, the itinerant school for sports leaders, the Olympic scholarship program, and the marketing program (Vipond, 1993).

Technical Sport Courses

Each NOC determines its coaches' and athletes' needs for training in the technical elements of particular sports. Working with their Continental Association of National Olympic Committees, the NOC prepares a technical training plan for the Olympiad. The relevant IFs then designate the requisite experts for training courses. Depending on need, the courses are funded in whole or in part by Olympic Solidarity, but are administered by the NOC.

The Itinerant School For Sport Leaders

Olympic Solidarity has developed and published (in English, French, and Spanish) sport administration training manuals, and has recruited and trained a nucleus of volunteer sport administration teachers. By 1992, that team consisted of 15 French-speaking, 14 English-speaking, and 15 Spanish-speaking instructors. The "sport leadership" courses are organized on a national level and are open to administrators who work at any level— club, NF, NOC, government, etc. Each course is taught by two instructors. Participants are chosen in consultation with the NOC.

The Olympic Scholarship Program

Olympic Solidarity's scholarship program is targeted at two distinct groups: young athletes and coaches.

The program for young athletes provides an opportunity for athletes from developing nations to train abroad. The program is limited to those who show promise of developing into elite competitors. Candidates are nominated by the NFs through their NOCs. Those who are selected are funded to train for 4 months at a training center selected by the NOC in consultation with the NF. If reports on the athlete's progress are favorable, the scholarship may be renewed in 4-month increments.

The program for coaches provides an opportunity for active coaches between the ages of 25 and 45 to participate and seminars and courses of between 1 and 6 months' duration. Candidates are nominated by their NFs through their NOCs. The training center is chosen by the NOC in consultation with the NF.

The Marketing Program

In response to NOC requests for help with sport marketing, Olympic Solidarity prepared a marketing manual to be used as the basis for instruction. Olympic Solidarity then trained a panel of experts to become consultants to the NOCs in all aspects of marketing. A continental seminar on sport marketing was held in Africa at the end of 1992, with each African NOC invited to send two or three representatives. One objective of the seminar was that Solidarity sport marketing consultants would meet with NOC officials to establish the basis for permanent consulting relationships. The program plan calls for each NOC to have one consultant assigned to it. The consultant will be available at all times to his or her designated NOC to resolve problems, answer queries, and make recommendations.

Other Activities

In addition to the four programs described above, Olympic Solidarity administers six activities on behalf of the IOC: (a) Olympic Solidarity coordinates the administration and financing of the national and regional sports medicine courses offered by the IOC Medical Commission; (b) Olympic Solidarity pays the travel and accommodation costs of one delegate per NOC to the annual meetings of continental NOC associations and to the biannual meetings of ANOC; (c) Olympic Solidarity pays each NOC a subsidy to cover costs of equipment, travel, and lodging in the Olympic village at each Olympic Games; (d) NOCs are encouraged to offer a 10 kilometer run open to the general population on Olympic Day (June 23) to celebrate the re-establishment of the Olympic Games, and Olympic Solidarity provides all NOCs organizing the run a US$1,500 subsidy, as well as certificates and T-shirts to be given to participants; (e) Olympic Solidarity pays 50% of the cost of air fare for one man and one woman from each NOC to attend the annual session of the International Olympic Academy (IOA), and Olympic Solidarity also provides a grant to the IOA to help defray the costs of accommodation; (f) IFs may apply to Olympic Solidarity for grants to fund development activities.

The Court of Arbitration for Sport

As the range and volume of international sport have grown, so too has the potential for strife. Contracts may be disputed; rule applications may be challenged; liabilities may be contested.

When compared to national systems of justice, the international system is relatively weak (Nafziger, 1988). However, there is a well-established legal tradition of settling disputes through private arbitration courts. In order to provide such an opportunity for sport, the IOC established the Court of Arbitration for Sport (CAS) in 1983. It became operational in 1985. It is recognized by the IOC and 15 IFs as the sole judicial authority to hear an appeal. Although it is funded by the IOC, it is administratively independent.

The CAS is composed of 60 lawyers chosen for their familiarity with sports issues. Members are appointed as follows: fifteen are appointed by the IOC; 15 are appointed by the IFs; 15 are appointed by the NOCs; 15 are appointed by the President of the IOC from outside the IFs and NOCs. Appointments, which are for 4 years, may be renewed. The President of the CAS is chosen from among its members by the President of the IOC, with the provision that the President of the CAS be a member of the IOC.

To arbitrate a dispute, the CAS sits in panels of three arbitrators, each of whom is one of the 60 CAS members. One arbitrator is chosen by each party to the dispute, and the third arbitrator, who becomes president of the panel, is appointed by mutual agreement of the two parties (sometimes under advice of the two arbitrators they have chosen initially). If no agreement is reached on the third arbitrator within 45 days, the third arbitrator is selected by the President of the Federal Tribunal of the Swiss Confederation. Unless there is an express agreement to the contrary, the panel applies Swiss law.

In order to submit a dispute to the CAS, the parties must first conclude a written arbitration agreement waiving any recourse to legal action before ordinary courts. The arbitration agreement may be drawn in response to an existing dispute or may be specified in advance of a dispute. In this latter case, it might appear in a contract, be included in a license, or be stipulated in statutes or regulations.

In addition to settling litigation, the CAS also gives advisory opinions. Any person or organization seeking such an opinion may forward a request through the Secretary General of the CAS. A consultative panel of between three and five members is then constituted to formulate the requested opinion.

International Federations

One of the three pillars of international sports is the international federations (IFs). More than the IOC and the NOCs, the IFs shepherd sport day-to-day year-round. The IOC holds an Olympics every 2 years. The NOCs work within their countries to develop sport and to promote the Olympic Movement. However, it is through the IFs that sport is contested -- they are on the front line of sport competition through their individual country organizations called national federations (NFs). For example, for track and field the International Amateur Athletic Federation (IAAF) is the international federation affiliated with the Malaysian Amateur Athletics Union being Malaysia's national federation for track and field.

All of the sports on the Olympic program, and many that wish to be, have an IF. Without an IF recognized by the IOC based on the *Olympic Charter*, that sport cannot participate in the Olympic Games. Even if an IF is recognized by the IOC, its sport(s) still may not be on the Olympic program. In 1992, there were 18 sports from 14 IFs that were IOC recognized but were not contested at the Olympic Games. These sports were aeronautics, bowling, curling, golf, karate, lawn bowling, orienteering, jai alai, racquetball, roller skating, sports acrobatics, squash, tae-kwon-do, pentathlon, underwater swimming, and water skiing. For the 1996 Games of the Olympiad in Atlanta, softball will become a medal sport for women, and tae-kwon-do and triathlon will be contested in Sydney in 2000.

Management Objectives

In order to bring order to its sport the IF must have objectives to which it subscribes. With these objectives, the IF can organize to meet goals for which to strive.

The following listings are common objectives for an IF:

1. To develop cooperation and encourage competitions between national federations and regional associations;
2. To ensure that competitions between the IF members (i.e. between countries) and regional groups are conducted under the IF rules;
3. To attempt the prevention of discrimination based on race, religion, and political affiliation for federations and competitions affiliated with the IFs;
4. To approve and distribute eligibility and competition rules and regulations for all groups under the IF affiliation;
5. To affiliate with the national federations recognized by each country's National Olympic Committee;
6. To mediate and/or rule on disputes between the IF's member NFs;
7. To cooperate with the Organizing Committee of the Olympic Games (OCOG) on venue preparation, equipment approval, and officiating within the parameters of the IOC; and
8. To establish rules for record performances and to verify record performances.

Management Structure

In order for the IFs to accomplish the objectives of their organizations, they must have both a permanent staff and volunteers. This is similar to any corporation because publically held companies have a full-time staff for administering the organization on a daily basis and a board of directors who receive little or no compensation for their time. The major difference with IFs, as well as the IOC, NOCs, and NFs, is that volunteers usually greatly outnumber the full-time employees and are called upon to advise and to administer a greater percentage of the IFs' duties than, for example, Exxon Corporation.

The number of full-time IF employees will vary depending on the financial resources of the federation. In general, if a sport has television appeal worldwide, then the television rights fees it receives allows it to address more programs for its members. These programs justify additional staff.

FIGURE 3.1
International Baseball Association Organizational Chart

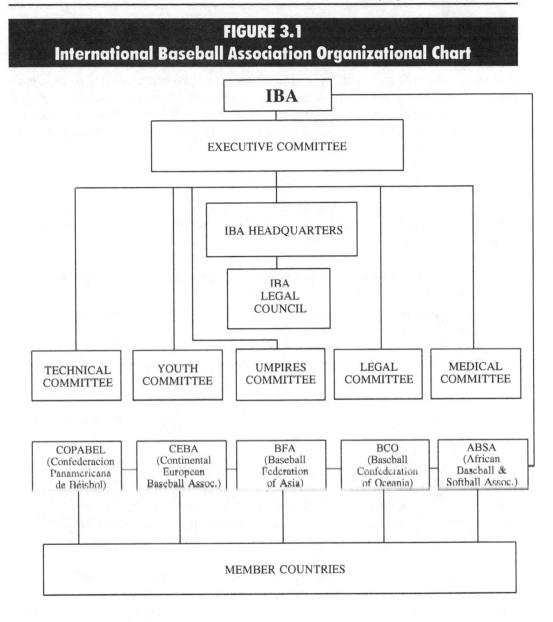

A look at Figure 3.1 shows the organizational structure of the International Baseball Association. This figure shows that there are five staff employees. This number is much smaller than the number of staff for a more widely followed sport, for example athletics, also known as track and field, which has greater financial resources due to its higher worldwide following, especially in the Olympic Games. At present baseball is played throughout the world but has gained a significant following only in North and Central America and parts of Europe and Asia. This should change now that baseball is an Olympic medal sport.

Executive Director

At the IF headquarters, there is one person who has the responsibility to manage the IF's daily business. This person is usually called the executive director, general secretary, or executive secretary with duties including

1. To ensure the implementation of the decisions of the federation Congress and committees;
2. To be responsible for the administration of federation-sanctioned contests, including the Olympics and world championships;
3. To ensure compliance with the federation regulations;
4. To organize the IF Congress, executive meetings, and committee meetings;
5. To distribute to its members the IF official communications, regulations, publications, and records,
6. To maintain public relations with the IOC, other IFs, official organizations, and the press;
7. To maintain an archives;
8. To ensure the receipt and distribution of funds in order to maintain accurate and current financial records;
9. To provide for the development of the sport and its administration; and
10. To represent the IF, as assigned by the president or the Executive Committee, at international congresses and meetings.

The number of IF staff with which the executive director works varies. What remains constant are the items that must be addressed: federation administration, public relations, marketing, event management, federation meetings, record keeping, financial control, banned substance control, and association communication.

Executive Council

By performing its daily duties the executive director and the IF staff implement the wishes of the federation president and executive council. The executive council usually consists of the president, vice presidents, treasurer, and other members chosen to represent their constituents. For example, the IAAF (the track and field/cross country/race walking international federation) Executive Council includes 6 different world area representatives and 11 individual electees (International Amateur Athletic Federation, 1990-1991).

Each executive council has specified duties it is elected to perform. Because the IFs have members from around the world, it is both time and cost prohibitive for them to check each member's wishes before a decision can be made. It is therefore the responsibility of the executive council to act in place of the entire membership for the benefit of the membership.

In order to act for the federation, the executive council is given specific power to act and duties to which these powers are specified. The executive council powers may include

1. To elect new national federation members, subject to congress or membership approval;
2. To sanction, suspend, or expel NF members;
3. To make urgent decisions that cannot wait until the next congress;
4. To call a special congress, if the need arises to approve special powers for the president in urgent situations;
5. To approve the financial statements and budgets, subject to congress ratification;
6. To govern and administer federation business;
7. To rule on federation constitutional interpretation and rules interpretation subject to congress ratification;
8. To appoint the General Secretary; and
9. To approve federation contracts.

Depending on the IF, more or less power is entrusted to the Executive Council. Other duties this group has in some IFs include deciding on honorary members, selection of a championship venue, and competition records approval. It is really up to each IF to decide how much power it wishes to entrust to its Executive Council.

President

The IF executive council is headed by the president of the federation. This is the highest official within a federation. In general, the more influential IFs have presidents who yield tremendous power granted by the constitution and bylaws within the organization. In addition, these presidents have risen to office through their ability to work within the federation political system. The federation members elect the president; the presidential candidates must convince the greatest number of member countries that they will lead the sport to greater glory.

As with any elected official, after winning the vote, the difficult job begins. Although the president is granted significant power, the elected person must still use his or her political acumen to serve the greater good of the sport -- not always easy!

Most IFs do not list a separate section in their constitution delineating the powers of their president. This can be misleading, however; the IF president does have the power to influence every aspect of the federation. However, the president's power is vested in the executive council. These powers were previously listed. In addition, as would be expected, the president presides over the IF congresses and council meetings, is ex-officio of committees, and represents the IF at functions and meetings outside of the federation. A few IFs designate specific duties; for example, the International Weightlifting Federation (IWF) president while at the Olympic Games and World Championships presides over Jury 1 and presents medals to the winners (International Weightlifting Federation, 1989).

Officers

In addition to the IF president, there is a complement of federation officers. These officers generally include one or more vice presidents, treasurer, or secretary-treasurer. Often there is no secretary because the day-to-day federation work and correspondence are handled through the executive director's office.

Continental Groupings

Throughout the world peoples come together for the benefit of their collective members, as with the Association of Southeast Asian Nations, or ASEAN. Likewise in sports there are groupings that come together. In general, the IFs have subdivisions called Continental Associations. Some IFs use a different term, such as continental areas, continental committees, continental federation or zone commissions. Some examples of these groupings are

1. International Basketball Federation (FIBA)
   - African Zone
   - Asian Zone
   - North American Zone
   - Central American Zone
   - South American Zone
   - Oceania Zone
   - European Zone (Federation Internationale de Basketball, 1990).

2. International Amateur Athletic Federation
   - African Area
   - Asia Area
   - Europe Area
   - North and Central America Area
   - Oceania Area
   - South America Area (International Amateur Athletic Federation, 1990-1991).

These continental associations have been formed to create a forum for discussion of regional interests and to promote competitions that are representative of their geographical area.

An important aspect of these groups' competitions is the qualification rounds for team competitions. It is impractical to expect 170 or 180 soccer teams to play a quality tournament in the 16 days of the summer Olympics or a world championship. Therefore, teams sports, such as soccer, basketball and baseball, have qualifying rounds. It is through these continental groupings that these qualifying rounds are played.

An important aspect of regional qualifying rounds needs to be mentioned here. It would seem natural that an equal number of countries would qualify from each continental association. However, this is not necessarily the case because of the number of countries in the continental groupings and the quality of team play within each region.

An example of this is the FIFA World Cup Soccer Championship. Although any

FIFA member country in good standing could qualify, the European region receives more qualifying slots than do the other regions. Although the Asian region has more countries than Europe, in general the quality of Asian soccer play does not match that of European teams. Of course, the number of qualifying teams can and will vary as the competitive quality of the regional teams changes.

Many IF councils also have representatives from the continental groupings. It is in this way the each world area is assured high-level representation within the federations.

Committees

Referring again to Figure 2 of the International Baseball Association (IBA), it is seen that there are a number of committees that handle specific IF duties. These committees, which vary from federation to federation, usually are composed of volunteers from the federation's NFs. These committees address specific aspects of the sport and its development. The IF executive director and president generally sit as members, with or without voting rights, on each committee. The IF committees may include

1. The Technical Committee addresses competition rules and their revisions. Some federations such as gymnastics may have specific technical committees to specify issues of different segments, that is, men's, women's, rhythmic, general.
2. The Medical Committee handles medical issues including banned substance/ doping, sex control, and competitor health, testing procedures, and education. Also, this group may appoint competition medical staffs, as needed.
3. The Officials/Referee/Judges Committee works to standardize and improve officiating through the education of the competition officials. Also, this group appoints or recommends officials for World Championships and the Olympic Games.
4. The Finance Committee oversees the budget preparation and its recommendation to the members.
5. The Youth/Development Committee addresses sport development programs, which often-times starts with young athletes but can grow to include mass-participation programs with athletes of any age.
6. The Veterans Committee handles all matters pertaining to veterans' (older athletes) competitions and competition records.
7. The Marketing/Business Committee seeks to effectively promote the sport and to advise on good business procedures.
8. The Legal Committee advises on conflict resolution and contractual legalities.
9. The Coaching Committee seeks to improve coaching though education programs. This task often is included within the Development Committee.

In addition to these committees, certain federations have specified groups that deal with equipment, discipline, and protocol.

Regional Sport Groupings

As was previously mentioned, countries group together for their mutual benefit to form regional sport organizations. This occurs within the IOC as well as the sport federations. The purpose of this section is to present the regional groups associated with the IOC. Their organizational structure, rules, and regulations are presented. These organizations vary in importance from country to country but are an important managerial level within the Olympic movement as well as a good vehicle for athlete development. Some of the multisport competitions sponsored by these regional organizations are presented in Appendix A.

The Olympic Council of Asia

The Olympic Council of Asia (OCA) was founded in 1982. According to its *Constitution and Rules* (1991, p.10) the OCA has three fundamental principles:

1. to "develop in the youth of Asia those moral and physical qualities that come from fair competition in sports and to promote the international respect, friendship and goodwill,"
2. to have no member discriminate in any way against any other member, and
3. to "apply and defend the Olympic principles as defined in the *Olympic Charter*."

It is through these principles that the OCA functions.

Fifteen general objectives are delineated in the OCA's *Constitution and Rules* (1991). However, these objectives can be synthesized into the OCA's being:

1. Asia's lone organization in charge of sport,
2. The coordinator of Asian sport for regional and international competitions,
3. The promoter of sport and physical education development to all the Asian peoples while promoting the Olympic movement principles,
4. The assurance that the Asian Games are well administrated every 4 years,
5. The arbitrator of disputes involving its members, to include discipline if need be.

As with most organizations, the OCA has rules by which it operates. The highlights of these include

1. An OCA member must include within its organization members of the NFs whose sports are included in the Asian Games.
2. The member must be independent so that it can not be influenced by outside pressures.
3. Approval of two-thirds of the members present is needed to admit a new member.
4. The office holders, all 4-year terms, shall be President; five Vice Presidents, one from each zone (Table 3.1) and the other from the Asian Games host country; Secretary-General; and Treasurer. The Senior Vice-President's post will rotate yearly among the four zonal Vice Presidents.

5. The OCA General Assembly will meet yearly with a quorum being 15 members.
6. The OCA authority and responsibilities will rest with the General Assembly, the Bureau, and the office-bearers. The General Assembly has the final authority on all matters concerning the OCA Council. The Bureau handles control, supervision, and administration of Council business. The office bearers' duties are similar to those of the IF office holders with respect to the OCA.
7. English shall be the official language.
8. The OCA will assign Olympic Solidarity courses in Asia.

TABLE 3.1
Olympic Council of Asia NOCs Zone Distribution

EAST ASIA
1. China
2. DPR Korea
3. Hong Kong
4. Japan
5. Korea
6. Macau
7. Mongolia
8. Chinese Taipei

SOUTH CENTRAL ASIA
1. Afghanistan
2. Bangladesh
3. Bhutan
4. India
5. Maldives
6. Nepal
7. Pakistan
8. Sri Lanka

SOUTHEAST ASIA
1. Brunei
2. Myanmar (Burma)
3. Indonesia
4. Laos
5. Malaysia
6. Philippines
7. Singapore
8. Thailand
9. Vietnam

WEST ASIA
1. Bahrain
2. Iran
3. Jordan
4. Kazakhstan
5. Kuwait
6. Kyrghyzstan
7. Lebanon
8. Oman
9. Palestine
10. Qatar
11. Saudi Arabia
12. Syria
13. Tadjikistan
14. Turkmenistan
15. United Arab Emirates
16. Uzbekistan
17. Yemen

There are five standing committees in the OCA:

1. Rules Committee examines the Rules and Bylaws for addition, change or amending.
2. Finance Committee does financial planning, creates budget estimates and account statements, audits major council expenditure, and raises funds.
3. Sports Development and Improvement Committee raises the sport standard in Asia for athletes, officials, and administrators through educational programs.
4. Information and Statistics Committee prepares and disseminates, as needed, statistics, media reports, and teaching materials relative to Asian sport.
5. Sports Medicine Committee improves Asian sport by conducting research on injuries, dietary requirements, training programs, and advising on medical needs and sanitary services at the Asian Games to include prohibited drugs (Olympic Council of Asia, 1991).

Association of Oceania National Olympic Committees

At the September 1981 meeting of the IOC in Baden Baden, Germany, IOC President Juan Antonio Samaranch encouraged sport development through regional organizations. It was at this meeting that the National Olympic Committee of Oceania was discussed. The first three goals of the organization would be the promotion of Olympism, the allocation of Olympic Solidarity funds, and the creation of a constitution. The NOCs present for this discussion were from Australia, Fiji, New Zealand, and New Guinea (Association of Oceania National Olympic Committees, 1992b).

On February 23, 1982, the first meeting of the Oceania National Olympic Committee (ONOC) was held in Melbourne, Australia. At this meeting the ONOC Constitution was adopted.

TABLE 3.2
Oceania National Olympic Committee Members

1. American Samoa	7. Papua New Guinea
2. Australia	8. Solomon Islands
3. Cook Islands	9. Tonga
4. Fiji	10. Vanuatu
5. Guam	11. Western Samoa
6. New Zealand	

Over the years the ONOC has grown to include 11 countries (Table 3.2). These countries are served by three commissions or committees. The Development Commission primarily sees to improving sport through the allocation of the Olympic Solidarity Programs for sport development, IOC Scholarships, and Oceania Olympic Training Center

Scholarships. In seeing to the efficient administration of these programs, the Development Commission helps to improve funding and increases the span of sport people serviced (Association of Oceania National Olympic Committees, 1992b).

Medical and Finance are the other ONOC Commissions. Although the authors do not have the listing of their responsibilities, it is fair to conjecture that each deals with similar topics of like committees in the IOC and the Olympic Council of Asia.

European Olympic Committees

On 17th October, 1975, the European Olympic Committees (OEC), formerly the Association of the European National Olympic Committees (AENOC), created statutes by which they today are organized and governed (Association of the European National Olympic Committees, 1992). The main aims of this nonprofit organization are

1. The spreading of the Olympic ideals throughout Europe in cooperation with the International Olympic Committee, the Association of National Olympic Committees and the continental Olympic associations;
2. Youth education through sport for the "construction of a better and more peaceful world" (p.2);
3. Enhancing cooperation between the European NOCs through cooperative educational pursuits and "the defence of common attitudes" (p.2); and
4. The Olympic Solidarity program development.

As with other Olympic continental associations, English is one of the official languages. For EOC French is the other official language and the language used relative to any translational disputes. In addition, at the General Assembly, simultaneous translation is also provided in German, Russian, and Spanish.

The EOC consists of the NOCs of the European continent. With the dissolution of the Soviet Union, Yugoslavia, and Czechoslovakia, this NOC list is growing. However, a new country does not automatically become an EOC member by achieving its sovereign independence. Remember, first the country must become a member of the IOC. Only then can it be considered for a continental Olympic association. For the EOC, two-thirds of the members attending the General Assembly must approve a country's membership request. Then, after its dues have been paid, the country's NOC becomes an EOC member. Currently there are 45 members (Table 3.3).

According to the EOC *Statutes* (1992), there are five official groups within the organization: General Assembly, Executive Committee, Permanent Commissions, Adhoc Commissions or Working Groups, and Auditors.

General Assembly

The highest authority of EOC is the General Assembly, which is composed of member representatives. The functions of this group include approving reports and account statements, approving budgets, and adopting activities. An important responsibility is to select its representative to the influential Association of National Olympic Committees from which the Olympic agenda is influenced.

Executive Committee

EOC's Executive Committee is composed of 11 members: President, Vice-President, Secretary-General, and 8 members. The members, with the exception of the Secretary-General, serve a maximum of two consecutive 4 year terms. The group meets at least twice yearly in order to conduct the business as decided upon by the General Assembly, including appointing ad hoc commissions and awarding honorary distinctions.

TABLE 3.3
European Olympic Committees Members

Albania	France	Monaco
Andorra	Georgia	The Netherlands
Armenia	Germany	Norway
Austria	Great Britian	Poland
Azerbaijan	Greece	Portugal
Belarus	Hungary	Romania
Belgium	Iceland	Russia
Bosnia and Herzegovina*	Ireland	San Marino
Bulgaria	Italy	Slovenia
Croatia	Latvia	Spain
Cyprus	Liechtenstein	Sweden
Czechoslovakia	Lithuania	Switzerland
Denmark	Luxembourg	Turkey
Estonia	Malta	Ukraine
Finland	Moldova	Yugoslavia

• Provisional Member as of November 2, 1992

From the Executive Committee, the President represents EOC in dealing with legal rights and duties, including signing EOC contracts. The Secretary-General is charged with administering the day-to-day operation of the Secretariat. In addition, this person may represent EOC at international meetings, as does the President.

Permanent Commissions

EOC permanent commissions are:

1. Preparation of the Olympic Games,
2. Marketing and Finances,
3. Technical Cooperation,
4. Medical and Scientific,
5. Juridical,
6. Press.

The Chairmen of the permanent commissions are Executive Committee members. This is advantageous because each commission is assured that it has a voice at the decision-making level, especially because it is the Executive Committee that dictates the functions and responsibilities of the Permanent Commissions.

Ad Hoc Commissions or Working Groups

The Executive Committee recommends ad hoc commissions to study and report on special questions not addressed by the permanent commissions.

Auditors

The General Assembly selects three auditors to check the finances as reported by the Secretary-General. The primary revenue sources to fund EOC work include membership fees and Olympic Solidarity subsidies.

Pan American Sports Organization

Serving North, South, and Central America for promotion of the Olympic movement is the Pan American Sports Organization (PASO). It was formed on August 3, 1948, to promote sport through the Americas' NOCs and to conduct the Pan American Games. PASO is a nondiscriminatory organization. Indeed, it specifies non-discrimination based on "sex," which the other regional Olympic associations do not. The Permanent Headquarters is in Mexico City with the PASO President hosting the Executive Offices wherever he or she lives (Pan American Sports Organization, 1989).

PASO functions and objectives are

1. To further the ideals of Olympism,
2. To work with the Americas' NOCs in order to promote sport education and access to sport consultants,
3. To promote the Pan American Games in accordance with the *Olympic Charter*,
4. To establish and promote "bonds of friendship" among the American peoples and with other regional Olympic organizations, IFs, and ANOC,
5. To coordinate the Olympic and the Pan American Solidarity Programs,
6. To advise and recommend rule changes to international sports organizations and to help them when needed.

PASO's official languages are Spanish and English. However, if there is a question of meaning, the Spanish version takes precedence. Interestingly, PASO has selected its motto to be "America, Espirito, Sport, Fraternite," two Spanish and two English words.

Membership in PASO shall be reserved for those national Olympic committees from the Americas that are recognized by the IOC. The PASO Executive Committee recommends and the General Assembly approves new members (Table 3.4).

TABLE 3.4
Pan American Sports Organization Members

NORTH ZONE	CENTER ZONE	SOUTH ZONE
1. Bahamas	1. Antigua	1. Argentina
2. Belize	2. Aruba	2. Bolivia
3. Bermuda	3. Barbados	3. Brazil
4. British Virgin Islands	4. Colombia	4. Chile
5. Canada	5. Costa Rica	5. Ecuador
6. Cayman Islands	6. El Salvador	6. Guyana
7. Cuba	7. Grenada	7. Paraguay
8. Dominican Republic	8. Honduras	8. Peru
9. Haiti	9. Netherlands Antilles	9. St. Vincent & The Grenadines
10. Jamaica	10. Nicaragua	10. Surinam
11. Mexico	11. Panama	11. Trinidad & Tobago
12. Puerto Rico	12. Venezuela	12. Uruguay
13. United States		
14. Virgin Islands		

Control and administration of PASO is held by the General Assembly, the Executive Committee, and the President with the executive authority given by the PASO *Statutes and Regulations* (Pan American Sports Organization, 1989).

The General Assembly can be Ordinary or Extraordinary. The Ordinary General Assembly meets to

1. Act for the "purposes and aims of PASO,"
2. Elect Honorary Members,
3. Invite special members to session meetings,
4. Warn, admonish, fine, or suspend the rights of a member,
5. Amend PASO statutes or regulations,
6. Accept or reject reports,
7. Elect Executive Committee members, and
8. Approve the next Pan American Games program.

The Extraordinary General Assembly can only address that (those) issue(s) for which it was called (Pan American Sports Organization, 1989).

The PASO Executive Committee, which meets twice yearly, consists of the President, three Vice-Presidents, Secretary General, Treasurer, and seven members. The three Vice-Presidents shall be elected to represent each of the North, Center, and South Zones, respectively. In order to ensure a continued equality of zone representation, the remaining nine positions must also be divided among evenly between the three zones. All office holders are elected for 4 years but may be re-elected. Interestingly, Honorary Members and Ex-Officio Members are members of the Executive Committee but have no voting rights.

In addition to the above, the PASO (1989) *Statutes* list the following powers and duties of the Executive Committee:

1. To enforce resolutions of the General Assembly,
2. To call General Assemblies,
3. To receive reports from special commissions, which it creates and dissolves,
4. To promote and check the planning and administration of the Pan American Games,
5. To promote the interests of PASO members through maintaining a good working relationship with the IOC and the IFs,
6. To administer PASO's financial affairs,
7. To promote sport education, including sport medicine,
8. To ensure press relations by providing adequate facilities for the mass media,
9. To decide on nontechnical controversies between PASO members, and
10. To regulate internal functioning including awards and honors.

An example of a PASO meeting called for a special situation generated the *Acapulco Charter* (Pan American Sports Organization, 1992). This document, signed in Acapulco, Mexico, on May 1, 1992, helped to delineate the power and responsibility of the Olympic family- IOC, IFs, NOCs, and NFs. Although nonbinding, the agreement also sought to strengthen the Pan American Games competition.

As would be expected, PASO's power and responsibility rests with the President -- by direct duties or as the presider of the Executive Committee and the General Assembly.

The additional power and duties of this office include

1. To sign necessary documents
2. To authorize PASO expenses and contracts
3. To monitor PASO rules and regulations
4. To represent PASO international meetings
5. To call Executive Committee meetings or General Assemblies
6. To designate special commissions
7. To handle emergencies as he or she sees necessary, and
8. To supervise the accounting of the Pan American Games organizing Committee.

The Secretary General has the duty to administer the daily PASO business affairs. This person's duties primary deal with maintaining accurate records of PASO's activities by attending Executive Committee Meetings and the General Assembly and ensuring that PASO's Secretariat performs the duties prescribed by the resolutions.

PASO (1989) duties are also performed by the other office holders:

1. The Vice-Presidents acts at the pleasure of the President.
2. The Treasurer keeps the accounting, presents the financial statements, and works with the President to increase PASO funding.

3. The zone members enforce PASO's Regulation and Statutes.

Association of National Olympic Committees of Africa

The Association of National Olympic Committees of Africa (ANOCA) is headquartered in Yaounde, Cameroon. As with other IOC regional associations, its primary aims are upholding the *Olympic Charter* and the promotion of sport in Africa (Association of National Olympic Committees of Africa, 1989a).

ANOCA's *Constitution* (1989a) is most specific about discrimination. Clause 4 has three references to this topic: 4.7 "right for all to practice sports and physical activities," 4.9 "help African NOCs combat all forms of racial, political and religious discrimination within the Olympic Movement", 4.10 "encourage the participation of women in the Olympic Movement" (p.2). Section 4.10 is particularly significant because many of ANOCA's member countries have followers of Islam whose religious and/or cultural beliefs do not encourage women's participation in many of the sports of the Olympic Games. One can foresee this being a problem in Africa, as well as the world over, as cultures mix.

ANOCA has three administrative bodies — the General Assembly, the Executive Committee, and the Secretariat General. The General Assembly is composed of NOC delegates, Executive Committee members, and IOC members from Africa (Association of National Olympic Committees of Africa, 1989a). It meets once every two years. An interesting aspect of the ANOCA *Constitution* (1989a) is that it mandates the General Assembly agenda to include various items, for example, adoption of minutes, auditor's report, budget approval, elections.

The Executive Committee of ANOCA consists of the president, three viceresidents, seven zonal representatives (Table 3.5), the secretary general, and the treasurer general. The Executive Committee is elected for 4 year terms which are renewable and members receive no salary. Their jobs, as expected, are to implement the General Assembly's decisions.

The Secretary General and his permanent administration manage the ongoing ANOCA business, for example, correspondence and distribution of minutes.

ANOCA has three official languages — Arabic, English and French. Unlike many organizations that have one language for interpretation purposes, if there is a disagreement, ANOCA's Executive Committee makes the final decision on exact meaning (Association of National Olympic Committees of Africa, 1989a). The Executive Committee meeting shall be conducted in English and French. In these two languages the minutes will also be published. However, any speaker may use the language of his or her choice provided translations are provided (Association of National Olympic Committees of Africa, 1989b).

Although not an IOC regional organization, mention must be made of the Supreme Council for Sport in Africa (SCSA). SCSA has long been a powerful force within the sport movement in Africa. Funded by the Organization for African Unity, SCSA has been a traditional force for enhancing society in Africa by promoting free sport (M. Whitfield, personal communication, February 21, 1995).

TABLE 3.5
Association of National Olympic Committees of Africa Zones

ZONE 1	ZONE 2	ZONE 3
Algeria	Gambia	Benin
Libya	Guinea	Burkina Faso
Morocco	Mauritania	Cote d'Ivoire
Tunisia	Senegal	Ghana
	Sierra Leone	Liberia
	(Cape Verde)	Niger
	(Guinea Bissau)	Nigeria
		Togo

ZONE 4	ZONE 5	ZONE 6
Angola	Egypt	Botswana
Cameroon	Ethiopia	Lesotho
Chad	Kenya	Malawi
Central African Republic	Uganda	Mozambique
Equatorial Guinea	Somalia	Swaziland
Gabon	Sudan	Zambia
Rwanda	Tanzania	Zimbabwe
Zaire		
Burundi		
(Sao Tome & Principe)		

ZONE 7
Djibouti
Madagascar
Mauritius
Seychelles
(Comores)

Concluding Summary

Many people who love sports, especially the Olympics, have very little knowledge of the entire realm of the Olympic Movement. Indeed, a prime motivator for this text was the realization that many of tomorrow's sport leaders had no idea what an international or national federation was, what Olympism meant or how throughout the world athletic development was fostered through Olympic regional organizations. Possibly this chapter alone will do more to further one's understanding of the governance of international sport than any other within this text.

Within the Olympic Movement the idealism of Olympism is the consideration. However, as with any movement, after the founder, Pierre de Coubertin, is gone the idealism must continue to work its way into the realism of an organization with a managerial structure with rules, regulations, general assemblies, and committees. With an understanding of the Olympic Movement's structure including national Olympic committees, international federations, national federations, and regional sport groupings, a more clear picture of governance will emerge.

Discussion, Analysis, Application, and Debate

Issues for Discussion

1. How would Coubertin's educational objectives for reviving the Olympics be viewed in today's world?
2. From what you know of the Olympics and the Olympic Movement, do present-day Olympic athletes subscribe to "the lofty aims of Olympism"?
3. Assuming you are a member of the International Olympic Committee, how would you promote the Olympic Movement in your country?
4. With American football growing in worldwide popularity, how would an amateur American football world championship be organized in order to achieve equitable representation from the continental associations?
5. Within the membership of an international federation, show how the president and the executive director would each establish powerful positions.

Matters for Analysis

1. The IOC president is continuously called upon to help ensure the continuation of the Olympic Movement and the Olympic Games. From what is presented in this text and from what you know from other sources, create the ideal credentials for the next IOC president.
2. If you were the IF executive director of your favorite sport, how would you organize your administrative staff in order to accomplish the tasks for which you are responsible?

Application

Contact your country's NOC in order to gather material on the programs it offers. After studying the programs, create and/or prescribe programs to further enhance its Olympic mission.

Ethical Debate

Olympism is presented here as an ideal that is to be sought for the good of sport. The success at obtaining this ideal has been questioned by some. Is Olympism obtainable in today's world, which requires monetary considerations be addressed in order to maintain the Olympics as they are conducted today?

References

Association of National Olympic Committees of Africa (1989a). *Constitution.* Yaounde, Cameroon: Association of National Committees of Africa.

Association of National Olympic Committees of Africa (1989b). *Rules of Procedure.* Yaounde, Cameroon: Association of National Olympic Committees of Africa.

Association of Oceania National Olympic Committees (1992a). *1991-1992 Yearbook.* Wellington, New Zealand: Association of Oceania National Olympic Committees.

Association of Oceania National Olympic Committees (1992b). *Annual Report and Statement of Accounts.* Wellington, New Zealand: Association of Oceania National Olympic Committees.

Association of the European National Olympic Committees (1992). *Statutes.* Rome, Italy: Association of the European National Olympic Committees.

Chalip, L. (1992). The revival of the modern Olympic Games and Pierre de Coubertin's thoughts on sport for all. *Proceedings of the 31st session of the International Olympic Academy* (pp. 65-71). Lausanne: International Olympic Committee.

Czula, R. (1978). Sport and Olympic idealism. *International Review of Sport Sociology, 13* (2), 67-79.

Czula, R., Flanagan, L., & Nasatir, D. (1976). A multidimensional analysis of Olympic idealism. *Review of Sport and Leisure, 1,* 1-14.

Federation Internationale de Basketball (1990), *General Bye-Laws and Internal Regulations.* Munich: Federation Internationale de Basketball.

Hoberman, J. (1986). *The Olympic crisis.* New Rochelle, NY: Aristide D. Caratzas.

International Amateur Athletic Federation (1990-1991). *Handbook,* 2nd ed. London, England: International Amateur Athletic Federation.

International Olympic Committee. (1993). *Olympic Charter.* Lausanne, Switzerland.

International Weightlifting Federation (1989). *Handbook.* Budapest, Hungary: International Weightlifting Federation.

Landry, F. (1990). The Olympic movement: Grandeurs and paradoxes of its development and successes. In B-I. Koh (Ed.), *Toward one world beyond all barriers* (Vol. 2) (pp. 51-69). Seoul: Poong Nam.

MacAlloon, J.J. (1987). Encountering our others: Social science and Olympic sport. In S-P. Kang, J. MacAloon, & R. DaMatta (Eds.), *The Olympics and cultural exchange* (pp. 1-41). Seoul: Hanyang University Institute for Ethnological Studies.

Nafziger, J.A.R. (1988). *International sports law*. Dobbs Ferry, NY: Transitional Publishers.

Olympic Council of Asia (1991). *Constitution and Rules*. Eastbourne, United Kingdom: Olympic Council of Asia.

Pan American Sports Organization (1989). *Statutes*. Mexico City, Mexico: Pan American Sports Organization.

Pan American Sports Organization (1992). *Acapulco Charter*. Mexico City, Mexico: Pan American Sports Organization.

Segrave, J.O. (1988). Toward a definition of Olympism. In J. Segrave & D. Chu (Eds.), *The Olympic Games in transition* (pp. 149-161). Champaign, IL: Human Kinetics.

Simson, V., & Jennings, A. (1992). *The lords of the rings: Power, money and drugs in the modern Olympics*. Toronto: Stoddart.

Vipond, P. (1993). Olympic Solidarity: Organization, objectives, activities. *Proceedings of the 32nd session of the International Olympic Committee* (pp. 178-185). Lausanne: International Olympic Committee.

CHAPTER FOUR

THE INTERNATIONAL

DEVELOPMENT OF SPORT

Overview

This chapter examines the relationship between sport and culture in order to probe the dynamics of sport diffusion. The chapter begins with a discussion of the Olympic sport program, Eurocentrism in Olympic-style sport, and sport growth outside an Olympic framework.

The discussion then turns to relations between sport and culture. It is observed that although a sport practice may be similar across cultures, its meaning may be quite different in different cultures. Consequently, developing a sport internationally is a matter of finding ways to fit a sport into new cultural settings.

The chapter then examines the dynamics of sport diffusion. It recommends three strategies for diffusing sport: adapting sports practices to fit new cultural settings, fostering the interest of elites, and working to kindle community interest. Implications for developing sport internationally are discussed.

Introduction

Although the governance of Olympic sports aptly illustrates the institutions that administer international sport, the vast majority of sports are not, in fact, included on the Olympic program. Sports governed by the International Federations (IFs) listed in Table 4-1 are designated in the *Olympic Charter* as Olympic sports. After each Olympic Games, the IOC reviews the program and determines whether new sports and/or new events can be added. At this time, IFs that are recognized by the IOC, but that are not included on the Olympic program can petition to be included.

No IF is obligated to keep the sport it governs on the Olympic program. In fact 11 sports that were once included in the Olympic Games are no longer represented on the program: cricket, croquet, golf, jeu de paume, lacrosse, motor boating, polo, rackets, roque, rugby, and tug of war. Tennis left the Olympic program after the 1924 Games, but returned 60 years later, in 1984. There has been some interest in recent years in

TABLE 4.1
IFs Governing Olympic Sports

Games of the Olympiad
International Amateur Athletic Federation (IAAF)
International Rowing Federation (FISA)
International Badminton Federation (IBF)
International Baseball Association (IBA)
International Basketball Federation (FIBA)
International Amateur Boxing Association (AIBA)
International Canoeing Federation (FIC)
International Amateur Cycling Federation (FIAC)
International Equestrian Federation (FEI)
International Fencing Federation (FIE)
International Association Football Federation (FIFA)
International Gymnastics Federation (FIG)
International Weightlifting Federation (IWF)
International Handball Federation (IHF)
International Hockey Federation (FIH)
International Judo Federation (IJF)
International Amateur Wrestling Federation (FILA)
International Amateur Swimming Federation (FINA)
International Modern Pentathlon and Biathlon Union (UIPMB)
International Tennis Federation (ITF)
International Table Tennis Federation (ITTF)
International Shooting Union (UIT)
International Archery Federation (FITA)
International Volleyball Federation (FIVB)
International Yacht Racing Union (IYRU)

Olympic Winter Games
International Bobsleigh and Tobogganing Federation (FIBT)
International Ice Hockey Federation (IIHF)
International Luge Federation (FIL)
International Modern Pentathlon and Biathlon Union (UIPMB)
International Skating Union (ISU)
International Skiing Federation (FIS)
World Curling Federation (WCF)

returning golf to the Olympic program. Motor boating would be unable to return to the Olympic program because current rules forbid inclusion of any sport that depends on mechanical propulsion.

In order for a sport to be included on the summer Olympic program, it must be practiced by men in at least 75 countries on four continents and by women in at least 40 countries on three continents. To be included on the winter Olympic program, it must be practiced in at least 25 countries on three continents.

As the size of the Games has grown and the number of participating non-European NOCs has expanded, two opposing forces have emerged regarding the Olympic program. One force presses for program growth to slow; the other force presses for inclusion of new sports.

The sheer size of the Olympic program has become a matter of increasing concern. On one day of summer Olympic competition, as many as 18 different sports may be contested, generating over 100 hours of competition (Chalip, 1987); and the number of events has grown with each successive Olympic Games. Consequently, the number of requisite venues and media sites has risen, as has the necessary size of the Olympic Village, which houses the athletes. Some argue that the Games are becoming too cumbersome and expensive. There has consequently been substantial support for limiting the number of sports on the Olympic program, although a precise formula for doing so has not been agreed upon (Lekarska, 1988).

Meanwhile, the preponderance of sports on the Olympic program have European origins. This has animated pressures for inclusion of non-Western sports. Critics of the current program note that the Olympic idea has its roots in Western civilization, and that modern Olympism emerges from European concepts of competition and victory (Seppanen, 1989). Not only are indigenous Asian, African, and American sports underrepresented, but there also is scant possibility for performances to be measured in terms other than "faster, higher, stronger." For example, Eichberg (1984) criticizes the inability of the "faster, higher, stronger" criteria to provide a basis for including expressive activities like dance (which are focal forms of physical activity in many cultures, particularly those of Africa), or meditative activities like tai chi or yoga (which are traditional forms of physical activity in Asia). The key point is that sport is a category whose boundaries vary substantially from one culture to the next.

The Eurocentrism of Olympic (and Olympic-style) sport has generated substantial controversy. Kidd (1989) worries that the emerging dominance of Olympic sports has precipitated declines in traditional (ethnic, non-Olympic) sports. Despite the decline of many ethnic sports, Cheska (1987) cites examples from Afghanistan and North America of traditional sports that have found renewed popularity as participants seek to reassert an ethnic identity not embodied by Olympic-style sport. Liponski (1987) reports a clandestine meeting of 30 Asian and African delegates to the International Olympic Academy in 1983. At that meeting, the delegates declared that "Olympism is basically a European idea, unacceptable for non-Europeans in its present form [and] the Olympic Games ... must be abandoned as an undesirable form of neo-colonialism" (p. 513).

Meanwhile, many sports continue to grow outside the framework of Olympic competition. For example, racquetball had a base of slightly over 50,000 players in 1968, almost all of whom were in the United States. By 1988, the sport claimed 14 million players in 75 countries on five continents. The International Racquetball Federation (IRF) was founded in 1979 to serve as the IF for the sport. The IRF was recognized by the IOC in 1981. Racquetball has since become a medal sport in the Pan American Games, the Central American Games, and the South American Games. The IRF seeks to have the sport included in other regional games (such as the Asian Games and the Mediterranean Games) and the Olympic Games.

Although the example of the IRF illustrates how rapidly a relatively new sport can grow, it should not be assumed that all (or even most) sports seek inclusion on the Olympic program. Consider the example of rugby, whose IF, the Rugby Football Union (RFU), founded in 1871, is older than the IOC. Rugby left the Olympic Movement after the 1924 Olympic Games. Since that time, the RFU has promoted development of the sport throughout the world. The game is now played on six continents. In 1987, the RFU established an international championship event, the Webb Ellis Cup, which is contested every 4 years.

It is beyond the scope of this text to describe the structure or progress of every sport. However, the discussion above highlights two related matters that managers seeking to promote or develop sport internationally must understand: (a) relations between sport and culture and (b) the dynamics of sport diffusion.

Sport and Culture

In standard English usage, sport typically refers to physical contests. Physical skills are compared socially, and there is typically a victorious contestant or team and one or more vanquished contestants or teams. However, the category sport is not a cultural universal. For example, Whiting (1989) notes:

> Before the Meiji restoration [1867-1912], the western concept of
> sport had been virtually unknown in Japan. There was sumo wres-
> tling, which had developed out of fourth-century Shinto [religious]
> rites, and horseback riding, swimming, and kendo, among others,
> which were done for military training purposes. The idea of athletics
> for fun, however, was an alien one. There was, in fact, no Japanese
> equivalent for the word sport. (p. 28)

Nor do all cultures measure the quality of sport performances in terms of winning and losing. It is useful to illustrate this point by reference to sports practice in three non-Western cultures: Eskimo, Pueblo, and Timbira.

Eskimo culture emphasizes the importance of cooperation. Thus, Eskimo physical contests are likely to emphasize communal esprit de corps, rather than winning or losing. For example, the game of marbles as practiced among the Tununak villagers of Nelson Island in Alaska, is really a cooperative test of skill. Each player arrives with one marble and leaves with one marble. It is the shared test of skill that is important; there are no winners or losers as in the typical Western case. When Tununak children were introduced to the Western version of the game--winner take all--they rejected it. One anthropologist describes the games of Nelson Island this way: "The kind of competition I saw was one in which everyone tried to do his best but not at anyone else's expense" (Ager, 1976, p. 82).

The notion of "sports hero" and the celebration of champions that is common in Olympic-style sport are rejected by many cultures. Ruth Benedict (1934) describes the attitude among Pueblo Indians, for whom foot races were an important form of competition:

> The ideal man ... is a person of dignity and affability who has never tried to lead, and who has never called forth comment from his neighbors... Even in contests of skill like their foot races, if a man wins habitually he is debarred from running. They are interested in a game that a number can play with even chances, and an outstanding runner spoils the game: they will have none of him. (p. 95)

In some cultures, the outcome of a sport performance may have scant significance. In this case, the occurrence of a sport event is more important than its outcome. For example, Hye-Kerkdal (1956) describes the social system of the Timbira in Brazil. Their society is organized in terms of religious and social polarities. Log racing symbolizes those polarities, and thus is significant. The symbolisms of the races are important to the Timbira, but the outcomes of the races are not. Although the races are vigorously contested, their outcomes have no effect on the status of participants or teams, nor is there any extrinsic reward.

These examples illustrate reasons that Olympic-style sport is rejected as "unacceptable" or "neo-colonial" by persons from some non-Western cultures. Sports practices that emphasize competitive individualism might seem inappropriate or even threatening to persons whose culture emphasizes cooperation over competition. Sport ceremonies that celebrate winners might threaten the egalitarian social customs that some cultures extol. The emphasis on sport result over sport performance might seem misdirected to spectators whose culture focuses their attention on the things a sport performance is intended to symbolize, rather than on outcomes.

Nevertheless, the practice of Western sports and Olympic-style sport competition continues to grow. It would seem easy, therefore, to dismiss illustrations like those above as aberrant, or as the residual behaviors of relatively primitive cultures. Yet those examples point the way to a more fundamental insight: The fact that a sport's *practice* may be similar across cultures does not imply that a sport's *meaning* is the same in different cultures. Since this insight is pivotal for the development and promotion of sport internationally, it is useful to illustrate it by briefly comparing baseball in Japan with baseball in the United States.

The game of baseball would seem to be almost identical in Japan and the United States--identical enough that American and Japanese teams frequently compete against each other. Yet analysts (e.g., Boersema, 1979; Obojski, 1975) have noted subtle differences in the expectations that management and the public have for players. For example, complaining, salary disputes, special treatment, and criticism of officials--which are all common to baseball in the United States--are simply not tolerated in Japanese baseball. Meanwhile, Japanese players are expected to undergo practice schedules that would not be tolerated by U.S. players. The difference in expectations for player behavior in the United States and Japan is typically understood by contrasting U.S. values of rugged individualism with Japanese emphases on politeness and selfless dedication to the team. Clearly, cultural differences have led to subtle differences in team management and training.

However, there is a less obvious difference in the meanings attached to baseball in the two cultures. In Japan, the game is understood to cultivate and measure the player's moral and spiritual character in ways that would seem foreign (and possibly even harsh) to U.S. players and fans. Suishu Tobita, who has been described as "the god of Japanese baseball" (Whiting, 1989, p. 3), wrote:

> The purpose of training is not health but the forging of the soul, and a strong soul is born from strong practice. To hit like a shooting star, to catch a ball beyond one's capabilities ... such beautiful plays are not the result of technique but the result of good deeds. For all these are made possible by a strong spiritual power. Student baseball must be the baseball of self-discipline, or trying to attain the truth, just as in Zen Buddhism. It must be much more than just a hobby. (quoted in Whiting, 1989, p. 38)

In the case of Japanese baseball, we see that the sport came to symbolize values that are central to Japanese culture. Consequently, the practice of baseball was readily adopted, though the meanings attached to that practice were somewhat different from those familiar to its American inventors. Whiting (1989) describes baseball's transmission to Japan this way:

> The Japanese found the one-on-one battle between pitcher and batter similar in psychology to sumo and the martial arts. It involved split-second timing and a special harmony of mental and physical strength. As such, the Ministry of Education deemed it good for the national character. (p. 28)

However, few sports are so easily reinterpreted. The task of developing a sport internationally and promoting its practice in diverse cultural settings requires more than the creation of organizational infrastructures and the distribution of promotional materials. Sport development requires the international sport manager to find ways to fit a sport into new cultural settings. It is a task of sport diffusion.

Sport Diffusion

How does a sport developed in one nation or culture come to be practiced in another? This section reviews key studies of sport diffusion to derive implications for the development of sport internationally. Three strategies can be identified: (a) adapting sports practices to fit new cultural settings, (b) fostering the interest of elites (i.e., persons who wield political, social, and/or economic power), and (c) working entrepreneurially in communities to kindle interest in a sport. Each of these strategies is reviewed below. Although they are described independently, the strategies are not autonomous. In practice, two or all three might be combined to address specific needs or opportunities.

Adapting Sports Practices

The martial arts are among the few Asian sports to have been enthusiastically adopted by Western countries. Yet the practice of those sports in the west has been adapted, in part, to Western cultural values. For example, in Japan the judoka (i.e., the practitioner of judo) has traditionally been taught to approach judo as a means by which to obtain self-awareness, mastery of the senses, and insight into human interactions. Competition is not the objective; competition is a path by which one learns a more perfect existence.

Yet, this objective is not commonly the focus of judo instruction in the West (Clark, 1986). Instead, the sport has been diffused into the West as a means of self-defense and as a form of competition. Its philosophical roots in Zen and Bushido are deemphasized in Western settings, at least until the practitioner has become fully committed to the sport.

> Nevertheless, Japanese cultural elements have not been purged: The rank-ordering structure, style of teaching, and ritualization of certain practices were seen as the vehicles of cultural transmission. The use of Japanese language, the explanation of "essence" of behavior (i.e., bowing, movements), and the constant and consistent referral to "respect" and "obligation" were seen as ways to socialize participants toward accepting judo (and thus Japanese) values. (Clark, 1986, p. 248)

In other words, Western participants are recruited into the sport in terms appropriate to Western cultures. They are allowed to approach judo as a sport and as a form of self-defense. However, the methods of instruction are designed to socialize the participant into a subculture wherein root Japanese values endure. Thus, as the practitioner advances in the sport, he or she is encouraged to reorient from a Western to a Japanese approach. The participant begins in a sport environment whose purposes seem consistent with those of Western sports. Training in the sport then teaches the participant to envision additional possibilities.

Allison and Luschen (1979) provide another example of a sport's adaptation to its cultural setting. They compared the ways basketball is played by Navaho and Anglo adolescents in the southwestern United States. They found that when Navahos play the game against Anglos, their play is consistent with Anglo styles and rules. However, when Navahos play the sport among themselves, they adapt it to a format that is consistent with their culture's cooperative and egalitarian social ethic. Among Navahos, the competition is less between players than with oneself. Consequently, Navaho players commonly allow each other to travel with the ball, double dribble, and step out of bounds-rule violations that are not tolerated among Anglo players. Similarly, in the Navaho version of the game, social sanctions are invoked against individual or team play that is deemed to flaunt skill. For example, one team will not run up the score against another; nor is play ever built around a "star" player. Skill is welcomed, but players are discouraged from seeking public recognition of that skill.

This example is instructive because it illustrates how competition in a sport can be adapted to a non-Western cultural setting. Although the version of basketball played within Navaho culture differs in important ways from the "standard" game, Navaho players are able to adjust their play when playing non-Navaho teams. Consequently, the sport can be developed in Navaho settings, and Navaho teams can compete with Anglo teams.

Fostering the Interest of Elites

Adapting a sport to a new cultural setting will not ensure that it will attract participants or spectators. When a sport is first introduced, it is nothing more than a curiosity. Public enthusiasm for the sport must be cultivated. The patronage of elite (i.e., politically, socially, or economically powerful) members of the target culture can promote public enthusiasm.

There are two reasons: (a) The public attention to elites focuses public attention on matters in which elites are interested; (b) elites often command the resources and influence required to develop the requisite infrastructure to foster the sport's growth.

Appadurai's (1987) study of cricket's diffusion into India provides a useful illustration. The sport was introduced into India during the 19th century by the British colonial administration. Initially, the sport was played among British residents. However, the sport rapidly captured the interest of the Indian aristocracy. Three reasons were important: (a) The sport allowed Indian aristocrats to link themselves to the British aristocracy; (b) patronage of the sport provided a means by which Indian aristocrats could ingratiate themselves with the colonial authorities; (c) cricket served as a relatively inexpensive spectacle that Indian aristocrats could provide their subjects.

By the early 20th century princes throughout India were constructing cricket grounds, sponsoring cricket teams, establishing tournaments, and importing coaches. Most importantly, the princes subsidized players, many of whom came from quite humble origins. The resulting social mobility for players furthered interest in the sport among peasants and laborers.

The consequent growth of cricket generated substantial interest in the sport among Indians. This, in turn, focused media attention on cricket. Public interest and media attention made corporate sponsorship of cricket attractive. As the aristocracy declined following Indian independence, Indian corporations took over development of the sport by sponsoring teams and subsidizing players.

An and Sage (1992) provide a contemporary example of ways in which the interest of elites can promote a sport's development. Their analysis of the golf boom in Korea shows how elite support can further a sport's development while simultaneously engendering some domestic opposition.

Prior to 1989, there were 54 golf courses in the Republic of Korea. By 1992, another 135 courses were being developed. Government and corporate elites have actively encouraged the sport's development:

> Golf courses are ... places for politicians to entertain friends and foster political support. They are sites for forming political and social networks and for cementing political and business interests; they are sites for informal political meetings; and, since their golf play is frequently reported in the media, politicians may obtain favorable publicity... Golf in South Korea is creating a new form of leisure activity for the elite, a form of leisure that gives them the feeling and pleasure of high social status. (An & Sage, 1992, p. 378-379)

However, An and Sage report increasing opposition to the golf boom from middle- and working-class Koreans who feel they are bearing a social cost for the sport's development, although reaping none of the rewards. Their opposition has three sources: (a) The construction of new golf courses eliminates land from agricultural and industrial use; (b) the extensive use of chemicals required to maintain the golf courses has intensified problems of pollution; (c) middle-class and working-class Koreans cannot afford to join golf clubs, and therefore do not benefit from the sport's growth.

The example of Korean golf contrasts usefully with the example of Indian cricket.

Elite involvement in Indian cricket served to promote opportunities for participation by most social classes. In fact, participation in cricket served as a means of social mobility. Consequently, public interest and participation grew rapidly, and development of the sport faced scant opposition. In contrast, elite involvement in Korean golf has served to highlight the relative deprivation of middle- and working-class Koreans. Consequently, public opposition to the sport's development intensified.

Working to Kindle Community Interest

Although it can be useful to obtain the commitment of elites to a sport's development, their commitment is not essential. Callede's (1993) study of the diffusion of Basque pelota provides a useful example. Pelota (which is related to jai alai) has long been played in the Basque villages of southern France and northern Spain. Practice of the sport has continued to grow throughout the 20th century. It is now played in at least 10 countries. Its IF, the International Federation of Basque Pelota (FIPB), was founded in 1930.

Initially, the sport spread in Europe and in the Americas as a consequence of contact with Basque communities and Basque migration. The game, long associated with Basque community spirit, was enthusiastically introduced by Basque players to neighboring villagers and to residents of communities to which the players immigrated. Clubs and leagues were organized, and local governments were lobbied to provide dedicated pelota facilities.

The case of Basque pelota is interesting because it illustrates the importance of local-level initiative to further a sport's development. Enthusiastic promotion of the sport by players stimulated creation local clubs and leagues. The consequent growth of participation provided the requisite political clout to compel communities to construct facilities specifically designed for the sport. The presence of dedicated pelota facilities and local clubs has, in turn, nurtured the sport's growth.

Management Implications

International federations (IFs) and their member national federations (NFs) work to promote participation in their respective sports. Meanwhile, an international movement (described in chapter 9) has emerged, independent of the IFs and NFs, to foster development of sports opportunities. Given the continuing concern to elevate sport participation internationally, it is constructive to review implications of what has been said so far.

When working in an unfamiliar culture, the manager must think flexibly about what the persons in the target culture may expect sport to entail. Ceremonies and rituals that are trivial or nonexistent in Western settings may be important elsewhere, as in Timbira log racing (Hye-Kerkdall, 1956) or Japanese baseball (Whiting, 1989). Sport may be expected to serve expressive goals (as in dance) or meditative functions (as in yoga) that are not common to Western sports practice (Eichberg, 1984; Herrigel, 1964; Liponski, 1987). The cooperative elements of sport may be more important in some settings than are its competitive elements, as in Eskimo games (Ager 1976), Navaho basketball (Allison & Luschen, 1979), and Pueblo running (Benedict, 1934).

It is not uncommon for cultural elites to be familiar with Western styles of interaction and Western sports practices. However, persons in the same culture whose experience is less cosmopolitan may not be so flexible. Indeed, the fact that cultural elites can function effectively in Western mode does not imply that they enjoy doing so. It is advantageous for the manager whose assignment requires work in other cultural settings to obtain appropriate training (Bhawuk, 1990; Chesanow, 1985). Many short-term programs designed to prepare the manager for work in other cultures are available. These include simulations, immersions, culture assimilators, role-playing exercises, and university courses. In sport settings, programs designed to train teachers to work with persons of other cultures may also be valuable (Thomas, 1992). The manager can often find appropriate programs through a local university or through state or federal agencies responsible for promoting international trade.

The ways in which a sport is practiced can vary subtly from culture to culture. As we have seen, these variations may play an important role in cultivating participation. In order to determine whether adaptations would be useful and to locate useful adjustments, it may be helpful to work closely with persons from the target population (cf. Rahman, 1985).

The recruitment of local and national elites into the sport development process can help to stimulate indigenous interest in a sport and development of the requisite infrastructure, as with Indian cricket (Appadurai, 1987). The interest of elites is furthered when they have a personal, political, and/or economic stake in the sport's development. However, if opportunities to participate and benefits from participation are not diffused to all social strata, political and social resistance may ensue, as with golf in Korea (An & Sage, 1992).

The creation of local-level clubs and leagues can produce the social and political influence needed to further the development of facilities--provided, of course, that there is sufficient participation (cf., Callede, 1993). Fine (1989) shows that sport organizations must undertake a number of promotional activities if participants are to be attracted and retained. He finds that participation is elevated when sport organizations publicize themselves, lobby for resources, disseminate information about their sport, and facilitate social intercourse among participants. He shows that it is not enough merely to provide a sports opportunity; rather, sport organizations must continually educate their participants, local media, and local officials about the sport--including its methods, needs, and activities. In addition, sports organizations must provide more than training and competition; they must provide opportunities for their members to interact socially.

It is sometimes difficult for the manager who is enthusiastic about a sport to recognize the stumbling blocks to a sport's growth. The manager's enthusiasm makes it difficult for him or her to fathom the reticence of others. This problem is exacerbated when the manager seeks to promote a sport in an unfamiliar culture. Nevertheless, the impact of cultural naivete can be reduced by working alongside persons from the target culture to design programs that meet local interests, needs, and expectations.

Concluding Summary

The majority of the world's sports, particularly those whose origin is not European, are excluded from the Olympic program. Nevertheless, many sports continue to grow and develop outside the framework of Olympic competition. In order to understand the dynamics of sport growth and development, it is useful to examine the relations between sport and culture and the dynamics of sport diffusion.

Cultures vary in what they include under the rubric of sport, and in the processes and outcomes they value. In some cultures, cooperative interaction may be emphasized over competitive outcome. In some cases, the celebration of exceptional sport skill is shunned. Sometimes, the symbolisms of a sport performance are more important than the performance's result. These differences from expectations common to Western sport can be subtle. The sport manager who works internationally should not be fooled into thinking that similarities in the *practice* of sport in different cultures implies any similarity in the *meanings* attached to sport by different cultures.

Three useful techniques to promote the diffusion of sport can be identified: (a) The ways in which a sport is taught and/or contested can be modified to enhance the fit of the sport into a local culture; (b) the interest of local and national elites can be solicited to focus public attention on the sport and to secure requisite resources for development of the sport; (c) local-level participation in the sport can be advanced if locals who already play the sport are helped to teach the sport to others and are aided in the process of establishing clubs and leagues.

Discussion, Analysis, Application, and Debate

Issues for Discussion

1. From the standpoint of a sport's IF, what do you see as the relative advantages and disadvantages for a sport to be included on the Olympic program?
2. What might be the dangers of "Eurocentrism" in international sport?
3. When working in a culture other than your own, how might you go about determining the kinds of expectations members of that culture have for sport? What differences from your own understandings or assumptions might you look for?
4. How would you go about using cultural information to adapt sports practices to the local culture?
5. If you were seeking to obtain the interest of local elites in your sport, what tactics might you employ?
6. What steps would you take to kindle community interest in a new sport?

Matters for Analysis

1. Some sports that are popular internationally have had difficulty establishing themselves in the presence of popular indigenous sports. For example, in the face of U.S. football's popularity, rugby has had difficulty establishing itself in the United States. What special problems are introduced when a popular international sport must compete for attention with a popular indigenous sport? What kinds of stakeholder problems might manifest themselves? How could sport administrators go about differentiating their sport from a popular indigenous one? How might sport administrators circumvent stakeholder resistance?

2. Some sports that are played internationally by both sexes manage to establish
    themselves with only one sex in particular countries. For example, field hockey is
    a popular game for men and women throughout much of the world. However, in
    North America, the men's game is poorly established in comparison to the women's
    game.
    What special problems of sport diffusion become manifest when a sport comes to be
    popularly considered as solely "a women's sport" or solely "a men's sport"? What
    means might sport administrators use to overcome the sex-based stereotyping of
    their sport?
    Overcoming the sex-based stereotyping of a sport is necessary but not sufficient for
    promoting its practice. What other development strategies should be applied? How
    would those be integrated with efforts to overcome sex-based stereotyping?

Application

Identify a sport that is played in your country primarily by a single ethnic group--for
example, bocce (Italians) or Jok'ku (Koreans). Familiarize yourself with any national or
international organizations for this sport. Then develop a strategy for diffusing play of
the sport nationally.

Ethical Debate

Some observers have lamented that international sport emphasizes competition over
cooperation. Some critics worry that the growth of international sports fosters the
expansion of competitiveness. Many traditional cultures value cooperation over
competition. Some analysts have suggested that international cooperation would be
healthier for our planet than international competition has been.

What do you see as the relative merits or drawbacks of developing sport internationally
if it represents and promotes competitiveness? What special concerns, if any, emerge
when sport is being encouraged in cultures that traditionally value cooperation over
competition?

References

Ager, L.P. (1976). The reflection of cultural values in Eskimo children's games.
In D.F. Lancy & B.A. Tindall (Eds.), *The study of play: Problems and prospects* (pp.92-
98). Champaign, IL: Leisure Press.

Allison, M., & Luschen, G. (1979). A comparative analysis of Navaho India and
Anglo basketball sport systems. *International Review of Sport Sociology, 14*(3-4), 75-
86.

An, M., & Sage, G.H. (1992). The golf boom in South Korea: Serving hegemonic
interests. *Sociology of Sport Journal, 9*, 372-384.

Appadurai, A. (1987). Decolonizing the production of culture: Cricket in contemporary India. In S-P. Kang, J. MacAloon, & R. DaMatta (Eds.), *The Olympics and cultural exchange* (pp. 163-190). Seoul: Hanyang University Institute for Ethnological Studies.

Benedict, R. (1934). *Patterns of culture*. New York: Mentor Books.

Bhawuk, D.P.S. (1990). Cross-cultural orientation programs. In R.W. Brislin (Ed.), *Applied cross-cultural psychology* (pp. 325-246). Newbury Park, CA: Sage.

Boersema, J. (1979). Baseball oriental style. *Soldiers, 34*, 28-31.

Callede, J-P. (1993). Basque pelota in the European space: Towards a sociological use of the notions of sporting evolution and diffusion. *International Review for the Sociology of Sport, 28*, 223-243.

Chalip, L. (1987). Multiple narratives, multiple hierarchies: Selective attention and the structure of the Olympic program. In S-P. Kang, J. MacAloon, & R. DaMatta (Eds.), *The Olympics and cultural exchange* (pp. 539-576). Seoul: Hanyang University Institute for Ethnological Studies.

Chesanow, N. (1985). *The world class executive: How to do business like a pro around the world*. New York: Rawson Associates.

Cheska, A.T. (1987). Revival, survival, and revisal: Ethnic identity through "traditional games." In G.A. Fine (Ed.), *Meaningful play, playful meaning* (pp. 145-154). Champaign, IL: Human Kinetics.

Clark, M.W. (1986). Delivery and receipt: Judo instruction in cross-cultural context. In M.L. Krotee & E.M. Jaeger (Eds.), *Comparative physical education and sport* (Vol. 3, pp. 243-251). Champaign, IL: Human Kinetics.

Eichberg, H. (1984). Olympic sport: Neocolonization and alternatives. *International Review for the Sociology of Sport, 19*, 97-106.

Fine, G.A. (1989). Mobilizing fun: Provisioning resources in leisure worlds. *Sociology of Sport Journal, 6*, 319-334.

Herrigel, E. (1964). *Zen in the art of archery*. New York: McGraw-Hill.

Hye-Kerkdal, K. (1956). Wettkampfspiel und dualorganisation bei den Timbira Brasiliens. In J. Haedel (Ed.), *Die wiener schule der volkerkunde* (pp. 504-533). Wein: Springer Verlag.

Kidd, B. (1989). Overview of the Olympic-media relationship. In R. Jackson (Ed.), *The Olympic Movement and the mass media: Past, present and future issues* (pp. 1/3-1/10). Calgary: Hurford.

Lekarska, N. (1988). Problems of the Olympic programme. *Proceedings of the 27th session of the International Olympic Academy* (pp. 93-99). Lausanne: IOC.

Liponski, W. (1987). Olympic universalism vs. Olympic pluralism: Problems of Eurocentrism. In S-P. Kang, J. MacAloon, & R. DaMatta (Eds.), *The Olympics and cultural exchange* (pp. 513-528). Seoul: Hanyang University Institute for Ethnological Studies.

Obojski, R. (1975). *The rise of Japanese baseball power*. Radnor, PA: Chilton.

Rahman, M.A. (1985). The theory and practice of participatory action research. In O.F. Borda (Ed.), *The challenge of social change* (pp. 107-132). Newbury Park, CA: Sage.

Seppanen, P. (1989). Competitive sport and sport success in the Olympic Games: A cross-cultural analysis of value systems. *International Review for the Sociology of Sport 24*, 275-282.

Thomas, D.R. (1992). *Culture, ethnicity and learning: Applications for educational policy and practice*. Hamilton, New Zealand: University of Waikato.

Whiting, R. (1989). *You gotta have wa*. New York: Vintage.

CHAPTER FIVE

NATIONAL SPORT POLICIES IN INTERNATIONAL CONTEXT

Overview

This chapter examines variations among national sport structures. It notes that they have emerged in response to each country's social, economic, and political history. Contrasting systems of national sport governance are explored through a comparison of the development of sport policies in Canada and the United States. The two countries provide an instructive contrast because the development of Canadian sport has been substantially influenced by a government agency (Sport Canada), whereas sport governance in the United States is explicitly nongovernmental. The chapter concludes by investigating potential conflicts of jurisdiction between national authorities and international federations.

Introduction

National sport policies provide the link between international sport governance and the national development of sport. The nature of funding for programs and facilities, as well as the specifics of program and facility administration, is determined, at least in part, by national sport policies. Just as forms of government differ (e.g., democracy, dictatorship, monarchy), so do national systems for administering sport. There is some relationship between the form of government and the structure of sport administration. For example, in countries where the government controls the economy (e.g., Cuba, China, North Korea), the government also exercises control over sport. This is not surprising, because there is no private sector in these countries to which to assign the task of sport administration. However, it is not the case that countries with similar forms of government necessarily administer sport similarly. Rather, policies that specify the structure of sport governance have emerged over time in response to each country's particular social, economic, and political history. When working internationally, it is helpful to have some appreciation of the variations among national sport structures.

It is not the purpose of this text to provide a comprehensive description and comparison of the entire array of sport policies from around the world. However, it is instructive to illustrate the development of contrasting systems of sport governance by comparing the evolution of U.S. and Canadian sport policies (with the Canadian model of government support being more closely followed worldwide). Although the two countries are neighbors sharing a common language and similar democratic traditions, their sport policies differ substantially. First, in order to establish the necessary background for a comparison, it is constructive to consider the different levels at which sport development takes place.

The pursuit of athletic excellence begins with youth and continues through elite levels, be they professional leagues, Olympic Games, or World Championships. At each level the control of sport is linked to its funding source. A common structure is depicted in Table 5-1.

TABLE 5.1
Levels Of Sport Development

Level	Governance	Primary Funding	Example
youth	local	taxes, donations	community youth soccer league
schools (primary and secondary)	local, state	taxes, booster clubs, ticket sales	high school basketball
clubs*	within the club	membership dues, fundraisers, corporate support	swimming club
college/ university	national organization, within the school, league affiliation	college general fund, booster club, ticket sales, licensing	Ohio State University
professional leagues	private	TV,ticket sales,licensing	Chicago Bulls

• Clubs may involve athletes at any age and skill level.

An objective of this text is to describe the management of sport internationally. Consequently, youth, school and college/university funding are noted only to the degree that they impact international sport governance. Indeed, not all sports are represented at every level of the structure described in Table 5-1. For example, although programs for youth are necessary for development of international class athletes in some sports, such as swimming and gymnastics, other sports, such as luge or shooting, are often developed without youth sports programs. Similarly, many countries, having little or no school or university sport, rely on club systems of sport almost exclusively.

Three factors commonly constrain the sport development strategies a country chooses: cost, resources, and historical circumstances. The requisite equipment, facilities, and staff each impact the cost of sport development. For example, the cost of constructing luge tracks has prevented the United States from developing a local-level or club infrastructure for the sport. International lugers are developed through programs at the Olympic Training Center in Lake Placid. The costs a country can manage for development of its sports depends, in part, on the country's resources. Wealthy nations can better afford to provide equipment, facilities, and program personnel. However, a country's ability to spend does not necessarily result in the choice to spend for sport. For example, even in a wealthy country like Negara Brunei Darussalam, sport development has required extensive volunteer labor.

Indeed, the choice of expenditures for sport depends, in part, on the country's institutional sport history. For example, the Republic of Korea (South Korea) was devastated by war during the early 1950s and spent the subsequent two decades rebuilding its cities, roads, and industry. As the country planned to host the 1988 Olympics, it had few sport clubs, and sport was not typically included in school or university curricula. In order to develop world-class athletes in the 23 sports that were then contested on the Olympic program, the Korean government chose to construct and staff a state-of-the-art sports training center at Taenung (on the outskirts of Seoul). Potential athletes were recruited and brought to the center for training.

It is common for sport programs to seek multiple sources of funding. For example, school sport programs often rely on taxes, and local sports clubs often use facilities that are constructed with public funds. However, clubs and schools may also seek private donations or even sponsorships from private companies.

In order to illustrate different ways public and private forms of governance and funding have arisen, it is instructive to compare U.S. and Canadian sport policies.

United States Governance of International Sport

The United States funds Olympic sports at national levels primarily through private contributions. However, at local levels, there is considerable public investment in sport. For example, schools and public recreation authorities invest tax dollars for the construction and maintenance of sports facilities and the provision of sports programs. Thus, in the United States, local-level sport is supported substantially (though not uniquely) via public investment. However, at the national level, sport is supported almost entirely by private investment.

The Amateur Sports Act of 1978 (36 U.S.C. sections 371-396) designates the USOC as the sole authority for supervision and development of sports contested in the Olympic and Pan American Games. (Formulation and content of the Amateur Sports Act are analyzed in Chalip, 1991; 1995.) Nevertheless, the USOC is explicitly nongovernmental. The only oversight requirement is that it annually provide a written report to Congress and to the President. However, no Congressional committee nor Executive Branch agency is provided any oversight authority. In fact, there is no committee or agency that is required to read or evaluate the USOC's annual report. Meanwhile, the USOC maintains an active lobbying program designed, in part, to protect its independence from government.

Since passage of the Amateur Sports Act, there have been two sources of federal funding: (a) a one-time grant of $10.2 million (appropriated on July 8, 1980) and (b) revenues from the sale of Olympic coins. The former has long since been spent, and the latter accounts for less than 7% of USOC revenues. The vast majority of USOC revenue is derived from private fundraising, licensing and sponsorship agreements. Thus, federal dollars do not now provide a practical means even for indirect control of U.S. sport. Sources of USOC funding are listed in Table 5-2.

TABLE 5.2
Sources of USOC Revenue*

42 %	Corporate Participation Licensing
28 %	Television Revenue
11 %	Direct Mail
8 %	Fund Raising
7 %	Olympic Coins
4 %	Olympic Spirit Stores

* Percentages vary somewhat annually; 1992 figures are reported here. (Source: USOC budget)

The primary governance tool of the USOC is its authority (conferred by the Amateur Sports Act) to determine which organization will serve as the national federation (NF) for each sport on the Olympic and Pan American Games programs. (In the United States, NFs are called "National Governing Bodies" [NGBs]; the acronym "NGB" is used throughout the remainder of this discussion.) Organizations governing sports that do not participate in these two events are free to choose to affiliate with the USOC, but are not required to do so. However, for sports on the Olympic and Pan American Games programs, the USOC has authority to select the organization to serve as NGB and the authority to place an NGB on probation or revoke its franchise. Thus, each sport is governed by a single NGB, and the NGBs are, in turn, governed by the USOC. Other organizations that provide sport programs (e.g., YMCA, NCAA, Special Olympics) are also able to apply for USOC membership. USOC policies are determined by vote of the member organizations (NGBs, YMCA, NCAA, etc.).

The Amateur Sports Act specifies 14 "objects and purposes" for the USOC: (a) to establish national goals for Olympic sports and to pursue attainment of those goals; (b) to coordinate and develop amateur sport activity; (c) to exercise jurisdiction over United States participation in the Olympic and Pan American Games; (d) to obtain the most competent representation in those Games; (e) to promote and support amateur sport; (f) to promote and encourage physical fitness and sport participation; (g) to assist in the development of amateur sports programs; (h) to provide for resolution of conflicts in amateur sports; (i) to foster development of facilities for amateur sports; (j) to provide and coordinate technical information on physical training, equipment design, coaching, and performance analysis; (k) to encourage and support sport research; (l) to promote sport for women; (m) to promote sport for the disabled; (n) to promote sport for minorities.

The Amateur Sports Act specifies seven derivative responsibilities of each NGB: (a) to represent the United States in the international federation (IF) that governs its sport internationally; (b) to establish national goals and foster attainment of those goals; (c) to serve as the coordinating body for national activity in its sport; (d) to exercise jurisdiction for international competition by U.S. citizens in its sport; (e) to conduct competitions in its sport; (f) to recommend to the USOC who should compete at the Olympic and Pan American Games in its sport; (g) to designate individuals and teams to compete in international competitions other than the Olympic and Pan American Games.

In order to protect Olympic symbols, as the *Olympic Charter* (the constitution of the International Olympic Committee) requires, the Amateur Sports Act grants the USOC exclusive U.S. rights to the symbol of the IOC (the five interlocking rings), the USOC emblem, and the words *Olympic, Olympiad,* and *Citius, Altius, Fortius*. These rights have allowed the USOC to obtain revenues via agreements that license one or more of these symbols to corporate sponsors.

In summary, the Amateur Sports Act specifies that U.S. governance of its international sports programs will be explicitly nongovernmental. Responsibility for administration and development of almost all international sports teams and programs is delegated to the USOC and its NGBs. The federal government has no direct authority over the USOC. In turn, the USOC obtains scant funding from federal sources. Meanwhile, sports outside the Olympic Movement or the Pan American Games (including professional teams and leagues) are subject to neither USOC nor federal oversight. They operate freely and independently while abiding by the laws of the land. The exception to this is Major League Baseball, which currently has an antitrust exemption in the United States.

Outside the United States, governments commonly assert some direct control over sport. Many countries exert that control through cabinet-level appointment of a Minister of Sport or Minister of Sport and Recreation or some variation thereof. The U.S. decision to have sport administered with no federal oversight is unusual. Why was this the choice?

An enduring principle of U.S. politics holds that government should govern minimally (King, 1973a, 1973b). This notion is aptly embodied in the U.S. dictum that claims, "That government is best that governs least." In fact, the principle was sufficient to keep the federal government out of sport governance until the 1970s.

Prior to 1978, there had been no U.S. legislation to mandate a governance structure for the country's international sport. However, in 1972 four incidents at the Summer Olympic Games in Munich set into motion a series of events that led directly to passage of the Amateur Sports Act (see Chalip, 1991, 1995): (a) Rick DeMont, a U.S. swimmer, was stripped of his gold medal because his asthma medication contained an ingredient on the IOC's list of banned substances. (b) Bob Seagren, a U.S. pole vaulter, was not allowed to use his preferred fiberglass pole, consequently jumping below his world record and finishing second to an East German. (c) U.S. sprinters Ray Robinson and Eddie Hart were not provided a correct schedule for their competition. Consequently, they were disqualified when they failed to arrive for the quarterfinal heat, and a Soviet sprinter won the gold medal. (d) The U.S. basketball team was defeated by the Soviet Union after a disputed ruling by the Secretary-General of the International Basketball Federation.

In and of themselves, these events might not have been sufficient to generate policy action by U.S. legislators. However, these events occurred in the context of increasing U.S. concerns about national prestige in the face of communist challenges--the Cold War. As early as 1954, Congressman Philip Philbin had wondered: "What is the meaning of this rapid advancement of Russia in the world of sports? ... To what extent is superiority in competitive athletics tied in with national success, prosperity, and invincibility in warfare?" (*Congressional Record*, 1954, p. 13763). Ten years later, as Soviet athletes became increasingly successful, Congress began to reconsider its laissez faire attitude toward international sport. Congressman Frank Morse explained the problem this way:

> The present situation is humiliating for the athletes involved and destructive of team performance and morale... The argument that we do not want to make our athletes political minions or adopt the practices of the Soviet Union does not reflect the realities of the situation. (*Congressional Record*, 1964, p. 5904)

By 1972, the fact that the U.S. team had for the first time fallen behind the Soviet team in the Olympic medal count made the incidents at Munich allthemore salient to U.S. policymakers. The situation was exacerbated by open warfare between the National Collegiate Athletic Association (NCAA) and the Amateur Athletics Union (AAU) over control of eight Olympic sports, particularly track and field. That dispute had already generated an ineffective federal mediation effort during the 1960s. In 1973, legislators' concern escalated as the NCAA threatened to keep college athletes out of the USA-USSR track meet, which was sanctioned through the AAU. This meet had been hailed as an opportunity for U.S. athletes to redeem lost luster. Although the NCAA relented under Congressional pressure and permitted college athletes to compete in the meet, the episode strengthened a growing sentiment that the governance of Olympic sports in the United States was in need of reform.

Nevertheless, although policymakers wanted reform, their concern that the United States not adopt Soviet methods remained pivotal. Consequently, direct government control of sport was vigorously opposed. In response to legislation proposing some federal oversight of sport, Senator Adlai Stevenson summarized the objections:

> I am deeply concerned about the future of amateur athletics and would hate to see the Federal government become involved in this aspect of American life. I urge the President to convene ... a conference, and I urge the organizations concerned with amateur sports to reconcile their differences and work together for the advancement of amateur sport. (*Congressional Record*, 1973, p. 16069)

White House staff agreed. A staff analysis sent to President Richard Nixon on May 24, 1973 (Memo, Jerry Jones to The President), urged him to forestall federal control of sport by establishing a commission to examine amateur sports problems and recommend reorganization of the USOC. A subsequent White House memo made the concerns explicit: "This Administration is committed to limiting--not expanding--the scope of Federal

Government, and Federal involvement in amateur athletics could well prove counterproductive" (Memo, Ken Cole to Staff Secretary, July 20, 1973).

On December 28, 1974, a presidential commission was established by executive order, precisely as recommended in earlier White House memoranda. That commission concluded that sport should be administered independently of government. It recommended that a private "Central Sports Organization" be given authority over sports on the Olympic and Pan American Games programs. Those recommendations became the basis for the Amateur Sports Act.

We see, then, that U.S. policies for international sport emerged from the convergence of ideological preference and a sense of national interest. In the context of the Cold War, it was arguably in the national interest to improve U.S. administration of its international sports. However, traditional U.S. values dictated that government should not take control. The situation was quite different in Canada.

Canadian Governance of International Sport

Since 1961, the Canadian federal government has exerted considerable influence over sports on the program of the Olympic and Pan American Games. It exercises that influence primarily through the distribution of funds (cf., MacIntosh, Bedecki, & Franks, 1987; MacIntosh & Whitson, 1990). Following passage of the Fitness and Amateur Sport Act (C-131) in 1961, the annual federal investment in sport rose steadily, reaching a high of Canadian $66.7 million in 1987 (Minister's Task Force on Federal Sport Policy, 1992). The growth of federal investment has been accompanied by expanded federal control.

The federal government has not shown comparable interest in professional sports leagues or franchises. It has, however, acted to protect the Canadian Football League through legislation preventing expansion of the National Football League (of the United States) into Canada.

The Canadian Olympic Association (COA) does not have authority over national federations (called "National Sport Organizations" [NSOs] in Canada) in a manner comparable to that granted to the USOC by the Amateur Sports Act. In keeping with requirements of the *Olympic Charter* that National Olympic Committees seek to remain independent of government, the COA has maintained an arm's-length relationship with the federal government. In response to criticisms by the Task Force on Sport for Canadians in 1969, the COA established the Olympic Trust in 1970 to raise funds from the private sector to cover costs of sending Canadian teams to the Olympic and Pan American Games. The Olympic Trust has helped the COA to retain its financial independence from government.

The NSOs have, however, developed substantial dependence on government funding. A survey by the Sport Marketing Council in 1986 found that 15 NSOs relied on the federal government for more than 85% of their funding, 35 NSOs relied on the federal government for between 50% and 85% of their funding, and only 15 NSOs obtained less than 50% of their funding from federal sources (cited in MacIntosh & Whitson, 1990, pp. 20-21). This dependence on federal funds has permitted increased federal control. For example, each NSO is required by the government to prepare a detailed 4-year plan for development of the sport that it governs.

Federal control of sport is implemented through Sport Canada, an agency within the government's Fitness and Amateur Sport Directorate. That directorate, in turn, is assigned its own government minister. Sport Canada's mission is to "provide Canadians with the opportunity to pursue excellence in competitive sport, and to improve the level of Canadian performances in international sport competitions" (MacIntosh, et al., 1987, p. 79).

Sport Canada asserts its authority by funding a range of sport undertakings. Perhaps its most significant application of control has been the payment of salaries for full-time NSO staff. NSO staff thus owe allegiance to Sport Canada.

Sport Canada also makes direct payments to athletes through its Athlete Assistance Program (AAP). By 1989, 800 Canadian athletes were subsidized by AAP at the following levels: "A" carded athletes (those ranked in the top eight in the world) obtained $650 per month, whereas "B", "C," "C-1," and "D" carded athletes secured $550, $450, $350, and $300 per month respectively. Reserve athletes in team sports received $250 monthly, and junior team athletes received $150 monthly. Criteria for carding and payments are established by Sport Canada, not the NSOs.

Through its Sport Marketing Council, Sport Canada brings NSOs together with potential corporate sponsors. It assists negotiation of sponsorship and licensing agreements. Its marketing support program provides funding and expertise for the preparation of marketing plans, implementation of those plans, and customer support.

In summary, the Canadian government exercises substantial control over its programs for international sport. That control is implemented through Sport Canada, which is an arm of the federal government. Sport Canada funds NSOs and athletes. Through its Sport Marketing Council, Sport Canada brokers the acquisition of funding from private industry. Thus, the government asserts its authority over sport through the funds that it provides directly and the funds that it helps to obtain from the private sector.

Clearly, the Canadian sport system differs radically from that of the United States. What prompted such extensive government intervention in sport?

As in the United States, a surprising defeat in international competition provoked federal action. However, in the Canadian case, national pride was more significant than Cold War anxiety.

In 1954 the Soviet ice hockey team defeated the Canadian team at the World Championships. Two years later, at the Winter Olympic Games in Italy, the Canadian ice hockey team finished third, behind teams from the Soviet Union and the United States. It was only the second time in Olympic history that Canada not won the gold medal in its national sport. That same year, in the Summer Olympic Games in Melbourne, Canada earned only three medals, finishing 17th in the medal tally. The relatively poor performances by Canadian athletes and teams, particularly in ice hockey, became a focus of national malaise. MacIntosh, Bedecki, and Franks (1987) describe the situation this way:

> This concern was evident in newspapers across Canada and in the House
> of Commons, where a number of members of parliament during the late
> 1950s urged the government to take action to provide support to Canada's
> elite athletes... The election ... of 1957 brought forward a prime minister
> with a strong belief in nationalism and the conviction that sport had an

important role to play in developing national unity and international prestige. (pp. 11, 23).

In Canada, government action was not forestalled by ideological beliefs, as it had been in the United States:

> The urbanization of Canada and the accompanying breakdown of the extended rural family contributed to a popular post-war belief that government could and should solve critical social problems... This ... coincided with an emerging view that the state had a responsibility to provide equal social-welfare and health opportunities for all Canadians... In this sense, the concept of government was much more interventionist than was that of [the United States]... Both [political] parties held a paternalistic view of government's role in Canadian society, one that was conducive to the provision of monies to agencies and organizations so that sport could be supported... (MacIntosh et al., 1987, pp. 22-23).

Canada's unique cultural and geographic position made the issues of national identity and prestige--as symbolized by the international performances of Canadian teams and athletes--particularly salient to Canadians (MacIntosh, et al., 1987; MacIntosh & Whitson, 1990). Regional identifications are considerably stronger in Canada than in the United States. Indeed, a substantial proportion of Canada's French-speaking minority advocates political independence from English-speaking Canada. Meanwhile, Canadians struggle to assert a cultural identity that remains independent from incursions by neighboring U.S. trends and media. Canada's international sports representation continues to provide a potent device for symbolizing national unity and a unique cultural status. In 1992, the Minister's Task Force on Federal Sport Policy put it this way:

> We are searching for common ground on which to build the future Canada. We are searching for shared identity, connectedness, a sense of belonging. Sport offers a common experience and a shared language relevant to our day-to-day lives. It offers pride in who we are and what we collectively accomplish. The thousands of sport events and media coverage every day across this country provide a cultural glue. The courage and performance of Canadians on the world stage gives Canadians a shared sense of pride. (p. 257)

The initial piece of legislation enabling government custody of sport passed Parliament in 1961, 17 years before the Amateur Sports Act of the United States. The Canadian legislation, Bill C-131, "An Act to Encourage Fitness and Amateur Sport," authorized the federal government to spend $5 million annually to support an administrative structure promoting Canadian sport. Since that time, federal involvement in sport has grown substantially. The intensity of federal focus on elite Canadian sport is evidenced by government's continuing formulations of policies to extend and amplify government's role in sport. These include two federal task forces (in 1969 and 1992), seven federal policy documents (in 1970, 1977, 1979, 1981, 1986, 1988, and 1990), and one national commission of inquiry (in 1990). By 1971, Sport Canada had been created as a government agency within the Fitness and Amateur Sport Directorate. In 1973, it was elevated to branch status and granted its own deputy minister.

Federal uses of sport were again elaborated during the 1980s as sport became a fundamental tool of Canadian foreign policy (MacIntosh & Hawes, 1993). In 1987, an International Relations Directorate was installed within Fitness and Amateur Sport. Working in cooperation with this new Directorate, the Department of External Affairs increased funding and staffing of the sport section of its own Cultural Affairs Division. Sport is used to project a positive image of Canadian society internationally and to enhance Canada's influence throughout the Commonwealth.

We see, then, that Canadian policymakers were not hampered by ideologies favoring small government in the way that U.S. policymakers were. Canadian policies for international sport enabled the government's efforts to use sport first as an instrument for nation building and later as a vehicle for projecting Canada's interests abroad. As we shall see in later chapters, motives like these are not unique to Canada.

National Sovereignty Versus International Governance

The extensive involvement of national governments in sport complicates issues of jurisdiction. The IFs establish the framework of rules for their sports, and the NFs are responsible to oversee appropriate application of those rules in their respective countries. Rules for matters of strictly domestic governance may be allowed to depart from international rules. For example, in the United States, swimming's stroke and turn rules have often differed in significant ways from the international rules. U.S. swimmers have been allowed to compete under those rules domestically, but are required to conform to international rules when competing internationally.

However, as governments become involved in sport, the apparatus of government also becomes involved. What happens when the IF and an arm of national government disagree? The problem is aptly illustrated by the dispute between the U.S. 400-meter world record holder and the International Amateur Athletic Federation (IAAF), the IF for track and field. In this instance, a U.S. court and the IAAF contested the right to determine the athlete's eligibility to compete (see Newman, 1994, for a discussion).

On August 12, 1990, at a meet in Monte Carlo, the IAAF randomly tested Butch Reynolds for use of banned substances (such as anabolic steroids). Seven days later, the IAAF informed Reynolds that his urine sample had tested positive for the steroid nandrolone. He was informed that that he was suspended until The Athletics Congress (TAC), the national governing body for track and field in the United States (now called USA Track and Field [USATF]), could conduct a hearing on the incident.

Reynolds claimed that the tests were flawed and therefore invalid. Rather than wait for TAC's hearing, Reynolds sued the IAAF and TAC in an Ohio District Court, claiming that they had no right to interfere with his participation. The court decided to postpone hearing the case until Reynolds had exhausted all of his administrative options, which included an American Arbitration Association (AAA) hearing and a TAC hearing.

The case began to take on a life of its won when the arbitration hearing found in favor of Reynolds' claims that the drug tests were flawed. TAC, upon evidence obtained from its own hearing, agreed with the AAA decision. However, despite two reports coming from these proceedings, the IAAF, after conducting yet a third hearing, concluded that

Reynolds should still be banned.

Reynolds felt pressed for time because he sought to qualify for the U.S. Olympic Trials. He again went to U.S. District Court in Ohio. On May 28, 1992, the court issued a temporary restraining order against the IAAF, prohibiting the IAAF from interfering with Reynolds' ability to compete in track and field competitions.

The IAAF ignored the order, contending that the U.S. courts had no jurisdiction over its authority to regulate athletes' eligibility. The IAAF informed meet directors that their events would be stripped of Grand Prix status if Reynolds was allowed to run in them. This would result in a loss of revenue and prestige because Grand Prix sponsors would no longer be available. Further, the IAAF threatened that any athlete who participated in an event with Reynolds would be disqualified. Within the United States, at least, meet directors and athletes were caught between the rulings of their IF and the rulings of their domestic courts.

Reynolds managed to qualify for the U.S. Olympic trials by racing in smaller (not Grand Prix) events where the risk to meet directors was minimal. However, because the IAAF continued to ban Reynolds from competition, he returned to court to obtain a preliminary injunction against TAC and the IAAF. The injunction would prevent both organizations from hindering Reynolds' right to compete. Reynolds won.

Now it was TAC's turn to use the courts. TAC appealed the preliminary injunction to the Sixth Court of Appeals. The appellate court determined that the district court should not have granted Reynolds the injunction. They ruled that the administrative proceedings in which Reynolds participated prior to his initial suit did not allow for court appeals.

Reynolds then appealed to the Chief Justice of the Sixth Circuit, who reinstated the injunction. TAC responded by appealing to the Supreme Court. TAC lost. The Supreme Court overruled TAC by determining that Reynolds was eligible to compete. In so doing, the court implicitly asserted its right to determine an athlete's eligibility. Nonetheless, the IAAF continued to ban Reynolds.

This incident highlights the essential contradiction between domestic sovereignty and international jurisdiction. As Newman (1994) writes:

> If American courts make track and field eligibility determinations, other countries will use their courts to determine athletes' eligibility as well. If many judges from many nations make eligibility decisions about track and field, chaos will result. There will be inconsistent eligibility standards around the world, making governance of sport unmanageable. (pp. 232-233)

A further complication is that the dispute between an athlete and a sport governing body has the potential to delay the start of international events. If athletes were allowed to appeal through already busy court systems, they could seek injunctions to prevent the start of competitions in their own countries until their own eligibility was decided (Nancy Raber, personal communication, October 7, 1994). International events like world championships, regional competitions (e.g., the Pan American Games), or global competitions (e.g., the World Student Games) might then have to be postponed. In an effort to prevent that outcome for any Olympic Games, the IOC announced plans at the end of 1994 to require Olympic athletes to sign a form agreeing to arbitrate disputes within the Olympic Movement, rather than filing lawsuits (Brown, 1994).

The case of Butch Reynolds highlights the increasing need to find means to resolve potential conflicts of jurisdiction between domestic and international authorities. One outcome has been that sport organizations increasingly seek to place arbitration authority over matters like eligibility in the hands of the Court of Arbitration for Sport (CAS). In some instances it is explicit in the IF and NF bylaws. Nevertheless, domestic sovereignty over matters of sport policy is curtailed to the degree that authority is conceded to an international organization like the CAS.

Concluding Summary

Just as forms of government differ, so do national systems for administering sport. Costs, resources, economic systems, and historical circumstances each impact a country's choice of sport development strategies. The impact of these factors is aptly illustrated by the contrast between the strongly private sport development strategies of the United States and the substantial government involvement in Canadian sport. Whereas the United States has delegated primary responsibility for development of international-level sport to the USOC, the Canadian government has become involved in sport development through government funding. In the United States, it was ideologically important to keep government out of sport. In Canada, the government chose to use sport as an instrument of nation building and foreign policy.

The complexity of relations between international sport governance and national sovereignty over sport is illustrated by Butch Reynolds' suit against the IAAF. The case involved an athlete suing in domestic court to secure his eligibility to compete. However, the degree to which eligibility matters are subject to domestic jurisdiction was simultaneously at stake. In order to reduce the probability of jurisdictional disputes of this kind, IFs and NFs are increasingly seeking to place the authority for dispute resolution into the hands of the CAS.

Discussion, Analysis, Application, and Debate

Issues for Discussion

1. Under what circumstances might an international sport manager need to work at local levels within a country?
2. What do you see as the relative advantages and disadvantages of using sport clubs rather than schools as venues for developing sport nationally?
3. What might be the relative pros and cons of private versus public funding of national sport programs? What conditions of national size, government, or economy might mediate those pros and cons?
4. Cold War anxieties served as a justification for U.S. policymakers to formulate the Amateur Sports Act. With the Cold War now over, what other justifications might be used as justifications for further federal legislation to regulated U.S. governance of its international sport?
5. What factors make sport an attractive tool for nation building?

Matters for Analysis

1. In most countries, sport is governed by a variety of organizations. These may include governments at various levels, private sport organizations, the country's National Olympic Committee, the national federations for each sport, and others. In a sense, then, the governance of sport requires a great deal of interorganization linkage and cooperation.

    How might the perspectives and interests of the various organizations converge? How might they differ? What particular problems and/or opportunities result? For which stakeholders? What implications do you draw for the administrators of the various organizations? For stakeholders who do not have administrative power (e.g., athletes)?

2. Consider the problem of integrating your country's sport system vertically--from the beginning local levels of sport to the creation of international-caliber athletes. Which organizations operate at which levels? What key tasks must each perform? How should those tasks and organizations be linked in order to optimize the development of athletic talent? What administrative mechanisms are required to facilitate the requisite linkages among the organizations? To what degree do those already exist in your country? What new programs or administrative actions are implicated by your analysis?

Application

Using library resources and/or interviews, develop an analysis of the ways that sport is governed in a country other than your own. At what levels is sport supported privately and publicly? What institutions are used to channel public and private resources into sport? Who are the key stakeholders? How do those stakeholders interact? What implications do you draw for development of sport programs or exchanges between your own country and the country you have analyzed?

Ethical Debate

It takes money to develop athletes. In most countries, some development of athletes is supported by tax dollars (e.g., publicly funded sport facilities, subsidies to athletes, salaries to coaches). It is sometimes claimed that this is unethical because it diverts public money into programs and facilities that only benefit a privileged (i.e., athletic) few. To what degree is public support of sport appropriate? What constraints should there be on public support of sport? Why?

References

The Amateur Sports Act of 1978 (36 U.S.C. sections 371-396).

Brown, B. (1994, December 6). Atlanta impresses big IOC gathering. *USA Today*, p. C3.

Chalip, L. (1991). Sport and the state: The case of the United States. In F. Landry, M. Landry, & M. Yerles (Eds.), *Sport ... The third millennium* (pp. 243-250). Sainte-Foy, Quebec: Les Presses de l'Universite Laval.

Chalip, L. (1995). Policy analysis in sport management. *Journal of Sport Management, 9,* 1-13.

King, A. (1973a). Ideas, institutions and the policies of governments: A comparative analysis: Parts 1 and II. *British Journal of Political Science, 3,* 291-313.

King, A. (1973b). Ideas, institutions and the policies of governments: A comparative analysis: Part III. *British Journal of Political Science, 3,* 409-423.

MacIntosh, D., Bedecki, T., & Franks, C.E.S. (1987). *Sport and politics in Canada: Federal government involvement since 1961.* Kingston, Ontario: McGill-Queen's University Press.

MacIntosh, D., & Hawes, M. (1993). *Sport and Canadian diplomacy.* Kingston, Ontario: McGill-Queen's University Press.

MacIntosh, D., & Whitson, D. (1990). *The games planners: Transforming Canada's sport system.* Kingston, Ontario: McGill-Queen's University Press.

Minister's Task Force of Federal Sport Policy (1992). *Sport: The way ahead.* Ottawa: Government of Canada.

Newman, J.J. (1994). The race does not always go to the stronger or faster man ... but to the one who goes to court! An examination of Reynolds v. International Amateur Athletic Fed'n, et al. *The Sport Lawyers Journal, 1,* 205-235.

CHAPTER SIX ─────────────────

BIDDING FOR AN INTERNATIONAL EVENT: THE OLYMPIC MODEL

Overview

This chapter describes bidding to host an international sporting event. The IOC format is described as a model which encompasses all aspects of the process. This model presents a thorough bidder self-examination through 23 themes such that the candidate organization will have fully examined its needs before presenting the bid. Included are the summary of recent IOC Olympic host city voting and the immediate needs following a successful bid.

Introduction

Long before an international athletic competition begins, the right to host the competition must be awarded to an organization. Hosting an event might, on the surface, appear to be a fairly obvious matter: Competitors play at a venue, a winner is declared, awards are presented, and everybody goes home. In a manner of speaking it is that simple. However, the nature of international competitions is such that culture, language, food, protocol, and weather conditions are but a few of the factors that need to be considered. Even the communication among individuals and organizations worldwide can and does cause serious problems when hosting an international event.

The idea of hosting an event usually germinates in the mind of an individual. That person's enthusiasm is then spread to others who see the possibility of making something out of nothing. After brainstorming the who, what, where, when, why, how, and how much, the next step is to contact the appropriate governing body for more information on the process to obtain an event.

As the Olympic Games are arguably the most exposed sporting event on the globe, the bidding process tends to be the most scrutinized and copied. Therefore, this text uses, primarily, the Olympic bidding model through which to illustrate the laborious nature of bidding for an international event. Much of the material presented is from the IOC *Manual for Cities Bidding for the Olympic Games* (1992). What is extremely important, however, is that the administrator(s) seeking to host an international event study carefully the IOC bidding model. Then, from this model that which is considered relevant can be addressed and implemented.

Each event presents its unique set of circumstances. For example, the World Cup of Soccer has over a year of qualifying rounds leading to a month-long final tournament. An interesting aspect is that the teams remaining in the tournament must be housed and fed, must practice and recreate for a month. Virtually each minute of each day has to be scripted before each team's arrival in the host country. However, after the first round, the teams do not know to which city they will be moving. Therefore, although the host country knows its role, having each team unsure of their status necessitates that each team be fully prepared.

The bid for an event for athletes with disabilities creates different difficulties. In general, most developed nations have facilities capable of handling the athletes. However, many host organizations would have to consider carefully their facilities and personnel before submitting a bid for an event for athletes with disabilities.

Olympic Bid Within a Country

The National Olympic Committees (NOCs) receive a letter from the International Olympic Committee (IOC) about 9 years prior to the given Olympic Games stating that the IOC wishes to be presented with candidate host cities within 6 months. (Only cities, not countries, may host the Olympics.) It is thus imperative that any city contact its NOC well in advance of this 9 year period so that proper and extensive thought is given and full preparation is established before a bid to the NOC is given. It is also during these early stages that the NOC and the country's IOC representatives(s) may counsel any city considering such an extensive endeavor as the Games of the Olympiad or the Winter Olympics (International Olympic Committee, 1992).

An NOC can only nominate one city from its country to host a particular Olympic Games (International Olympic Committee, 1993). When that country's representative city has been selected the city's official authorities and its NOC present themselves as a candidate to host the Olympic Games. It is at this time that the city's candidature becomes official (International Olympic Committee, 1993).

As with any major event, usually there is more than one group enthusiastic to host. It thus becomes the responsibility of the governing body within the country to select the representing city. For countries with fewer resources, the major city within the country is the only location with the infrastructure to host.

For the Olympic candidate cities an informational meeting with the IOC will be held. It is at this meeting that all aspects of the candidate's bid are explained so that the officials from the candidate city know exactly what is expected of them and when. At this time also, a 10-minute presentation is made to the IOC Executive Board about the prospective bidder's abilities, support, and desire to host the Olympic Games. This will be the only presentation to an IOC meeting until the IOC Session at which the Olympic host city is selected (International Olympic Committee, 1993).

By this time candidate cities should have a good sense of the commitment and responsibility required to host the Olympics. Of particular importance is the impact on the bidding city itself. Does the city have the commitment not only from the bid committee and city officials but also from the people in order to host the Olympic Games? In 1976 Denver, Colorado, backed out as host city for the Winter Olympics after having been awarded the Games. The value to the city, in the eyes of the voters, was overwhelmed by the negative consequences that might have evolved.

For the 1996 Games of the Olympiad, Toronto was thought to have the early lead as the favorite to host the Games. The Toronto organization felt that Athens would be the sentimental favorite for the modern Olympic centennial, but Athens did not have the total infrastructural package to win the bid. Also, Toronto thought that it was time to have the Games of the Olympiad in North America again. With the experience of bidding for the 1976 Olympics, which was won by Montreal, the Toronto Ontario Olympic Council (TOOC) felt that they had the proper ingredients of experienced, capable personnel, quality venues, a developed infrastructure, and a committed community. However, during the bidding process a problem developed.

During the meetings with various civic groups in the Toronto area, some members of City Hall, knowing the significance of hosting an Olympic Games, realized the impact the Games would have on the "social agenda" of Toronto well into the next century. This group created the Olympic Task Force (OTF) to examine Toronto's bid before it went to the IOC. The OTF did a social impact assessment and held several meetings in order to hear from all interested parties on their areas of concern.

At the same time as the OTF was working, an organization called Bread Not Circus (BNC) was formed to "shift the focus of the city's politics away from mega-projects and unchecked development to the challenges of poverty and homelessness" (Kidd, 1992, p.157).BNC "demonstrated against IOC members, staged an 'anti-Olympic' torch relay through the poor neighborhoods of the inner city, and flooded the media with flyers about Olympic movement embarrassments" (Kidd, 1992, p. 157). Both of these situations emphasize the need of the organizers to gain the support of local citizens before proceeding with bidding to host the Olympics or any other major event that will require the cooperation of the local populace.

There has been some criticism of the bidding process and the "official promotional campaign" waged by the bidding cities that want to host the Olympic Games. In order to address this matter, the IOC published the *Manual for Cities Bidding for the Olympic Games* (International Olympic Committee, 1992). These regulations came into force February 7, 1992. Therefore, the Olympic Games held after 1998, beginning with Sydney in 2000, will have been bid according to these guidelines. The new guidelines stress the importance of financial awareness and responsibility when considering an Olympic bid. The basic expenditures mentioned include

1. Pre-candidature studies,
2. Candidate visitations (travel costs, housing, meals, etc),
3. Creation and presentation of the candidature file,
4. Promotional and communications campaign, and
5. The guarantee deposit.

The guarantee deposit is US$100,000, which must be forwarded to the IOC upon the presentation of the candidature file. The cities that are not awarded the Games will have their deposit returned with interest.

In addition to the considerations in the previous paragraph, the IOC gives specific instructions to the bidding cities on limiting expenditures:

1. The candidature file must be on A4 format paper stapled, not bound; the use of pre-existing brochures and materials is encouraged; video and/or audio works may accompany the file but are to be limited in expenditure to produce.
2. Maximum of six persons from the bidding city may attend Olympic meetings as official accredited delegates. Olympic meetings include those of the IOC, IFs, and NOCs.
3. Candidates must refrain from organizing special events, exhibitions, parties, or meals during an Olympic meeting, unless all the bidding cities jointly agree to host one of the above.
4. A city may reserve a room or suite in the hotel housing the participants at the Olympic meetings to discuss its bid with IOC meeting delegates.
5. Candidates cannot send representatives to IOC members in their home countries unless the IOC member did not visit the candidature city.
6. Each IOC member and one guest may visit each candidature city with the following conditions:
   a. expenses covered by the host city include international travel and accommodations for 3 days (nonrefundable to the recipient),
   b. the IOC Executive Board may authorize "certain qualified persons" to visit the candidature city with the expenses borne by the bidding city,
   c. any gift or remembrance presented to the IOC member and guest may not exceed US$200 in value (later changed to no gifts),
   d. candidate cities are "forbidden to conclude with IOC members, their relations, relatives by marriage, their guests or companions, agreements, transactions or any other contracts; the same applies to all juridical persons represented by such persons or in which such persons hold an interest". (International Olympic Committee, 1992, p.80)

These regulations include not only candidature cities but also third parties working on their behalf. Should these regulations be violated the bidding city may be eliminated from consideration for hosting the Olympics.

Candidature File

The information presented here is to be used as reference for those organizations or individuals contemplating hosting an international contest. Not every governing body will require the same procedures, but administrators have to be aware that this detail may be expected of their group. Thus, as this material is studied, imagine how any international event bidder can adapt these themes to its own circumstances and purposes.

In order to standardize better the bids submitted for hosting the Olympic Games, a reply to a questionnaire covering 23 themes must be submitted by each bidding city. The themes are to be replied to in order of their presentation and explanation in the IOC's *Manual for Cities Bidding foe the Olympic Games* (1992). The questionnaire themes, in order, with a synopsis of the information requested include

TABLE 6.1
International Olympic Committee Candidature File Themes

1. National and international characteristics of the country
2. Candidate city
3. Customs and immigration formalities
4. Meteorological conditions
5. Environmental protection
6. Security
7. Health/Medical system
8. Olympic village
9. Accommodation (with the exception of the Olympic village)
10. Transport
11. Program of the Olympic Games
12. Proposed competition sites
13. Cultural program and youth camp
14. IOC Session
15. Ceremonies
16. Media
17. Telecommunications
18. Data processing services and links
19. Financial
20. Marketing
21. Communication, image and Olympism
22. Legal aspects
23. Sports experience

Theme 1. National and international characteristics of the country

The IOC requests information about the political system, political parties, topics of debate, election years for each government level and sport policies of each. Of particular note is the IOC's desire to know with which countries each candidate city's country does not have diplomatic relations.

Theme 2. Candidate city

Of vital importance to successfully hosting the Olympics is community support. In the bid, the IOC wants the candidate to have thoroughly examined the will of the people, not only locally but also nationally. In order to accomplish this self-examination and to establish its legal status, the bidder presents a city and regional history; profile of economic development; description of the political process, parties involved and their autonomy from the regional and national institution; documentation of support from each governmental level; surveys showing local citizen support for the bid and a listing of possible opposition groups; involvement of local authorities with the organizers; committee members' names and functions; and documents providing verification of the committee's legal status.

Theme 3. Customs and immigration formalities.

Because so many people will be visiting the host city from the world over, it is imperative that that country have customs and immigration procedures in place that will allow for this flow of athletes, officials, and spectators into the country.

As a result of these concerns, candidate cities must provide information about immigration and entry visa regulations, guarantees for Olympic identity-card holders to move freely, equipment import regulations, tax regulations, health and vaccination regulations, and entry of horses regulations. Note that the *Olympic Charter* (International Olympic Committee, 1993) states,

> The Olympic identity card establishes the identity of its holder and constitutes a document which, together with the passport or other official travel document of the holder, authorizes the entry into the country in which the city organizing the Olympic Games is situated. (p.100)

Theme 4. Meteorological conditions

Climatic conditions play a vital role in sport. High altitude conditions, as in Mexico City, can play a significant role in aerobic and anaerobic event results. Additionally, an Olympics should not be held during the monsoon season.

In order to satisfy the IOC's commitment to holding a quality Games, the candidate cities must supply data for the completion period about general climatic conditions, air pollution data, altitude in meters; tide, water temperature, and depth for sailing events; and respective IF approval for these conditions for their events.

Theme 5. Environmental protection

The Olympic Movement has adopted the philosophy that the environment must be protected. The IOC even sent a representative to the 1992 World Environmental Conference in Brazil.

The hosting of the Olympic Games often requires massive building projects for event venues, the athletes' village, and transportation networks. In addition to the thousands of athletes, administration, press, and visitors infused into a confined area for a short period can overload a waste disposal system not adequately planned. Because of this, the bidding cities must supply guarantees to comply with environmental protection regulations, environmental impact studies, planned use of recycling event material, and opinions of ecological organizations.

Theme 6. Security

The massacre of Israeli athletes at the 1972 Munich Olympics was a turning point in the Olympics. Never again would cursory security measures be adequate. The Olympics now commands such pervasive media attention that it is indeed an inviting target for any group seeking to gain international attention.

In order to limit the potential for a negative incident occurring, the bid cities must provide data that indicates measures to address risks of activists, city crime statistics, public and private security organizations, and guarantees to take "all possible measures that the Olympic Games run smoothly and without incident" (International Olympic Committee, 1992, p.31). It is important to understand that the IOC requires security measures not only at the sporting venues and the Olympic village but also throughout the host city, the Olympic Family accommodations, training sites, opening and closing ceremonies, during Olympic-related travel, at Olympic-affiliated cultural events, the Olympic torch relay, the Main Press Center (MPC) and International Broadcast Center (IBC), and for visiting delegations and VIPs.

Theme 7. Health/Medical System

When hundreds of thousands of visitors converge on a host city, with them comes the possibility of their needing medical assistance. This is particularly true of the athletes' village inhabitants because of the high density of their living conditions. As result the IOC requires the bidding cities to closely examine their health and medical care system. Therefore, the following topics need addressed.

Theme 7.1 Health service in the candidate city

Current and historical medical procedures for emergency care, drinking water and food safety, and disease control are discussed. The payment method and billing procedure for medical assistance need to be explained.

Theme 7.2 Arrangements planned for the Games

Medical care, first aid, and emergency evacuation for the events need to be explained. Statements from those people and organizations providing these services are required.

Theme 7.3 Anti-doping control

A delineation of doping-control collection centers and laboratories is required, including those for horses during the athletic contest.

Theme 8. Olympic village

The Olympic village is home to the visiting Olympic teams -- athletics, coaches, medical personnel, and administrators. Because this mini-world is such a focal point of the Games, with all the nations represented, extra care must be taken to provide for the athletes' safety, meals, and daily needs, before their athletic achievements can be addressed. To this end the IOC pays particular attention to the proper planning of the Olympic village. The bidder must include site plans, work schedule, catering plan, cultural andsecurity measures, and post-Olympic use. Even the less glamorous but important everyday items need to be addressed: laundry services, recreation and relaxation areas, places of worship, bank, post office, hair dressers/barber shop, telecommunications facilities, and training sites within the village.

Theme 9. Accommodation (with the exception of the Olympic village)
Because there are so many other people, other than athletes and team officials, coming to the host city, plans must be made to accommodate each group.

1. The IOC, the Presidents, and Secretaries General of the international federations and national Olympic committees, guests
2. The media
3. Officials of the international federations (foreign judges and referees)
4. Sponsors
5. Volunteers and local personnel
6. Spectators.

With the dissolution of the Soviet Union, Yugoslavia, Czechoslovakia, etc., the increase in the number of visiting officials is a factor not only in the Olympic village but also in these accommodations. It is anticipated that soon there will be 200 members of the IOC.
This part of the Olympic Games bidding manual is delineated into four sections.

Theme 9.1 General framework of accommodation
Included within this requirement is details concerning contract details with local hotels for room guarantees (number and price); current available rooms and location; construction plans delineated into what will be built, by whom and their references; and use of new accommodation construction after the Games.

Theme 9.2 The IOC, The Presidents and Secretaries General of the international federations and the national Olympic committees, guests
The description and prices for present and planned accommodations are needed. In addition, meeting rooms are required for IOC meetings as well as IFs, which may schedule meetings during the Olympics. Table 6.2 indicates the guidelines and number of rooms needed for this grouping.

Theme 9.3 The Media
Because the media will be under constant press deadlines, which vary depending on the country or information serviced, most media members will require private rooms with direct internationaltelephone access and television. Laundry and catering services are needed 24 hours a day because of the time constraints.
The Barcelona Olympic organizers estimated 7,600 rooms would be needed, 80% of which would be single rooms, with many media members staying 4 to 5 weeks. It is also important to note the location and access of the housing relative to the sport venues, the main press center, and press satellite centers.

TABLE 6.2
Olympic Games Hotel/Motel Room Requirements

Games of the Olympiad

IOC members	180
IF Presidents and Secretaries General	60
NOC Presidents and Secretaries General	360
Members of IOC commission	100
Guests of the IOC	100
	800

This includes 20 suites

IOC staff	100
Persons with B/C acceditations	200
Observers for next Olympic Games and candidate cities	300
	600
	1400

Winter Olympics

IOC members	150
IF Presidents and Secretaries General	15
NOC Presidents and Secretaries General	120
IOC Commission members	55
Guests of the IOC	60
	400

This includes 20 suites

IOC staff	80
Observers for next Olympic Games and candidate cities	200
	280

Theme 9.4 Other Accommodations Needs

For the international federations approximately 900-1,000 rooms are needed. Since each IF will have a headquarters, several hotels may be needed.

The foreign judges' and referees' accommodations must be located within easy access of the venue in which they will officiate. Approximately 1,000 rooms are needed for the Summer Olympics and 200 rooms for the Winter Olympics. The IFs, with a "contribution" from the IOC, pay for these accommodations.

IOC sponsors and host committee sponsors and suppliers will need about 3,000 double rooms for the Winter Olympics and 4,000-5,000 double rooms for the Summer Olympics. The Olympic broadcasters will be included in this group.

Each host city needs to consider how many volunteers and staff will be needed and whether they are local or will need housing.

Many visitors will be expected. Due consideration is relevant when realizing that many of these visitors will be foreign and will have the same special needs as any foreign visitors, that is, language difficulties, cultural differences, food, banking, or medical needs.

For all the aforementioned groups descriptions of existing and planned housing are required relative to capacity, comfort, price, availability, and location.

Theme 10. Transport

During the Olympics there can be great strain placed upon the host city's transportation system. Without proper planning a breakdown in this system can cause major problems with efficient event management, press coverage, and spectator enjoyment of the Games. The IOC requires the bidding cities to provide historical verification of their international airport's accessibility and capacity; official verification of existing and planned ground transportation capabilities, including parking; distances in kilometers and travel times between housing units and the venues; and types of vehicles available, especially to transport the athletes' and the media's equipment. Specific rules dictate which IOC and NOC members and officials must be supplied with chauffeur-driven cars.

Theme 11. Program of the Olympic Games

In general, the sports and disciplines program is set with the awarding of the Games to a candidate city, normally 7 years in advance. The host city must consider IF requests, national and school holidays, and city/regional events planned during this period (International Olympic Committee, 1993).

In the bid document, the candidates must have written statements from the IFs that they have been consulted, verification that no other local or regional events will be planned from a week before through a week after the Olympics, that the city is capable of staging all the sports involved, and, if desired, the same information for the Paralympic Games immediately following the Olympics.

Theme 12. Proposed competition sites

The facilities associated with an Olympic Games become a lasting reminder of that special occasion. The IOC wants this memory to be positive in the host city and leave a positive legacy. Therefore, in preparing to bid for the Olympics, the following topics need to be addressed very early:

1. Public relation in the community and region
2. Construction planning and costs
3. Infrastructure (transportation, housing, etc.)

4. Financial support and resources
5. Post-Olympic use of the facilities.

From these initial considerations, the Olympic bid must address the following: descriptions of the venues and reasons for their selections; statements of whether the facilities are existing, new, or renovated; guarantees from authorized authorities condoning the facility projects; post-Olympic use; detailed descriptions of each facility; and guarantees that no publicity or propaganda will appear within the competition venues. In addition, early on there must be close cooperation with the IF of each competition venue because the *Olympic Charter* (International Olympic Committee, 1990) states that the IFs will be the technical organizers of their respective sports. Therefore, each IF must be satisfied that the venue is appropriate for its sport.

Theme 13. Cultural program and youth camp
The host city must organize a cultural program during the Olympic Games. (This has become popular at other sporting events as well.) The host's culture as well as international flavor should be included in "entertainment, dance, music, theater and the arts." (International Olympic Committee, 1992, p.55) Additionally, the host city may sponsor a youth camp for 18- to 22-year-olds in order to bring the world's youth together to promote Olympism to the next generation of leaders.
For the bid, the candidate city must describe its proposed cultural program, when and where it will be held and what the budget will be. Should a youth camp be planned, its specifics must also be stated.

Theme 14. IOC Session
The host city must provide facilities for the IOC Session. The Session is a meeting of the entire International Olympic Committee with associated administrators and service personnel. This meeting lasts 3 days with approximately 150 people in attendance, including interpreters. In bidding for the Games, cities must describe the facility to be used and its location relative to IOC member housing.

Theme 15. Ceremonies
There are five ceremonies recognized by the IOC that must be organized by the host city.

Theme 15.1. Opening ceremony of the IOC Session.
As with the IOC Session, the IOC provides organizing guidelines when preparing for this affair. When arranging for this occasion a 1,500-person minimum capacity is required.

Theme 15.2. Olympic Village Arrivals
The candidate city must submit its plan for welcoming each country's contingent to the Olympic village. This ceremony is to include a parade, raising of the country's flag, and playing its national anthem.

Theme 15.3. Olympic Games Opening and Closing

In the bid, the prospective host city must describe where these two ceremonies will be held and approximately the other activities included, other than the official ceremonies.

The spectator capacities for the Games of the Olympiad are 70,000 and 25,000 for the Winter Games. The *Olympic Charter* entitles about 15,000 athletes and team officials for the Games of the Olympiad and 3,000 for the Winter Olympics to attend.

The ceremonies must also allow for other Olympic Games accredited personnel, approximately 20,000 for the Games of the Olympiad and 10,000 for the Winter Games.

The opening and closing of the Olympic Games are carefully choreographed. The *Olympic Charter* dictates what will happen (parade of participants, Olympic flag and torch movement, protocol speeches) and in what order these will occur. This ceremony is so important that the host country's head of state is required to say, "I declare open the Games of...(name of city) celebrating the ... Olympiad of the modern era (or the ....the Olympic Winter Games").The closing ceremony is likewise arranged.

Theme 15.4. Medal Ceremony

Each venue must provide for medals to be awarded to the top athletes/teams in each event. The bid must describe the medal ceremony for each competition site.

Theme 15.5. The Olympic Torch Relay

The bidding cities must describe the Olympic flame journey from Olympia, Greece, to the Olympic Stadium and the lighting of the Olympic flame at the opening ceremonies. The description needs to include the cities through which the torch relay will proceed, dates, and other activities planned in conjunction with the Olympic Torch Relay.

In all the ceremonies, protocol is the operative word. The Olympics stand on prestige and ceremony, foreshadowing the athletes' best efforts. Because these ceremonies are as much a part of the Olympics as the competition itself, the host city must show that each ceremony is in accordance with the Olympic tradition.

Theme 16. Media

With about 12,000 journalists accredited at the Games of the Olympiad and 7,000 for the Winter Games, there is a significant task in providing for their needs. Because these people are the eyes and ears for the world, not only during the Games but also inpreparation and review, every effort to accommodate their needs should be expended. The candidate cities must provide a Main Press Center (MPC) and an International Broadcasting Center (IBC). In the bid, these centers, as well as subcenters, must be located and described.

A television company experienced (see Theme 17) in major events needs to be recognized. In addition the IOC wants to know that at least one organization wants to be the host broadcaster.

Theme 17. Telecommunications

The modern Olympics has become a media spectacle. For that reason, the bidding cities are to provide a guarantee that the media will have access to telecommunications systems. In addition the information in the bid must include present telecommunications system specifics, improvements projected, national and international communication rates, and a written statement from the appropriate national authority guaranteeing that existing technical services will be available to the media.

Theme 18. Data Processing Services and Links

International contests require a significant amount of data processing. Fortunately, modern computers with the appropriate software have simplified accreditation, volunteers scheduling, ticket and housing reservations, timing, and event results, etc. Because subsequent host cities may benefit from previously written software and its use, the bidding cities are required in their bid to submit a technical description of the data processing system each intends to use.

Theme 19. Financial

The financial aspects of hosting an Olympic Games have become critical. With the great debt incurred in Montreal in 1976, the Games of the Olympiad, as we know them, were thought to be nearly extinct. However, Los Angeles in 1984 showed the world that a significant revenue in excess of expenses could be garnered if costs were kept under control (particularly with facility construction) and significant revenue generated, primarily from television rights and marketing programs. As such, each bidding city must assure the IOC of its fiscal viability (1993).

The other information required with the bid includes the annual inflation rate for the past 5 years along with future projections, host city financial status, price control procedures (particularly for hotels and special services), and price control agreements from trade or professional associations. In addition, a detailed budget to include the following items needs to be included:

- investments in infrastructures,
- investments in sites,
- investments in services:
   • public participation
   • private participation
- budgeted expenditure for operating costs:
   • public participation
   • private participation
- expected income:
   • television rights
   • marketing
   • ticketing, etc.
- expected profit (if any). Specify how your share of this will be used.
- loss (if any). Explain how you will compensate for this (International Olympic Committee, 1992, p.66).

Theme 20. Marketing

Because of the 1984 Los Angeles Olympics, marketing of sporting events has changed considerably. The two major sources of revenue, and those most specifically addressed in the bid, are from television and radio rights and sponsor programs. In the bid, the IOC requires that the host carefully examine the potential for the electronic media rights with respect to revenue and services required. The sponsors' programs that need addressing include the TOP Programme (the IOC program that combines the OCOG, the NOCs, and the IOC), and the host city's national sponsors' program of awarding special affiliation and logo rights to companies supplying services and financial support. The candidate city should also detail other marketing programs that will generate financial and public support.

Theme 21. Communication, image, and Olympism

Mention the term Olympic Games and most people will have a vivid image, strong feeling a special moment to which they can relate. The IOC carefully cultivates the Olympic experience to include the ideals of the Olympic Movement. Therefore, each candidate city must present in its bids surveys conducted dealing with the "image of the Olympic Movement and the Games," not only for that city but also for its region and country. Also, the bid must include a statement that "define(s) the communication concept or concepts which, in your opinion, best link the Olympic spirit and the distinctive features of your city, your country, in its Olympic calling,..." (International Olympic Committee, 1992, p.69).

Theme 22. Legal Aspects

With the number of people and organizations affiliated in some manner with the hosting of the international sporting events, the legal aspects, particularly contract implementation, become very important. The IOC is particularly cognizant of a candidate city binding itself with a legal commitment *before* the city has won the rights to the Games.

With the candidate's bid, the following legal aspects must be addressed:

1. Any promises made during the bid process will be binding and must be fulfilled. This provision is intended to assure that the candidate does not make promises in order to win the Games hosting, that it knows it can not provide.
2. The candidate city guarantees that an athlete with a valid passport, or its equivalent, and the Olympic identity card will be permitted entry into the host country.
3. Legal measures must be assured to protect Olympic and host city property rights, including protection from ambush marketing.
4. A method to quickly resolve legal disputes involving the Games or the IOC must be presented.
5. Candidate cities must indicate any other legal problems that may occur and how they would be resolved.

Theme 23. Sports Experience

When desiring to host the largest international sporting event, experiences of the candidate city are very important. Therefore, the IOC requires that the bidders provide information relative to its city's and country's history in hosting international sport competitions. Of particular note is the candidate city's personnel and their relationship with its national Olympic committee.

Upon examining the 23 themes, one can easily understand that a great deal of time, effort, creativity and cooperation is needed when submitting an international sporting event bid. Although each event will have its own bid criteria, with the exception of hosting the handicapped or physically/mentally challenged athlete, this listing provides a good framework from which a bid could be created.

Candidate File Examination

Each city wishing to submit its bid to host the Olympics must give the IOC 20 copies, in English and in French. The IOC studies the file and may request additional information. Only after the IOC permits, may the candidate city release the bid file to the public.

In addition to distributing the candidature file to the IOC and releasing it to the press and general public, the candidate cities must also send one copy of the file to

1. IOC members,
2. Each international federation directly affected,
3. The Association of the Summer Olympic International Federations (ASOIF) or the Association of the International Winter Sports Federations (AIWF), respectively,
4. The Association of National Olympic Committees (ANOC),
5. The five NOC continental associations (ANOCA, OCA, PASO, EOC and, ONOC), and
6. The Olympic museum in Lausanne.

After studying the submitted files, the IOC assigns a Study Commission to visit each city. The Study Commission will discuss with the bidding organization specifics of the bid, visit proposed sites and venues, and evaluate the merits of each city. From this visit, a report is sent to the IOC members for their examination. This report is sent at least 2 months prior to the IOC session at which the host city will be selected.

For the 2002 Winter Games the IOC has appointed an Evaluation Commission to recommend four possible hosts from the nine bids received. Thus, the IOC decided that its membership would be better served by concentrating on what appear to be the four best Olympic host cities. These four cities will then be visited by up to 70 IOC members before the final vote is taken (Huba, 1994).

Candidate Presentation

At the IOC session at which the Olympic host city will be selected, each city is given one hour to present its bid and to answer questions of the IOC members. The order of presentation is by a blind draw several months before the session. Each city is limited to 6 presenters, 4 advisors, 2 technicians and 10 observers. Use of audiovisual equipment is permitted. After each city has presented, the IOC Study Commission presents its findings from its visits to the candidate cities. After answering any questions, the voting commences.

TABLE 6.3
Recent Olympic Host City Voting

1988: Lillehammer 1994

Lillehammer	25	30	45
Oestersund	19	33	39
Anchorage	23	20	
Sofia	17		

1990: Atlanta 1996

Atlanta	19	20	26	34	51
Athens	23	23	26	30	35
Toronto	14	17	18	22	
Melbourne	12	21	16		
Manchester	11	5			
Belgrade	7				

1991: Nagano 1998

Nagano	21		30	36	46
Salt Lake City	15	(59)	27	29	42
Oestersund	18		25	23	
Jaca	19		5		
Aosta	15	(29)			

1993: Sydney 2000

Sydney	30	30	37	45
Beijing	32	37	40	43
Manchester	11	13	11	
Berlin	9	9		
Istanbul	7			

1995: Salt Lake City 2002

Salt Lake City	55
Sion	14
Ostersund	14
Quebec	7

Olympic Candidate Voting

After the presentations and discussions are concluded, the IOC voting begins. In this secret ballot, the city with a simple majority wins. However, it normally takes several rounds before a city gains that simple majority. The city with the least votes in a given round is dropped from the succeeding rounds. Table 6.3 shows the recent round-by-round voting (Scott, 1992).

When the voting is completed, the IOC president makes the announcement, usually before live television coverage to the candidate cities. Immediately thereafter, the winning city signs the "Host City Contract" with the IOC.

The "Host City Contract" specifies that the new host Olympic city create an Organizing Committee of the Olympic Games (OCOG) within 6 months and within 10 days pay an additional sum to the IOC of US $900,000 for the Games of the Olympiad or US $400,000 additional for the Winter Olympics. The OCOG members must include the host country IOC member(s), the NOC's president and secretary general, and at least one member from the host city. Other members may be added as needed. It is the duty of this OCOG to manage and administer according to the *Olympic Charter* and the instructions of the IOC Executive Board, and to see the host city carries out its contractual obligations (International Olympic Committee, 1993). The IOC specifies that the OCOG, host city, and the host country NOC will be "jointly and severally liable" for the provisions of the "Host City Contract" (International Olympic Committee, 1993).

With other international events the presentation and voting procedures will vary. What will remain constant is the desire of the international federation or other awarding body to have the successful bidder bind itself to fulfilling its obligation to provide for the quality event envisioned in its bid.

Concluding Summary

A city wishing to host an international sporting event needs many years in which to prepare. This chapter used the Olympic bid format to illustrate the thoroughness that is needed in examining the potential host's desire, resources, and ability to stage a successful event.

Critical thinking for potential host organizations is systematized through response to the 23 themes presented in the *Manual for Cities Bidding for the Olympic Games*. Using this format those seeking the bid must be able to show that they have examined and are able to address successfully topics as infrastructure, medical, transportation, housing, venues, global communications, personnel, and security. Critical to this process is the local, regional, and national commitment that is needed in order that the people most affected, the city's citizens, enthusiastically support the event.

When a potential host organization has completed its bid document, it should know whether it has the desire and ability to host an international sporting event. With this information in hand the bidder can seek the support of the event organization, in this chapter the IOC, in order to be the successful host bidder.

Discussion, Analysis, Application, and Debate

Issues for Discussion

1. The Olympic bidding model presented is quite extensive. Do you believe that model should be followed for your favorite sport's international championship?
2. When bidding to host an international sporting event, there is always the possibility that revenue will not exceed expenses. How would you respond to a local group that would rather have the city's money spent on social programs?
3. Do you believe an international sporting event is an appropriate venue to have a cultural program? Explain your answer.

Matter for Analysis

1. Using the Olympic bid model, what themes might be different for a single-event international competition?
2. When evaluating an Olympic host bid, what are the pros and cons of financing the event with governmental and nongovernmental funds? Why would the IOC be concerned which method is used?

Applications

1. Based on the IOC's 23 themes create a bid for an international event in a city near you.
2. Examine the IOC's 23 themes. For each theme, describe criteria for each that would reflect negatively on a host's bid.

Ethical Debate

Bidding to host a major international sporting event requires great planning in order to assure proper allocation of resources, such as personnel, facilities, and capital. After being awarded the Olympic Games, the organizing committee often becomes the target of social protest. Could the millions of dollars spent in Olympic preparation be better used on social programs, for example, Montreal's Bread not Circus? Be sure to consider long-term and short-term effects.

References

Huba, K.-H. (1994). *Sport intern.* (Vol 26, Issue 15) August 15. Muenchen, Federal Republic of Germany.

International Olympic Committee (1992). *Manual for cities bidding for the Olympic Games*. Lausanne: International Olympic Committee.

International Olympic Committee (1993). *Olympic charter*. Lausanne: International Olympic Committee.

Kidd, B. (1992). The Toronto Olympic commitment: Towards a social contract for the Olympic Games. *Olympika, The International Journal of Olympic Studies, 1,* 154-167.

Scott, R. (1992). *Is it the dollar or the spirit that inspires cities to bid to host the Olympic Games?* Paper presented at the International Olympic Academy, Ancient Olympia, Greece.

CHAPTER SEVEN —————————

Hosting an

INTERNATIONAL EVENT

Overview

This chapter follows naturally from Chapter 6. Again the Olympics are modeled. The majority of the chapter deals with pre-event organization as this is the key to understanding the host's responsibilities and, ultimately, the successful event hosting. The Calgary Olympics illustrate what transpires during the event itself. After the competition ends the post event phase is examined. This phase may take years with venue hand-over and contract completion. Finally, the event's legacy, which was considered at the initial bid stage, is examined.

Introduction

One of life's heaviest burdens is being awarded a major international event. From that moment onward the whole world will be focusing its attention on the development of the host's organization, venues, management, marketing, and goodwill. This section will present the organization needed for hosting an international sporting event. **For the sake of relevance, the Olympic Games will be presented primarily.** However, it must be understood that each event -- Games of the Olympiad, Winter Olympics, Goodwill Games, Asian Games, etc. -- is unique. The strengths and weaknesses of each host organization, venues, transportation network, and infrastructure must be combined to produce the desired results. Each host organization can learn from the others. However, one mold will not produce identical successful events.

Pre-Event Organization

Atlanta was awarded the 1996 Games of the Olympiad on September 18, 1990. On January 28, 1991, the Atlanta Committee for the Olympic Games (ACOG) was incorporated. Normally a host organization would work with the international governing body and the host city to prepare for the event. However, the Olympics function under rules established by the IOC. The *Olympic Charter* mandates that the host city enter into a contract with the IOC and the host city's National Olympic Committee (International

FIGURE 7.1
Atlanta Committee for the Olympic Games Organizational Chart

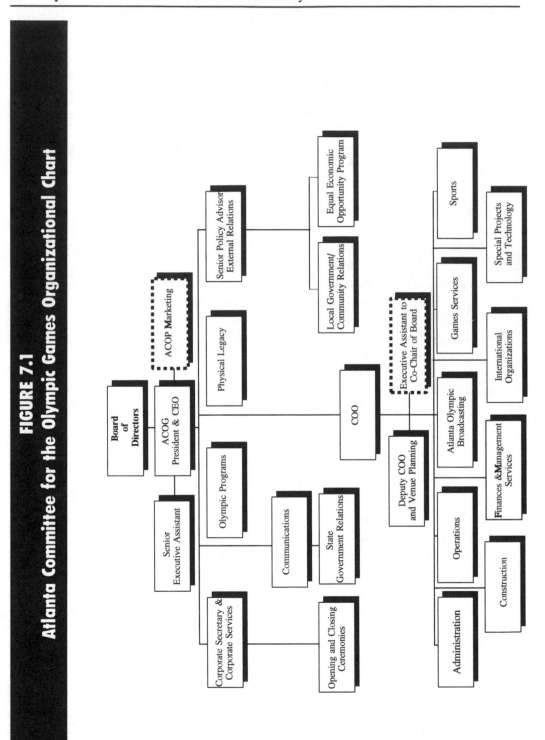

Olympic Committee, 1993). In the case of Atlanta, this is the United States Olympic Committee. ACOG also has agreements with the city of Atlanta and Metropolitan Atlanta Olympic Games Authority (MAOGA). "MAOGA is a public authority responsible for review of ACOG construction contracts, financial statements and budgets; approval of venue changes; and construction of the Olympic Stadium" (Atlanta Committee for the Olympic Games, 1992a, p.9). MAOGA will act as a check on ACOG's legal and financial dealings since the city of Atlanta, primarily, will inherit the remnants of the Olympics. No city wants to carry the heavy financial debt Montreal inherited following the 1976 Games.

Responsibilities

Primary responsibilities of the organizing committee include establishing an organization and delegating responsibilities. A well-crafted bid document will prompt a bid city to critically analyze its abilities. Therefore, the city that does win the competitive bid process is very much along in its way to a quality organization and games presentation.

In analyzing ACOG's organization as of September 1994 (Figure 7.1, Atlanta Committee for the Olympic Games, 1992b), the President and Chief Executive Officer (CEO) has a number of departments reporting directly to him. Each of the departments obviously is very important to the success of the Olympic celebration. Upon further inspection, however, one can see that the Chief Operating Officer, who reports to the CEO is responsible for the administration and management of the aspects directing the competition.

By comparison to ACOG's organization, the organizational chart for the 1988 Seoul Olympic Organizing Committee (SLOOC) is shown on Figure 7.2 (Seoul Olympic Organizing Committee, 1989). This organization had three vice presidents reporting directly to the president. By inspection one can see that the major domestic matters were handled by the Secretary General, who also was a vice president. However, two of the most public aspects of the international event -- international relations and the sport contests -- were each assigned their own vice president reporting directly to the president. In contrast, ACOG has decided that these two administrative areas fall within the reporting line through the Chief Operating Officer to the CEO.

As one inspects these two organizational charts, two important aspects must be emphasized. First, the complexity of each area is not evident from the figures. For example, although ACOG built some facilities and a Games' village, it had a metropolitan region with a well established infrastructure. Seoul, however, was a city that accelerated a national rebuilding program as a developing nation growing out of the Korean War. Therefore, the construction in Seoul was more widespread and complex than Atlanta.

Second, organizational charts illustrate formal lines of authority and communication. However, within each organization the informal lines of communication are often more important than the formal channels. The informal lines can only be known by those individuals whose personalities mesh within the organization.

An important aspect that is not evident in Seoul's organizational chart is the ex-officio members of the Executive Board and the ex-officio members of SLOOC, Tables 7.1 and 7.2, respectively. Also, because Korea is a much smaller country than the United

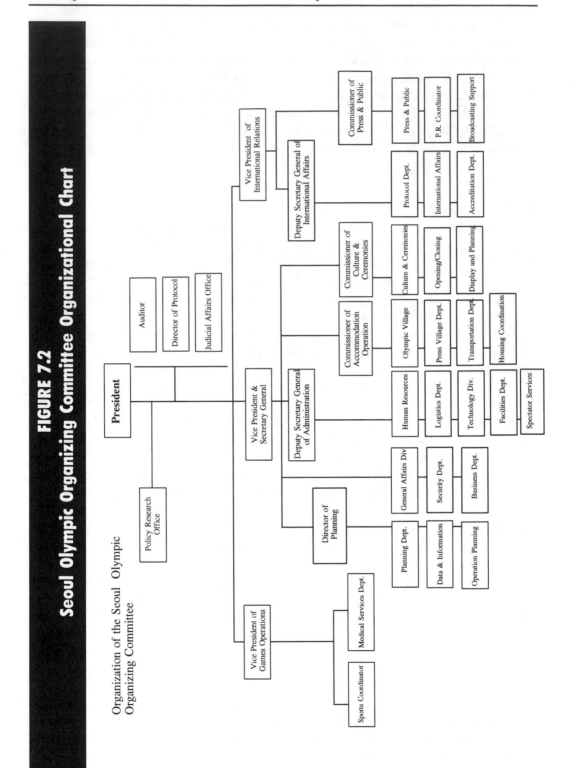

FIGURE 7.2

Seoul Olympic Organizing Committee Organizational Chart

Organization of the Seoul Olympic Organizing Committee

TABLE 7.1
Ex-Officio Members of the SLOOC Executive Board

- Chairman, National Assembly Education and Public Information Committee
- Minister of Home Affairs
- Minister of Finance
- Minister of National Defense
- Minister of Education
- Minister of Sports
- Minister of Construction
- Minister of Communications
- Minister of Culture and Information
- Minister of Government Administration
- Seoul mayor
- President, Federation of Korean Industries
- President, Korean Broadcasting Association
- IOC Member
- President, Korean Olympic Committee
- Secretary-general, National Supporting Committee for Seoul Olympic
- Secretary-general of the SLOOC

Note: A minister in the Parlimentary government system is equivalent to the United States' cabinet secretaries: for example Minister of Education is equivalent to the Secretary of Education.
Note: From Official Report: Games of the XXIVth Olympiad Seoul 1988 (p. 82). Seoul Olympic Organizing Committee, 1989.

States, SLOOC would need much closer cooperation from a greater cross-section of the nation's resources (Table 7.2)

Figure 7.2 illuminates Korea's more centralized sport organization, as most countries would have. Table 7.2 also indicates the diversity of a greater span of resources and support needed by Korea. Of particular note is the inclusion of political parties and trade union leadership on the organizing committee. These two constituencies, although important in Atlanta, would more likely be represented on a local or regional level as opposed to a national level.

A major task of any such organization is to select qualified, competent personnel to administer each position. In addition, each additional position added must have a person capable of handling the tasks assigned. The major problem with filling positions for an international event is that few of the staff will have experienced what it will take to host the event, and few will have the experience organizing or directing whatever activity is assigned. As a result, the people selected for each position must have skills that can be adapted to the organization. Recognizing the importance of qualified personnel, the IOC requires that bid cities indicate the experience and qualifications of key organizing committee members.

TABLE 7.2
Ex-Officio Members of the SLOOC

- Floor leaders of political parties
- Superintendent, Seoul Education Board
- President, Korea University Sports Committee
- President, Korea Chamber of Commerce and Industry
- President, Korea Traders Association
- President, Federation of Korean Culture and Arts Association
- President, Korea Newspaper Publishers Association
- President-publisher, Yonhap News Agency
- President, Federation of Korean Trade Unions
- President, Korean National Tourism Corporation
- Deputy secretary-general of the SLOOC in charge of administration
- Deputy secretary-general of the SLOOC in charge of sports
- Deputy secretary-general of the SLOOC in charge of international relations

Note: From *Official Report: Games of the XXIVth Olympiad Seoul 1988* (p. 82). Seoul Olympic Organizing Committee, 1989.

It should be recognized that primary importance when hosting an international event is that all organizing committee members and workers, from the chairperson to the volunteers, must present a friendly face to the public. Goodwill, pleasant demeanor, and a helpful attitude will go a long way to creating an enjoyable experience for everyone concerned with a sporting event. This attitude must begin from day one and continue until the books are closed on the event, which will be long after those particular games terminate. This attitude becomes part of the corporate climate. Any visiting dignitary, business executive, reporter, scholar, or whoever should experience this good feeling. For example, ACOG exhibits this feeling in the form of "Southern Hospitality," thus achieving one of its major objectives: to "Show Atlanta's personality to the world through the people" (Atlanta Committee for the Olympic Games, 1992b, p.73).

Community Outreach

When hosting an international event one of the great opportunities, as well as challenges, is to secure the support of the local and regional citizens. This can weigh heavily in bid evaluations. Kidd (1992) pointed to the lack of this support in Toronto by the group Bread Not Circus as a possible reason why Toronto did not win the 1996 Olympics.

Atlanta, in its bid quest, began a campaign in July 1989 to solicit 100,000 volunteers for the hosting of the Games. By January 1990, that 100,000-person mark was surpassed. This accomplishment occurred even before Atlanta submitted its formal bid to the IOC in Lausanne on February 1, 1990. This showed the Atlanta organizing committee's understanding of the need for citizen involvement and, by reaching its goal in half a year, the public's support for Atlanta's bid.

One of the key principles of gaining support for a venture such as staging an international sport event is to have a broad base of community support. ACOG recognized this principle by creating four "Community Outreach Organizations" (Atlanta Committee for the Olympic Games, 1992a). The groups are Advisory Councils, Support Groups, Task Forces, and the ACOG Advisory. They are shown in Table 7.3.

It is through these Outreach Organizations that ACOG seeks the council and support of the Atlanta area citizens. These organizations may be compared to quality circles; each group contains experts in the subject. Through their sharing of the "the way it is," the host organization can make more educated decisions by having eyes and ears in the heart of what will become the Olympic stage. In addition, the citizens involved provide that community link that can prevent a problem or can diffuse one before it becomes too serious.

Governance

When an organizing committee is instituted there must be a mandate and authority to govern. In ACOG's situation, its Board of Directors governs by

1. ACOG's charter and bylaws - documents that provide legality to ACOG and provide a method of internal operation.
2. The *Olympic Charter* - rules and regulations of the IOC.
3. The Host City Contract - an agreement between the IOC, USOC, the city of Atlanta, and the Metropolitan Atlanta Olympic Games Authority (MAOGA) specifying each party's responsibilities.
4. The Tri-Party Agreement- a document specifying the "roles, authorities and obligations" (Atlanta Committee to Organize the Games b, 1992, p.5) of the city of Atlanta, ACOG and MAOGA. In this document, ACOG is charged with staging the Games.
5. The ACOG/USOC Joint Venture Agreement - agreement between the host city and the USOC to market the 1996 Olympics and specifying the division of revenues and expense (Atlanta Committee for the Olympic Games, 1992b).

ACOG's Boards of Directors has five committees as specified in the bylaws:

1. Executive Committee - Acts in the absence of the full Board.
2. Audit Committee - Reviews financial information.
3. Compensation & Executive Resources Committee - Reviews and approves compensation and benefits for ACOG's staff members.
4. Equal Economic Opportunity Committee - Oversees compliance with ACOG's Equal Economic Opportunity plan to provide non-discriminatory employment practices and a voluntary affirmative action plan.
5. Finance & Administration Committee - Monitors the finances and administration of ACOG.

TABLE 7.3
ACOG Community Outreach Organizations

Advisory Councils
Provide community input relating to specific areas.

- Athletes Advisory Council
- Consolidated Neighborhood Advisory Council
- Construction Services Advisory Council
- Communications Advisory Council
- Cultural Advisory Council
- Disabled Access Advisory Council
- Design Services Advisory Council
- Financial Advisory Council
- Interfaith Advisory Council
- Savannah Olympic Support Council
- Youth Development Advisory Council

Support Groups
Provide expert advice and implementation with respect to required services.

- Accommodations Support Group
- Environmental Support Group
- Human Resources Support Group
- Olympic Medical Support Group
- Olympic Security Support Group
- Olympic Transportation Support Group
- Risk Management Support Group

Task Forces
Provide consultation with respect to specific decisions.

- Atlanta University Neighborhood Task Force
- Education Task Force
- Youth Advisory Task Force
- Olympic Stadium Neighborhood Task Force
- Olympic Village Neighborhood Task Force
- Stone Mountain Neighborhood Task Force
- Volunteer Task Force

ACOG Advisory
Community leadership group organized to consult with ACOG; chaired by Atlanta's mayor.

TABLE 7.4 **Olympic Games Roles**		
IOC	**USOC**	**ACOG**
Oversees the Olympic Movement	Is responsible for Olympic sports in the U.S.	Is the Organizing Committee for the Olympic Games
Grants rights to stage the Olympic Games	Must endorse and support the application of the Bid City	Organize and stage the 1996 Games
Markets to selected worldwide sponsors, providing a share of revenues to ACOG	Serves as partner in marketing joint venture providing a share of revenue to ACOG	Serves as partner, marketing joint venture, providing of share of revenue to USOC

Tables 7.4 and 7.5 summarize the responsibilities of ACOG and its respective partners based of the aforementioned agreements (Atlanta Committee for the Olympic Games, 1992b).

Throughout the building to an international event, the host has developed a timetable by which its goals and objectives are to be met. ACOG calls this its Critical Tasks (Figure 7.3). By using this general timetable, more specific timetables are developed. In this manner an organization can maintain its time perspective as well as being able to pinpoint short-, medium-, and long-term goal achievement (Atlanta Committee for the Olympic Games, 1992b). Figure 7.4 provides a pictorial display for the four general areas of tasks that need to be completed leading to a successful staging of the 1996 Games of the Olympiad.

Operations

Seeing that an international sporting event is conducted as prescribed is a Herculean task. The actual events themselves generally are of lesser problem for the host because the officials and administrators for the events are provided through the international federation or the country's affiliate; for instance, the IAAF or USA Track and Field will provide the officials for track and field at sanctioned international events held in the United States. The greater problems are in supporting these events. ACOG addresses these issues accordingly:

TABLE 7.5
Roles Under The Tri-Party Agreement

ACOG	MAOGA	City of Atlanta
Organize, promote, market, manage and operate Games; receive all revenues and pay all costs in connection therewith		
Provide or construct venues, training sites, Olympic Village and Media Village	Approve venue changes and changes in plans for Olympic and Media Villages	Receive notice of proposed change of any venue in City; right to find alternate city site within 120 days
Financially support at least one City-designated employee secretary	Finance, acquire and construct facilities when requested by ACOG	Assist zoning, MAOGA permits and other governmental approvals and consent to and his/her condemnations; transfer city property
Design and develop plans for Olympic Stadium	Own and construct Olympic Stadium	Receive Olympic Stadium after Games
Receive City Services from MAOGA	Enter intergovernmental contracts and make City Services available to ACOG	Enter City Services Agreement with MAOGA
Indemnify MAOGA and City and maintain sufficient insurance	Indemnify City	
Distribute surplus pursuant to Contract		Designate a foundation Host City receive 50 of surplus proceeds
Submit initial detailed financial plan	Receive initial detailed financial plan	Receive initial detail financial plan
Prepare and submit quarterly and annual financial statements	Receive quarterly and annual financial statements	Receive quarterly and annual financial statements
Prepare and submit annual budget	Receive annual budget	Receive annual budget
Submit construction contracts over $250,000 to MAOGA for approval	Approve construction contracts over $250,000	
Permit inspection of books and records	Right to examine ACOG books and records	Right to examine ACOG books and records
Prepare and submit Facility Impact Report to City	Prepare and submit Facility Impact Report	Receive Facility Impact Report
Submit proposed amendments to Articles and Bylaws	Approve amendments to ACOG Articles and Bylaws	Approve amendments to ACOG Articles and Bylaws

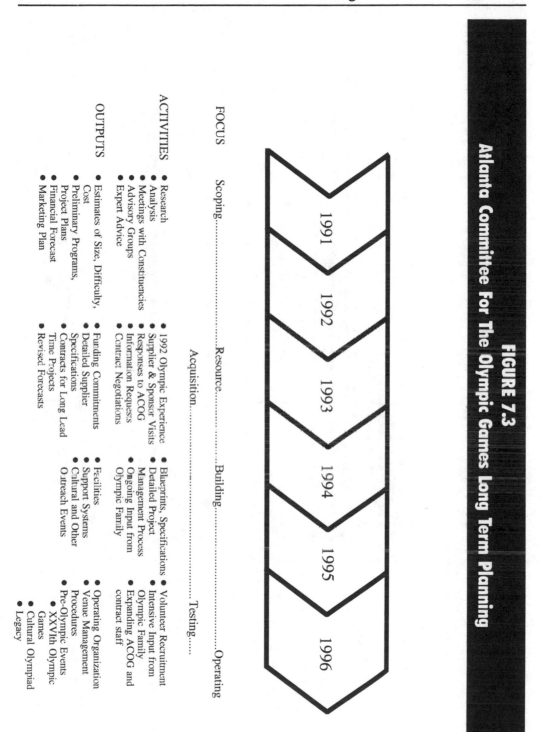

FIGURE 7.3
Atlanta Committee For The Olympic Games Long Term Planning

FIGURE 7.4
ACOG 6-Year Planning Summary

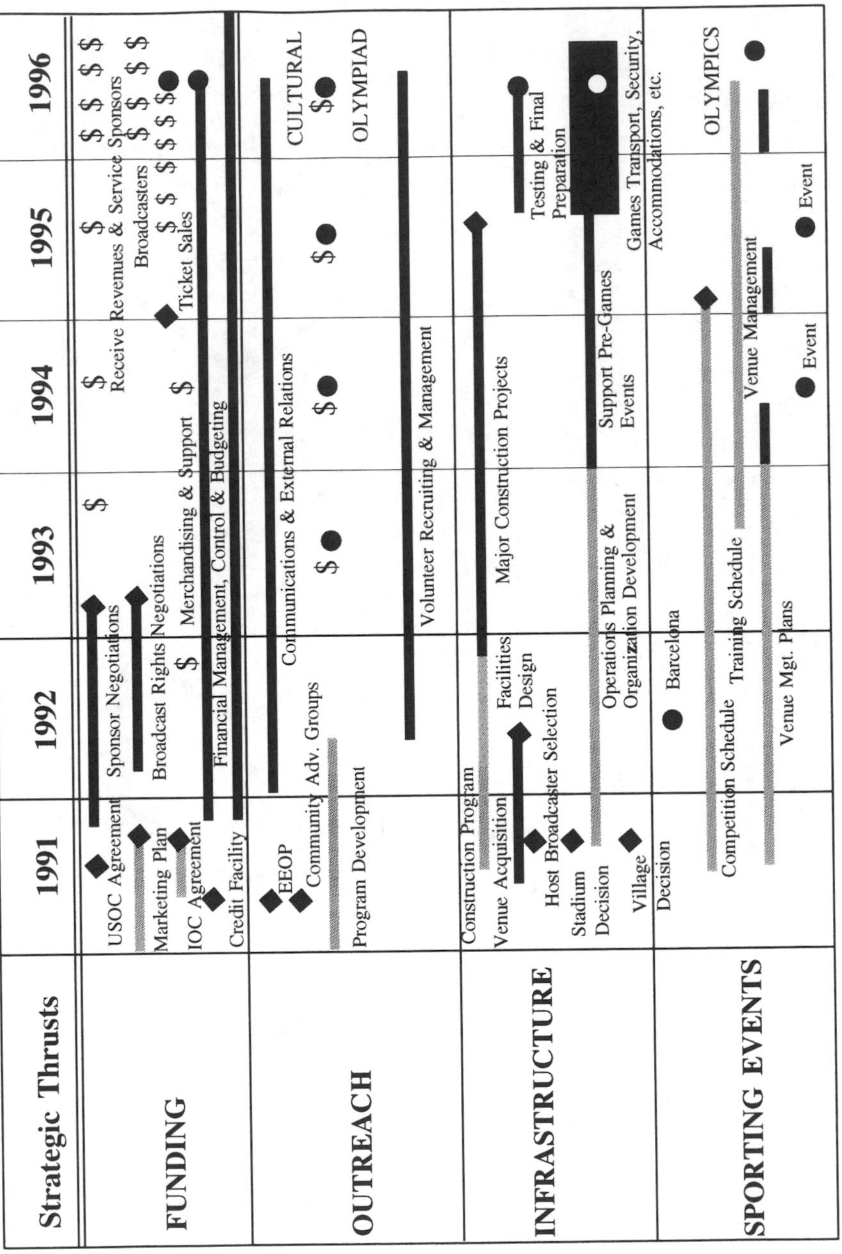

Strategic Thrusts	1991	1992	1993	1994	1995	1996
FUNDING	USOC Agreement / Marketing Plan / IOC Agreement / Credit Facility	Sponsor Negotiations / Broadcast Rights Negotiations / Merchandising & Support / Financial Management, Control & Budgeting	$	Receive Revenues & Service Sponsors / Broadcasters / $ Ticket Sales	$ $ / $ $	$ $ $ / $ $ $
OUTREACH	EEOP / Community Adv. Groups / Program Development		Communications & External Relations / $ / Volunteer Recruiting & Management	$	$	CULTURAL / $ OLYMPIAD
INFRASTRUCTURE	Construction Program / Venue Acquisition / Host Broadcaster Selection / Stadium Decision / Village	Facilities Design / Operations Planning & Organization Development	Major Construction Projects	Support Pre-Games Events	Testing & Final Preparation / Games Transport, Security, Accommodations, etc.	
SPORTING EVENTS	Decision / Competition Schedule / Venue Mgt. Plans	Barcelona / Training Schedule		Venue Management / Event	Event	OLYMPICS

Accommodations

ACOG is attempting to reach a comprehensive contractual agreement with 260 hotels/motels in the Atlanta/Savannah (venue for sailing) areas for at least 40,000 rooms reserved and controlled by ACOG at a fixed rate. Also, housing will be made available for the media at colleges and universities in the respective areas.

Accreditation

Accreditation is generally specified by the international governing body hosting the event. The IOC defines the credentials for the Olympic Games only. However, the IOC format is the model the international federations generally follow. Through this identification process, security control is enhanced for entrance to sport venues, housing areas, press centers, and administrative areas. The ACOG accreditation system will include an identification card that will have the bearer's photograph, signature, and access privileges. ACOG's system will

a.   Pre-screen all operating personnel and guests,
b.   Provide access to restricted areas,
c.   Provide identification,
d.   Verify access credentials,
e.   Aid in tracking the Olympic Family.

Logistics

Logistics is the function that is invisible if performed properly but handled improperly becomes a major headache quickly. ACOG's program of logistical support includes "food and spectator service, warehousing, trucking, waste management (remember in the bid package the IOC wants to know the planned recycling program), and maintenance" (Atlanta Committee for the Olympic Games, 1992b, p.113). This program addresses these needs for all the venues and spectators.

Host broadcasting

Because the mass media contribute so greatly to supporting major international events, the host has a great responsibility to provide the best support for the media's presentation. It is through the media of television, radio, periodicals, and newspapers that the host's heritage will be recorded. As such, the host broadcaster will be evaluating broadcast sites and assembling experts to administer production, finance, logistics, telecommunications, budget development, and necessary construction. ACOG's experts include procedures from the Olympics in Calgary, Tokyo, Barcelona, and the Goodwill Games.

Television rights

Since the Los Angeles Olympic Organizing Committee showed the world how powerful television revenue could be in presenting the Olympic Games, this has become the greatest income source for the Olympic host city. The European Broadcast Union has extended a letter of intent to purchase the European rights to the Atlanta Olympic Games for US $275 million. The much anticipated contract for the United States rights has been awarded for US $456 million. (Note that the IOC negotiates Olympic television contracts with the host city receiving a percentage of the amount agreed upon.) Also, there will be agreements with electronic media in other parts of the world; that is, Japan, Australia, New Zealand, and the Middle East.

Medical

It is important that quality medical care be available expeditiously to the athletes, officials, and visitors at sporting events. ACOG has developed a plan that allows for around-the-clock medical attention. There will be a 30-bed medical clinic in the Olympic village as well as care provided at each venue. Each country that does not bring its own medical personnel will have a medical staff, including a physician assigned to it.

Doping control and gender verification provisions will be organized according to the IOC standards that all international federations must abide by for participation in the Olympics.

Olympic Village

The Olympic village will be located on the campus of the Georgia Institute of Technology (Georgia Tech). Plans call for housing for 15,500 athletes and officials. The yachting athletes and officials, tentatively, will be housed in Savannah, Georgia, the satellite Olympic village.

Within a Games village the personal needs of the athletes take precedence. Remember that the athletes spend much more time away from the competition venue than in competition. ACOG will have the Olympic Village Festival Center. This area will house games, a disco, shopping, and movies. In addition an International Zone will be provided for friends and family to visit on a temporary basis.

An excellent example of the early planning is exhibited with the ACOG's Olympic village. They plan to expand the use of the Olympic village to include parts of two housing areas. In order to accomplish this ACOG officials had to receive the cooperation of local developers, architects, city of Atlanta, the Atlanta Housing Authority, the United States Department of Housing and Urban Development, and public housing residents. This process obviously can be very time consuming and requires years of lead time to secure approval.

Interfaith Services

Having a religious faith means many things to different people. To many, faith equates to lifestyle. At the Olympic Games, maintaining as normal a lifestyle as possible for the athletes in preparation for their events is imperative. To that end the Interfaith Advisory Council has been formed by ACOG. This group will provide religious observances in different languages and advise on religious matters, such as dietary laws, housing issues, and social activities.

Security

Security is a major function of any event. The attention garnered by the Olympics and the masses of people drawn to the Olympic venues and villages create many security problems.

ACOG is addressing this situation by creating the Olympic Security Support Group (OSSG), which is composed of federal, state, and local law enforcement agencies. This group is planning the security measures in consultation with the Barcelona Olympic security officials and officials from other major events. The security planned includes armed Olympic guards, patrols, full-time surveillance and 12-foot-high fences around the Olympic village.

OSSG has received a $1-million grant from the United States government's National Institute of Justice to develop this security plan. Because of the nature and size of the Olympic Games, the study results will act as a model for international event security throughout the United States (Atlanta Committee for the Olympic Games, 1992c). It should be reiterated that security has become a prime consideration at international competitions since the tragedy at the Munich Olympics in 1972. Barcelona created a 50,000-member joint security force of national and civil police forces and the Spanish military (Woodward, 1992). Seoul's Olympic security force included "112,009 police, military troops and volunteer security workers" (Seoul Olympic Organizing Committee, 1989, p.797). Table 7.6 and Table 7.7 shows the detection equipment and control equipment used by Seoul's security forces.

TABLE 7.6	
Detection Equipment Used At The Seoul Olympics	
Motorized air masks	9
X-ray scanners	10
Door-shaped metal detectors	74
Hand-held metal detectors	229
Explosive and bomb detectors	7
Vehicle screening mirrors	81
Stick mine detectors	44
Inspection device sets	110
Inspection sticks	920

Note: From *Official Report: Games of the XXIVth Olympiad Seoul 1988* (p. 801). Seoul Olympic Organizing Committee, 1989.

TABLE 7.7
Control Equipment Used At The Seoul Olympics

Barricades	1,008
Iron spike pads	258
Road blocks	415
Movable flower stands	344
Movable rope supporters	2,687
Movable checkpoints	240
Magnetic Stripe Readers (MSR)	312
Inspection stands	265
Card containers	167
Sunshades	53
Ropes	16km

Note: From *Official Report: Games of the XXIVth Olympiad 1988* (p. 801). Seoul Olympic Organizing Committee, 1989.

Technology

Because an international athletic event can generate significant worldwide attention, the event host must be prepared to project its image globally through the most modern technology available. In addition a great deal of administrative communication must be addressed in order to successfully plan and administrate the event. AT&T signed an agreement with ACOG to provide state-of-the-art communications not only in Atlanta but also to extend the "AT&T Global Olympic Network" to connect the Olympic family worldwide (AT&T, 1994).

Tickets

When hosting a major international event, the hosts always worry about the events' acceptance manifested through ticket sales. One only needed to watch the 1994 Goodwill Games from St. Petersburg, Russia, to realize that great athletes do not always translate into great attendance. However, in the case of the Olympics the host has a reliable expectation that most of the tickets will be sold. In fact, for the Olympics, many of the tickets are distributed to the Olympic family, Olympic sponsors, and hotel/travel agencies for promotional packages.

Transportation

Because of the difficulty in moving a great number of people during an event, having the means to move these people becomes a major administrative task. When Cleveland, Ohio, was awarded the triathlon world championships, a major factor was the ease of the athletes' moving their bicycles and gear from the airport to the downtown race location via the metro system, thus avoiding the hassles of buses and taxis.

Under the IOC host city contract, the host must provide transportation for the athletes, IOC members, sport federation personnel, sponsors and media. Atlanta has one of the busiest airports in the world and a high-capacity rapid-rail system. More significantly, however, is that 16 of 25 sports venues will be within ACOG's Olympic Ring (1.5 miles/ 2.5 km in radius). With this proximity, many spectators, officials, athletes, and members of the press will be able to walk from venue to venue or to the Olympic village as needed. Within the Olympic Village a tramway will provide free transportation.

Also included within the Olympic Ring will be housing for the Olympic family, ACOG Headquarters, many hotels, and the media center. With this concentration of sporting and support venues contiguous to the housing, transportation problems should be limited.

Sport Competitions

Of primary concern to the hosts and athletes is that the competition be conducted properly. Though the public rarely sees a major flaw in competition administration at major events, examples are known, for example, the swimming venue at the 1994 Goodwill Games that had cloudy water. This lack of obvious problems is a direct result of the planning and preparation long before the actual event. For the Olympics all the venues are to be completed well in advance so that preliminary competitions can be used to test the facilities, personnel, officials, and technological equipment. In addition, the athletes appreciate being able to compete in the venue prior to the event.

As in any successful endeavor, the planning is the most important aspect. This is particularly true with an international event because of the different expectations born of different cultures. Atlanta's Olympic preparations have been used extensively here as examples. However, nearly any international event management team can use this model in order to facilitate its own competition.

During the Event

Management duties are often described as planning, organizing, administering, and controlling. With the first tasks coming long before any athletic event is contested, management must prepare to address the day-to-day, minute-to-minute administration of the event and the controlling of the event's scenarios, whether anticipated or not.

Important here is that the planning and organizing directly affect administering and controlling. Without the anticipation in the early preparation stages, control can be lost. Because of the complexity of hosting an international event, the importance of an experienced, quality management team cannot be overemphasized.

For our purposes, a look at the event administration of the 1988 Calgary Olympic Games is appropriate. A look at its management during the Games indicates how important preparation is.

After years of preparation, the event commences. However, the event begins long before the first competition. For an international event, competition begins several weeks before with the arrival of the world press and officials. These people serve to retest those venue services, housing accommodations, technical support, transportation plans, security arrangements, medical preparation, and meal preparation. Most of the imagined managerial concerns can be anticipated and controlled. It is the unexpected that creates problems.

The Calgary Organizing Committee prepared for the unexpected by careful planning and personnel training. A month before the Games, a top management task force was created. This task force created scenarios for its venue supervisors. It then became the supervisor's duty to decide how to handle each situation. The following illustrates how the sessions went:

> We asked one venue chairman: "What would you do if it was 10 minutes before an event was scheduled to start and only 10,000 people were in the venue while 40,000 were still lined up outside trying to pass through the ticket turnstiles?"
>
> The chairman replied without hesitation, "I'd open up the gates and tell the people to come on in!" "Great," we replied, "you're here to serve the people, not to make life miserable for them. For many people attending the Games will come only once in their lifetime."
>
> We asked another: "What would you do if a truck backed into a fire hydrant at your venue and water was spraying everywhere?"
>
> He said, "I'd call Bill Pratt and ask for help."
>
> We said, "Why would you call Pratt - he's not a plumber? Call the public works department or a plumber yourself and get it fixed. Then call Pratt and tell him that everything is under control."
>
> At the end of several days of focus on roles and responsibilities we had a team meeting to review what we had learned. The feedback proved that the exercise had been valuable. By direct and frequent contact we had reduced or eliminated doubt and fear that could have crippled our team in times of emergency. We had divided the project into manageable parts and assigned responsibility to capable people. And we had been able to identify where the gaps were in our detailed planning and training.
>
> We were prepared for the XVth Olympic Winter Games. We now awaited the results of our efforts. When the Games came and the wind blew or accidents happened, our team responded professionally, applying their leadership skills with confidence.
>
> There was no mental gridlock because the organization had competent leaders throughout (King, 1991, pp. 244-245).

Even with the best planning, unexpected situations occur that require decisive action. In Calgary, Frank King (1991) related that the organizers' planned IOC member transportation system differed from the one member-one car system demanded by the IOC. After explaining what King and Bill Pratt, president of the Olympiques Calgary Olympics '88, had planned with knowledge of the city of Calgary, IOC President Juan Antonio Samaranch "raged," "Listen to me. If you aren't going to keep your promises then I will not use your transport and neither will anyone else in the IOC. We will rent our own cars and drivers and you will pay the bills" (p. 261). King backed away from his system and accepted the IOC's transportation method.

It is fair to say that King acceded to Samaranch's request because of the compromise that is needed in order to present an event. Later in Calgary Samaranch asked that the medal ceremonies location at the Olympic Plaza be changed. However, after King showed

Samaranch the people's fervor at the presentations, Samaranch compromised.

As King relates in his book, *It's How You Play the Game* (1991), there were a number of experiences during the Calgary Winter Olympics that careful planning prepared them to handle:

1. Each morning at the management team met to handle last-minute ticket distribution and accreditation requests.
2. The warm chinook west winds blew during much of the Games. This could have caused serious problems with the skiing events. However, so much snow base had been created that there was plenty of snow, even with the warm weather.
3. The opening ceremonies site engineer helped avert what could have been a major disaster. The winds, during the outdoor opening ceremonies, were causing a decorative 15-story tepee to vibrate nearly to collapse. However, the engineer lowered the wind blown banners that were causing the tepee vibration, avoiding a possible incident had the tepee fallen on the athletes and spectators.
4. Alberta ranchers with manure spreaders were hired to spread snow along the 50-kilometer Nordic race trail.
5. The Royal Canadian Mounted Police provided an escort for King Carl Gustaf of Sweden when he wanted to go cross-country skiing. However, the king was so good that the police officer could not stay with him.
6. During a test to check the Cauldron Bowl for the Olympic flame, apparently gas had not been purged properly. An explosion occurred. Fortunately, no one was injured, but the incident created a more stressful period in preparation for the lighting of the flame during the opening ceremonies. The correction was made, and the opening went as planned. (The lighting of the flame to open the Barcelona Olympic Games must have caused the same anticipation as the archer's arrow arced through the night sky.)
7. The former Soviet Olympic pairs figure skaters, the Protopopovs, were removed from the closing ceremonies because of the Soviet's protest. The Protopopovs had defected from the Soviet Union.
8. International Ice Hockey President, Gunther Sabetski's request for compensation payments for scheduling changes was rejected.
9. Due to the warm, chinook winds, 33 events were rescheduled. Rescheduling was done through a conference telephone call between the IFs affected, venue chairmen, sports chairmen, host broadcaster, television rights holders, ticket managers, security, transportation, manager of volunteers, and Bill Pratt or Frank King. Because each area was directly affected and thus would need to enact changes if an event were rescheduled, all were consulted. Cooperation and compromise were essential when rescheduling.

It is interesting to see the daily schedule of King, chairman of Calgary's Olympic organizing committee, during the Games:

6:30 a.m.   Meeting to release the emergency pool of tickets.

7:30 a.m.   OCO '88 management team meets to review the previous day's problems and to anticipate today's events, and primarily on the weather forecast.

8:30 a.m.   Meeting including OCO '88 management and the IOC Executive Board to address IOC concerns weather related schedule adjustments.

9:30 a.m.   Meeting with OCO '88 Board of Directors to exchange information and discuss problems. The board spent their days at the venues and could meet directly with the staff there.

10:00 a.m.   Traveling with Samaranch to competition venues. Early evening preparation for obligatory evening social events and medal ceremonies.

With this schedule daily, King was able to address in an organized manner, the anticipated and unforeseen problems that occur. These same problems, or variations depending on the event, will occur again and again. Anticipation and preparation are the keys to avoiding a major problem during the event.

Post-Event

After the television cameras are off, after the reporters have packed their bags, after the athletes are gone, to most people the event is over. However, as Catherwood and Van Kirk (1992, p.183) state, "Shutdown: It's Not Over When It's Over." The 1984 Los Angeles Olympic Games was not closed officially until 1991 -- 7 years later. The major obstacle to closing the books for good was lawsuits. This can be particularly true in the United States where suing has become a sport unto itself. With the possibility of a multimillion-dollar surplus in Atlanta in 1996, shutdown will not occur until years after the closing ceremonies.

Catherwood and Van Kirk (1992) state that shutting down an event involves:

1. Venue closedown;
2. Insurance settlement/claims;
3. Legal claims;
4. Human resources and outplacement activities;
5. Contract finalization;
6. Debriefings;
7. Final accounting;
8. Final media communications; and
9. Closing celebrations and follow-on events. (p.185)

Catherwood and Van Kirk's event shutdown topology has significant relevance in international sport.

Venue Closedown

The hosting of an international event often-times mandates the building or renovating of facilities, be they sporting venues, dormitories, communications centers, etc. Often, closing a venue after the event means handing the keys over to the new user. For example, in Atlanta the Olympic village will return to Georgia Tech dormitories. The 1992 Albertville Olympics Village town of Brides-Les-Bains funded new housing for the athletes, refurbishment of the Grand Hotel de Thermes, a new water purification system, cinema, and a casino enlargement; the 1980 Winter Olympics athletes' housing became a prison; and Los Angeles saw a number of sport training facilities renovated and then returned to the local communities after the Games.

Understanding that the event will end is fundamental in order to turn over venues. It is in the bid stage, possibly a decade earlier, that the ultimate use of the venues is determined. In accordance with the axiom FORM FOLLOWS FUNCTION, it is at the bid stage that the event venue functions marry with the venue's ultimate use, thus creating a facility that closes down or hands over more easily.

Insurance Settlement/Claims

Although the event management team tries to anticipate difficult areas in order to lessen the chance of a problem, insurance is secured in order to handle the liability inherent with any event, for instance, a person's tripping on steps while departing a facility. It is only when these claims are settled that this managerial concern is finished.

Legal Claims

In any event where there are a great deal of money and people involved, there will be lawsuits. It should be anticipated that some of these cases will take years to work their way through the courts. Before the event closes its financial books, all of these costs need to be resolved.

Human Resources And Outplacement Activities

Major international events involve thousands of personnel. If these people are volunteers, they are not as concerned with "what will I do after this is over." However, possibly thousands of others will become full-time employees. If these employees are on loan from other companies, as for the Atlanta Olympics IBM and Bell South are loaning some top level administrations to ACOG, these employees know they have a job to return to on completion of the event. The problem arises when the employees have devoted years to creating a successful games. Some will have established sufficient contracts and skills in order to network into a job. However, many will need career counseling for the job search -- resume writing, interviewing, lifestyle change. In order to get the maximum commitment from these employees, an organization should make a firm, visual commitment to help these people acquire and/or sharpen the skills that made them quality employees for the event. The host organization has a moral duty to reward loyal employees with the transition to post-event life.

Contract Finalization

With international sports, bigger means more complicated. Fortunately, most international sport organizations have a standard operating procedure that dictates, within parameters, how an event is to be organized and administered. However, excluding the competition itself, the host organization has a lot of leeway in which to organize the activites.

To administer the event takes the cooperation of many companies and organizations. In doing so, many contracts must be signed in order to secure compliance with what is required. Many of these contracts are performance graded. In other words, the payment exchanged for services rendered may not be determined until after the last sporting events. For example, a sport television contract normally guarantees a certain television rating. After the event is completed and the final ratings are known, only then can the contract remuneration be met. Another example may be the retrofitting expense of converting an Olympic venue to another status; the work must be completed before the contract is satisfied.

Debriefings

Assessing what happened is vital after any event. Because of the unique nature of international sporting events, subsequent hosts need and want to know what worked for an organizer. The best time to debrief event personnel is immediately after the completion of their responsibility. If the administrator has kept a detailed log during the event, the decisions relative to the administrative procedures should be easily recalled. From these debriefings, the final report can be written. For the Olympic Games, a two-volume tome is submitted detailing the results and the organization and planning.

In addition to the final reports, hosts of subsequent sporting events frequently work closely with current event hosts in "learning the ropes" of administering the events. ACOG sent over 100 observers to Barcelona to learn how the Catalonians organized the Games. In fact, the technical systems used during the Olympics become the product of the IOC in order to have their availability for subsequent Games.

Final Accounting

When all the lawsuits are settled, the lawyers paid, the venues handed over, etc., the final financial numbers must be crunched. Catherwood and Van Kirk (1992) state that the final accounting may include

1. Comparing actual financial results to original (or revised) budgetary amounts.
2. Preparing tailored reports for various parties (e.g., governmental entities, economic assessment reports, contract resolutions, and licensee/concessionaire finally payments).
3. Final tax returns, including final release from federal and state taxing authorities if the entity is to be shutdown.
4. Processing dissolution legal papers if the entity is to be disbanded.
5. Payoff of any debts (or possible resolution through bankruptcy process).
6. Asset disposition - What to sell, give away, or destroy. This also included resolution of in-kind contributions to the entity that possibly might require return to the person or organization that provided them (e.g., donated computers that require return). It is hoped that the resolution of in-kind assets will not result in payment for lost items.

7. Decision as to whether and when a final audit by outside accountants might occur. This might also entail royalty audits for various licensees. This final audit must be started ahead of the final days of the event to enable interaction with the remaining accounting personnel and records.

Final Media Communications

Depending on the fame of the event, the mass media will convey the press releases to a greater or lesser extent. Of course, much of the coverage received will be due to the management's own press organization.

At a major international event, after the last athlete has returned home, many people are still interested in the legacy, statistics, and human interest stories surrounding the event. It is therefore, important to maintain a media relations person to release positive aspects of the event. When all is said and done, the last person out the door is the media person releasing the story of the close down.

Closing Celebrations and Follow-on Events

After months or years of event organization, the staff members deserve to be recognized for their efforts. This recognition can take many forms. The 1984 Los Angeles Olympics created an alumni group in order to keep many of the vital personnel together for subsequent events. King (1991) "celebrated" the many staff from the 1988 Calgary Olympics by placing all their names at the bottom of each page of his book, *It's How You Play the Game* -- a nice tribute.

Together this delineation serves as a good framework from which the post-event closure can be modeled.

Evaluation

In order to examine the presentation of an international event, some type of evaluation is needed. Every organization begins with goals and objectives that it feels must be met in order for it to have staged a successful event. In some manner management must provide for evaluating its efforts.

Typically international sport events require years of preparation. Therefore, it is logical that periodic evaluations be made at least yearly for the master plan. However, within each administrative unit more frequent appraisals would be needed.

As the event approaches the frequency of evaluations will naturally increase. These checks may come within a meeting, through written reports, or by the hosting of preliminary competitions. No matter the method, preset criteria must be established so that an objective appraisal can be made. Examples of these reports are clearly evident in newspaper reports of the Olympic hosts presenting to the IOC their organization's progress. In this manner a host organization has not only its internal but also an external evaluation.

A good example of an event evaluation by external means is gained by examining the Seoul Olympic Games of 1988. These Olympics were evaluated by means of an independent committee of "international experts" (Kane, 1990). It was felt that this group could give an independent and objective evaluation of the Seoul Olympic Organizing Committee's efforts. The Organizing Committee felt that through this effort, it could establish a model that subsequent Olympic Games could use for their evaluation.

The Evaluation Committee agreed to the following Terms of Reference:

> To investigate and evaluate the overall effectiveness of the Seoul Olympic Organizing Committee's work in planning and carrying out the task of mounting the XXIVth Olympiad with specific reference to both the needs of the athletes and the public at large having in mind, in particular, services and facilities and the Charter purposes of the Olympics. Without in any way limiting the scope of this task, the Committee should have in mind both the specific and general aspects of   its work which will embrace among others the following areas:

Specifically: Planning and organization; accreditation, transportation, security, technology, medical, the conduct of the competitions, protocol, the sports facilities and the sports competitions.

Generally: The impact of the Games on athletes, the citizens of Seoul and the wider public attending or associated with the Games. The ambiance of the Games and its immediately and extended effects. The "extended" Olympics, e.g. the associated social, cultural and scientific programmes. The communication process during the Games (Kane, 1990, p. 4).

Following an extensive review based on the Terms of Reference, the Evaluation Committee concluded:

1. The Olympic Games have arrived at a point of development where the greatest care must be taken to avoid disaster by controlling the overall size and complexity of future undertakings.
2. The Guide - *The Administration of the Olympic Games* - needs urgent and radical up-dating.
3. The host organization needs to establish early and effective links with the International Federations of Sport and with the international professional organizations for sport and physical education in order to mount the most effective procedures for operating the Games and the Extended Olympics. (Kane, 1990, pp. 39-40)

In addition to the Seoul Evaluation Committee report, the Olympic Organizing Committee (1989) reviewed their accomplishments in their *Official Report*. The attainment of five goals are explained:

1. Largest participation of countries (160) and athletes (13,304) in Olympic history,
2. Optimum harmony of the countries from East and West,
3. Achievement of cultural, athletic and economic development,
4. Security and Service provided an "Olympics free of trouble" through the use of "...about 110,000 volunteers and the world's security officers...", (p.832)
5. A surplus of 341.4 billion won (South Korean currency)was generated through

"efficient operation and the development of revenue- generation programs..."
and "The emphasis on multi-purpose, post Games utilization of facilities and
equipment, tight control of (the) budget and minimization of new
investments..."(p.832)

It is important to have preset evaluation criteria. In this manner, the event management
can evaluate its success but more importantly, the successful management techniques
used can be left to future event organizers.

Legacy

Because an international event requires years of preparation, thousands of contracts,
thousands of employees, multiple revenue sources, many venues, and a lasting legacy,
closure is complicated; but this is not so unique unto itself. What makes the Olympics,
the Goodwill Games, the World Student Games, etc. unique in closure are the facts that
the years of planning are done by a corporation that will cease to exist when the event
finishes, and that the event is multinational. Each of these events, because of the
community/regional commitment and the sporting venues required, leaves a legacy.

At the Montreal Olympics in 1976, the legacy left for the citizens was greater world
exposure, beautiful facilities, and a billion-dollar debt. It was this debt that nearly changed
the traditional Olympic format for the summer games.

The Los Angeles Olympics of 1984 found that after the lawsuits were settled and the
bills paid, a surplus of US$222.7 million was achieved. This money was split 40% to the
IOC, 20% to the national federations, and 40% to the Amateur Sports Foundation, a
nonprofit organization to promote amateur sports in the Southern California area. It is
through this money that the legacy of Los Angeles lives on, especially through early
funding of the Olympic Solidarity Program and the Amateur Sports Foundation.

The 1988 Seoul Olympics legacy, following the model of Tokyo in 1964, dealt with
world exposure. Both Seoul and Tokyo used the Games of the Olympiad to showcase
modern cities of international stature that grew out of the ravages of war -- Seoul, the
Korean War and Tokyo, the Second World War.

Both cities showed the world that they had rebuilt not only their superstructure but
also their business acumen. They were and would continue to be significant players on
the world economic scene. Seoul also considered its legacy to be the movement of Korea
closer to the

> ranks of the advanced countries on the strength of bolstered national
> development and the enhancement of [the] general level of awareness
> among the [Korean] people. The economic growth and the enhancement
> of [the] civic spirit of the public bolstered Korea's stature in the
> international community. (Seoul OlympicOrganizing Committee, 1989,
> p.832)

Further, the Koreans as citizens of a developing nation, believed that through the
successful staging of the Olympics, other developing nations would find inspiration "to
make an active commitment to the international community" (Seoul Olympic Organizing
Committee, 1989, p.832).

Concluding Summary

Hosting an international athletic event will prove to be more difficult and time consuming than most could imagine. The myriad of details needed to be addressed seems never to end. However, with a proper state of mind, the organizers can succeed.

Preparing for such an event requires being ready for three major phases: pre-event, during the event, and post-event. The most critical time is the pre-event stage. It is here that the host organization creates a management team that can communicate and coordinate private, government, community, and international organizations and agencies. It is also at this phase that careful planning prepares the event administration for the transition to the post-event organizational shutdown.

During the event the most important aspect is crisis management. Actually through careful preparation, including rehearsing procedures for possible crises, most trouble can be eliminated.

The post-event period is primarily a matter of pre-event preparation. Catherwood and Van Kirk's (1992) nine aspects to address when closing an event provide an excellent framework from which pre-event preparation can begin. The most important aspect is to assist the loyal staff, who worked so hard to create a quality event, into the transition to another career or organization.

From the bidding to closedown, the organizers must be keenly aware of the event's legacy. Again, pre-event preparation is critical in leaving a positive legacy like youth sports in Southern California being funded from the 1994 Los Angeles Olympics or a negative image created by Montreal's billion-dollar debt at the 1976 Games of the Olympiad.

Hosting an international event is exciting and difficult; the two are connected. Good management understands this and prepares to deal with all event aspects from bidding through closedown.

Discussion, Analysis, Applications, and Debate

Issues for Discussion

1. What qualifications would you specify for the Chief Executive Officer of an Olympic host organization?
2. If you were to solicit public support for a continental multievent competition (e.g., Asian Games), how would you proceed and what groups would be included?
3. What complications could occur with medical coverage at an international event due to language differences? cultural differences? religious beliefs?
4. Had Beijing been awarded the 2000 Olympic Games, how would you expect the Olympic village to differ from Sydney?

Matters for Analysis

1. Examine the Olympic Games roles of the IOC, host organization and host country NOC. Based on what you know of different sport governance models worldwide, create the scenario for Olympic Games governance in a governmentally controlled sport system.

2. Assume you are in charge of issuing credentials for an Olympic Games. You have
    been approached by a nation with a large delegation that would like to have more
    administrators credentialed. It is common knowledge that a smaller nation will not
    be using its credential allotment. However, the two nations have no diplomatic
    relations. How would you negotiate between the countries in order to reallocate
    the credentials to assist the country in need?

Application

At this point in time, you have seen the coming and going of a few Olympic Games,
Summer and Winter. Select one of these Games and illustrate what would have been
involved in shutting down the event based on the delineation of Catherwood and VanKirk.

Ethical Debate

Countries and cities use international sporting events to showcase their culture and
achievements. Periodically reports have stated that just prior to a major event, people
who live on the streets (e.g., the homeless, prostitutes, beggars) are forcibly removed so
that they do not detract from the positive face the organizers want to project to the world.
Is this a good idea? If it is, should this not be a standard procedure on a regular basis? If
it is not, will these people detract from the visitors' enjoyment of the sporting event
experience?

References

AT&T (1994, January 11). news release. Atlanta: Atlanta Committee for the Olympic
Games.

Atlanta Committee for the Olympic Games (May 1992a). *Press Information Guide*.
Atlanta: Atlanta Committee for the Olympic Games.

Atlanta Committee for the Olympic Games (January 1992b). *Master Plan Summary*.
Atlanta: Atlanta Committee for the Olympic Games.

Atlanta Committee for the Olympic Games (1992c, September 17). News release.
Atlanta: Atlanta Committee to Organize the Games.

Catherwood, D.W., & Van Kirk, R.L. (1992). *The complete guide to special event
management*. New York: John Wiley & Sons.

International Olympic Committee (1993). *Olympic Charter*. Lausanne: International
Olympic Committee.

Kane, J., (1990). Evaluation committee for the Seoul Olympics. In B.I. Koh (Ed.),
Toward One World Beyond All Barriers (Vol. 2, pp. 3-40). Seoul: Poong Nom.

Kidd, B., (1992). The Toronto Olympic commitment: Towards a social contract for the Olympic Games. In *Olympika, The International Journal of Olympic Studies. 1*, 154-167.

King, F.W. (1991). *It's how you play the game*. Calgary: Script: the writer's group inc.

Seoul Olympic Organizing Committee (1989). *Official report: Games of the XXIVth Olympiad Seoul 1988*. Seoul: Seoul Olympic Organizing Committee.

Woodward, S. (1992, June 24). Barcelona puts centuries of culture on display. *USA Today*, p. C12.

CHAPTER EIGHT ───────────

Nᴀᴛɪᴏɴᴀʟ ᴛᴇᴀᴍs

Overview

Most people have little knowledge or understanding of the athlete selection process and event attendance for international sporting events. The selection process is presented for sports within one country, the United States, and for one sport, swimming, from three countries. These examples serve to illustrate the selection criteria and procedure. The latter part of the chapter discusses team staff selection for international events. Of particular note are the extensive duties entrusted to the chief of the mission, the head coach, and the head manager. The chapter concludes with examples of the situations that athletes and staffs encounter during an international tour.

Introduction

When competing in an international event, the athletes have reached the pinnacle of their sport. People throughout the world admire that they are the best from their countries. What most people do not comprehend is the process through which the athlete is selected for the international team and the details that go into having that person arrive at the competition, ready for a peak performance.

In this chapter two major topics will be presented: team selection and event attendance. Team selection will address how athletes are selected by national federations and/or national Olympic committees to represent their country in international competition. Event attendance will examine the processing of the athletes from the time they are selected for the international team until they return to their home country or are released from the sport governing body's responsibility.

Team Selection

Each national federation selects its team for international competition. The level of the competition (i.e., dual meet or world championship) may, however, create more or less complexity within the selection process. In addition, the ultimate goal for which the team is selected may dictate which athletes compete. Consider these examples:

1. The 1992 United States women's basketball team took the bronze medal at the Barcelona Olympics. Because some people considered this group to be the finest collection of women's basketball talent ever assembled on one team, there was considerable disappointment in the United States. One result of this disappointment is that the U.S. team for the 1996 Olympics is to be selected one year in advance of the Atlanta Olympics. These players will train and play together until going to Atlanta. In order to compensate the players for foregoing their salaries from non-U.S. teams, each women will be paid US$50,000 (Becker, 1994).

2. In Negara Brunei Darussalam the number of selected athletes to represent their country will decrease as the standards of competition rise for the Borneo Games, Southeast Asian Games, Asian Championships, World Championships, and the Olympic Games. In each competition, to compete is important, but also "exposure" and athletic development are considered along each step up in the competitive level.

3. The Winter Olympics or the Games of the Olympiad are held every 4 years. This schedule provides an athlete a natural training cycle

    Year 1: Base building, try new techniques
    Year 2: Continued base building, refine techniques
    Year 3: Focused training, sharpen techniques
    Year 4: Olympic year peak.

    With this schedule an elite athlete can decide on the competitions that will best meet his or her needs leading to the pinnacle competition. This is not to assume that all athletes train with the Olympics in mind; however, it does seem reasonable that that would be the goal for Olympic sport athletes. If the sport is not on the Olympic program, the schedule would be adjusted for the major competition, for instance, World Championships.
    A caveat to this schedule would be those athletes who support themselves through their participation as elite athletes. In that case a great deal of money can be made the year after the Olympic medal has been won. Therefore, the athlete would not necessarily experiment too much with a new training routine or technique change.

4. In the year prior to the Olympic Games, the Olympic city will host competitions in order to test its facilities, personnel, administrative procedures, communications, and infrastructure. Where normally a nonchampionship competition might draw little notice from many athletes, an opportunity to compete at the Olympic venue will be highly sought by most athletes. As a result, team selection for an Olympic venue event can be much more prized and competitive than would be expected in a mere pre-Olympic competition.

Team Selection Worldwide

As was discussed in chapter 5, each country has its own sport governance system. In like regard each national federation within each country will have its own system to select athletes and team officials for international competition. Obviously, many selection systems will be similar from national federation to national federation and country to country. There are just so many methods by which the selection process can be handled.

The two primary selection models are Objective and Subjective. The Objective model has athletes selected based solely on the time or distance from the qualifying competition(s). The Subjective model bases the athletes' selection on the recommendation of a panel of experts, be they coaches or administrators. A third model is a Combination of the previous two. This model has a quantification as in diving scores and placement, but only to select the group of athletes who are eligible for the team. Then, the experts select for the team from the qualified athletes who they believe will ultimately perform best at the international competition.

The following examples are illustrative of the selection methods used throughout the world for selecting national teams. For each example it is good to remember that team selection is a continuously evolving process. Therefore, what is current today might necessitate changing or fine tuning so that the best athletes truly represent their country.

United States

In the United States the Amateur Sports Act of 1978 gave the United States Olympic Committee (USOC) the responsibility of sending American athletes to the Olympic Games. The USOC then delegated the responsibility of selecting the athletes to the NFs. Prior to the Olympic Games, each national federation informs the USOC of its selection procedure. Prior to the USOC's submitting its athletes roster to the Olympic host organization, it must verify that each athlete is (a) eligible to compete given the rules of the national federation and its international federation and (b) has met the qualifying standards, if any, set by the international federation for the competition. Only if these criteria are met can the host allow the athlete into the competition village and certify each as competitors.

Athletics/Track and Field

Track and field is governed by USA Track and Field. Its duty is to conduct and promote track and field in the United States. This duty includes selecting teams for international competition.

In order to qualify for an international track and field team from the United States,

1. An athlete must meet the qualifying event standard is established by the Men's and Women's Track and Field committees for the indoor or outdoor national championship. In an Olympic year, the athlete must qualify for the Olympic Trials. These standards are based on times or distances (Objective) for running or field events, respectively.
2. At the championships or the Olympic Trials, the athlete must finish in the top places for the designated international event, for example, the top three places qualify for the Olympic team, if they each also meet the Olympic standard. If

no athlete meets the Olympic standard, only the top finisher is invited to the
Olympics.

3.   The top 10 finishers in each event become the National Team. It is from this list
     that competitors are chosen for any international competition in the subsequent
     year, provided the athlete is fit for competition.

4.   For the Olympic 4 x 100 meters and 4 x 400 meters relay teams, the top finishers
     in each 100 meters and 400 meters, respectively, will receive the primary
     consideration (Combination). Additionally, the women's team may choose
     any other athlete who competed in the Olympic Trials for a relay; the men may
     pick non-100 meter/400 meter athletes who have qualified for the Olympic
     Team, no matter the event. Carl Lewis ran on the gold medal-winning 4x100
     meters relay at the Barcelona Olympics because he was available based on his
     long jump event qualification (P. D. Mahoney, personal communication, June
     27, 1992).

The salient point is that the athletes "select themselves" by their finish placing, except
for the relays. Administrators and coaches have little chance to affect the international
team composition, except when the international event takes place at an unusual time in
the United States competitive calendar. Then, from the National Team list, athletes are
listed by their order of national championship meet finish to join an international team.
The caveat is that the athlete must be competitively fit in order to be a team member for
a particular competition.

Gymnastics

The United States Gymnastics Federation (USGF) sanctions competitions by private
clubs and organizations through competitions at the state, regional, and national levels.
It is through this gymnastic meet system that the athletes qualify to compete at the United
States National Championships.

At the U.S. National Championships, the national teams are selected for men, women,
and rhythmic all-around. The selection (Objective) is based on the athletes' scores, 60%
for compulsory routine and 40% for optional routine, at that national championship
event. The best athletes then become members of the Senior Elite National Team, if they
are old enough. Age eligibility for men is 18 years and above and for the women's and
rhythmic teams, 15 years and above. (Because events between two or more national
federation must be sanctioned by the Federation Internationale de Gymnastique [FIG],
the world governing body for gymnastics, FIG's age eligibility standards set the limit for
international competition. This is common practice in the international federation-national
federation relationship throughout the world.) It is from these teams that the athletes are
selected for competition at the Olympic Games, World Championships, Goodwill Games,
and the Pan American Games (United States Gymnastics Federation, no date).

For the 1992 Barcelona Olympics, the USGF instituted a new team selection process.
This process involved combining scores from the national championship meet and the
United States Olympic Trials in order to select the Olympic competitors. However, because
of injuries two of the eight women selected for the Olympic training team were placed on

the team based on their outstanding performances at the national championships alone or at the 1991 World Championships. The final Olympic team was selected based on a vote of the coaches and officials selection committee after observing the athletes' training just prior to the Olympic Games.

The USGF made a change to this selection process (Combination) from the "top six at the Olympic Trials make the team" because it was felt that the best team to compete at the Olympic Games may not be the top six athletes from the Olympic trials. Each system has its good and bad points, but the membership of the USGF felt that the best team could be selected in this manner. See Table 8-1 (Retton, 1992).

TABLE 8.1
USGF Olympic Team Selection Critique

Pros
1. Limits mental and physical regression
2. Allows an injured athlete to recuperate without the pressure of pre-Olympic qualifying

Cons
1. Teams are selected by a committee, instead of strictly by competition results.
2. May not allow the athlete to focus fully on the Olympic games knowing that he or she may not be on the Olympic team.

Baseball

Team selection for the USA Baseball presents a few different wrinkles than does selection for the previously discussed track and field and gymnastics. Because baseball is best known for its professional players, the amateur athletes are not media stars as Carl Lewis and Mary Lou Retton were. Most, if not all, of the USA Baseball team for any competition will be unrecognizable to baseball fans. This was clearly discussed in a *Wall Street Journal* article by Roger Lowenstein, "The National Pastime, Passed Over in Prime Time" (1992). Therefore, the selection process (Subjective) to make a USA Baseball team has little likelihood of becoming a media event, as the 1992 Olympic trials were to track and field with Butch Reynolds, or in gymnastics with coach Bela Karolyi and gymnasts Kim Zmeskal and Shannon Miller.

Initially, USA Baseball creates a list of potential team members from three sources:

1. A national tryout camp.
2. Consultation with coaches and professional baseball scouts.
3. Player lists from established teams or organizations like colleges, summer leagues, and the U.S. Olympic Festival.

With the many professional baseball teams in North America, most quality players are known to the professional scouts. Many of these players are selected (drafted) by a professional team after finishing their secondary school eligibility. Some, however, forgo the immediate minor league route in favor of collegiate competition in order to continue their formal education while playing baseball. This is significant because once a baseball player accepts compensation as a professional, he is no longer eligible for USA Baseball- or International Baseball Association-sponsored competitions.

Preparation of player selection lists begins in November with the week-long USA Baseball Team Fall Trials held in Homestead, Florida. Seventy two players attend these trials. The USA team coaches use this week to evaluate and assist in selection of a maximum of 40 players to the national team tryouts. The coaches' invitees number 35 from the National Collegiate Athletic Association (NCAA) Division I universities. Five players will be nominated from the following group as a whole:

1. National Association of Intercollegiate Athletics (NAIA)
2. National Junior College Athletics Association (NJCAA)
3. National Collegiate Athletic Association Divisions II and III (NCAA)
4. California Association of Community Colleges (CACC).

Just prior to the 40 invitees' arriving at the Millington, Tennessee, training site, an open walk-on tryout will be held. At least one player is selected from this tryout to attend the selection camp.

The prospective team roster will initially be cut to 30 players for the first series of games at the training site. A 26-player traveling squad will then be selected for games leading to the major event of the year. The USA Baseball team is eligible to play in the Olympic Games, Pan American Games, World Championships, Intercontinental Cup, and the Goodwill Games. The roster must be cut to 22 players for these major competitions (United States Baseball Federation, 1992). This 22 person roster limit thus creates a team on which a player with multiposition skills is prized (Lawes, 1992).

A major factor in this process is professional sports. According to the USA Baseball rules,

> To be eligible for the USA Team, players must be amateurs (they may sign a professional contract but not accept money or play for the organization until after released from the USA Team) and a U.S. citizen (if naturalized citizen, the naturalization must have occurred three years before the competition) (United States Baseball Federation, 1992, p.8).

With this ruling, there can be no "Dream Team" as was seen in the United States Olympic basketball team at the 1992 Olympics. Because each international federation is permitted to define amateur in its own way, baseball, at least for the present, will use nonprofessional athletes.

In addition to the ruling on professional status, USA Baseball specifically states the time period for a naturalized citizen to be eligible to compete for the U.S. team. This stipulation clearly restricts the movement of a player from one country to another with the immediate effect of being eligible for international competition while representing the United States. However, it is worth remembering that any rule can be challenged or changed, especially within the jurisdiction of the United States legal system. It is not as easy to question a rule by the international federation as any country's legal system does not overrule an international organization when dealing with multinational competition, as previously discussed in chapter 5 (P. Seiler, personal communication, February 8, 1995).

Figure Skating

Selection to an Olympic team in figure skating is a dramatic event and selection for an international team is indeed prestigious. Because figure skating is favored by television viewers, many competitions are broadcast on United States television. When watching these broadcasts, it is inevitable that the announcer will explain the scoring system. Yet, nobody viewing the judges' scores really knows who the winner is until the ice dancing or skating scores are adjusted for technical merit and composition + style. It is not the object of this book to explain this process but to show how these results translate into the figure skaters' and dancers' making an international team.

In order to make the United States Figure Skating Association (USFSA) national team, an athlete must be a USFSA Registered Skater. Then, the Registered Skater must qualify for the USFSA National Championships in order to have the possibility for international team membership.

Selection as a competitor to the U.S. Team, U.S. Alternate Team, and the U.S. Developmental Team is based on the athlete's performance in the two most recent National Championships and sanctioned competitions held between these two events. For the world championships, the current National Champion is automatically selected to represent the United States. The remaining selectee(s) is(are) decided by a majority vote of the International Committee.

The USFSA International Committee also selects the Olympic figure skating team. However, as with other NFs, the Olympic team selection process must be approved by the NOC, in this case the United States Olympic Committee (United States Figure Skating Association, 1994).

The USFSA International Committee retains the right to select competitors for international competitions who did not compete in the most recent National Championships, especially in pairs and dance couples when a couple change has been made (United States Figure Skating Association, 1994). Nancy Kerrigan's place on the 1994 Olympic team was a good example of an exception being made for extenuating circumstances.

One aspect of competing in the Winter Olympics is that the skater must be an "amateur." A skater who has become a professional competitor has only one opportunity to be reinstated for Olympic eligibility. This option was used by Katarina Witt, Brian Boitano, Viktor Petrenko, Ekaterina Gordeeva, and Sergei Grinkov in order to compete in the 1994 Winter Olympics. Because the rule is so new there is likely to be much discussion in the International Skating Union about this rule (Becker, 1995).

World View: Swimming

In order to understand some of the similarities and differences in the national team selection within a sport, swimming provides a good medium. Within the competitive swimming realm, this process will be illustrated for Canada, Brazil, and Belgium.

Canada

The primary swimming competitions for Canadian athletes are the Olympic Games, World Championships, Commonwealth Games, Pan Pacific Meet, and the Pan American Games. To make the Olympic Games team requires qualifying on time standards (Objective). FINA, the international federation for swimming, sets Olympic Games qualifying time standards. However, these standards are relatively easy for world class swimmers. Therefore, Swimming Canada, the Canadian national federation for swimming, has created, as many national federations do, more difficult standards for its athletes. The Canadian qualification process for the Olympic team incorporates these standards in this manner:

1. If an athlete "beats" a very fast standard in a present period, the athlete automatically qualifies for the Olympic team and does not have to prove himself or herself during the Olympic trials.
2. If an athlete does not automatically qualify during the present period, then the Olympic trials qualifying standard must be met.
3. During the Olympic Trials, the athlete must finish in the top two in the event (FINA allows two swimmers per team per Olympic event) and beat the Olympic team qualifying time.

An interesting caveat of the Canadian methods is that at the Olympic trials, the qualifying time must be beaten during the event final. This is required in order to better simulate the Olympic Games event final. Thus a first place finisher in the event final would not qualify for the Olympic team unless the qualifying standard time was beaten in that race. This current Canadian system is being evaluated because some thought that more swimmers should have represented Canada in the 1992 Olympic Games.

In order to qualify for the World Championships or the Commonwealth Games, time standards have to be beaten at a qualifying competition. The standards for the World Championships are normally of a higher standard than for the Commonwealth Games.

Qualifying for the 1991 Pan Pacific competition was held at the Summer National Championships. Since Canada considers the Pan Pacific meet of higher caliber than the Pan American Games, the top two event placers in the Summer Nationals, if they have world caliber times, will more likely be selected for the Pan Pacific Competition than for the Pan American Games. If a swimmer swam in the World Championship he or she would then go to the Pan Pacific meet, not the Pan American Games (J. Jay, personal communication, November 15, 1992).

As with other sports, because international events change venues and dates to correspond to the host's needs, the qualifying competitions and the order of major competitions will affect team selections.

Brazil

As with most countries, being selected for an international swim team representing Brazil means beating a time standard (Objective). For 1992, selection to the Olympics was the major goal for the top swimmers. Because only 10 men and no women were selected to swim for Brazil in Barcelona, it follows that the Olympic Games can be the goal for only a few Brazilians.

Selection to the Brazilian Olympic team and other international teams followed this sequence:

1. If a swimmer qualified for the Olympic Games based on he time established by the Brazilian Olympic Committee (Comite Olimpico Brasileiro, or COB), then that swimmer definitely made the Olympic Team.
2. If a swimmer earned a medal in the Pan American Games, and met the COB qualifying standard, the Olympic team position was secure.
3. If the athlete did not qualify based on 1 and 2, the athlete could qualify at the Olympic Trials Competition, which was held May 30, 1992. If an athlete was unable to be at the Brazilian Olympic Trials because he or she was living and training elsewhere (i.e., student attending college in the United States), that athlete had to choose one designated competition before May 30 at which the qualifying time would be attempted. COB felt that this allowed some of its better swimmers who were on the United States collegiate training cycle to qualify without having to come to Brazil.

Qualifying for other international competitions from Brazil meant meeting the following requirements:

1. For the Latin Cup in May 1992, qualifiers were the event winners at the Summer National and the four fastest 100m and 200m swimmers for the relays.
2. For the South American Championship the qualifiers are the two fastest at whichever competition is designated, usually the Summer Nationals. Again, the relay teams consist of the four fastest athletes from the 100m and 200m.
3. The two fastest qualifiers at the Pan American Games trials qualify for that competition. The relays are as previously stated (J. Costa, personal communications, November 15, 1992).

Belgium

The major swimming competitions for elite swimmers from Belgium follow the cycle of Olympic Games - European Championships - World Championships - European Championships - Olympic Games.

Qualifying for the Belgium Olympic swim team does not occur at one competition, such as an Olympic trials, because so few swimmers can meet the Belgian Olympic Committee Olympic qualifying standards. Instead the qualifying standard for the 1992 Olympic Games had to have been met between September 1, 1991, and June 1, 1992. If the athlete met the qualifying time only once, the swimmer might have been selected for the Olympic team, but there was no guarantee (Combination). If, however, a swimmer reached the time standard only once, by swimming to an eighth place at the 1990 World Championships or fourth at the 1991 European Championships, making the Olympic team was still a possibility. With this system three women and four men made the Belgium Olympic swim team.

It is important to understand the significance of meeting the qualifying standard twice. In Belgium there are two national teams representing the Flemish and the French languages, respectively. These two groups have a fierce rivalry. For example, in 1991 a dispute arose on the composition of a women's relay team for the European Championships. No agreement could be reached between the sides. As a result the Belgian team that, on paper, could have taken a silver medal did not even enter the competition. Therefore, in order to avoid this potential problem Belgian swimmers seek automatic qualification based on twice reaching the standard.

Qualifying for the World or European Championships is based on time standards. For the European Championships held prior to the Olympic year, one need only meet the Olympic qualifying standard once, instead of twice as for the Olympic team. However, as previously mentioned, making a non-Olympic team can be difficult because the Flemish and French "ligues" must agree on the team composition. This difficulty does not seem to arise at the Olympic team level.

The Belgian team generally does not attend the World University Games because the European Championships take precedence (B. Vrancken, personal communication, November 15, 1992).

Review

When national team selection is viewed from different federation view points, the following methods are most common worldwide:

1. For time and distance events, a qualifying standard is created. In order to make the team, these Objective standards must be met, sometimes more than once within a specified period. If many athletes can surpass the standard, a qualifying competition, head-to-head competition, is used to select the team members.
2. For judgment events (Subjective model), athletes qualify for the team based on their performance, which is not directly quantifiable.
3. Some sports have a Combination model selection process. These sports select a training team based on the results of preliminary competitions. For the final team a panel of experts selects what they believe will be the best performers at the major competition.

International Linkages in Training and Selection

A related matter that needs to be discussed is selection of athletes who are training in another nation. This is important in three ways: (a) athletes in school in another country (e.g., on scholarship in a U.S. university); (b) athletes in residence in another country (e.g., those who train with a coach in another country); (c) athletes who have been sent overseas for better training conditions (e.g., skiers looking for better snow, or runners looking for milder winter weather).

In many instances, the foreign training has been important for the development of top international talent. However, the key issue has been how to make these athletes eligible for their national teams. The policy debates have centered on matters of sport development, team development, athlete preparation, and procedural justice:

1. When the best athletes are overseas training, it creates a gap in the national sporting scene. The best athletes are not present for developing athletes to use as role models or to compete against. This has been a particular problem for many developing nations.

2. When athletes are training overseas, it becomes harder to put together a cohesive national squad. For example, many of the top U.S. volleyball and soccer players have been attracted to play in European professional leagues. Consequently, the U.S. men's volleyball team to the 1992 Barcelona Olympics (which included U.S. players from the European leagues) had only trained together as a team for 2 months prior to the Games. Some critics argued that this was an inadequate period for full development of the team's potential. Others criticized the detrimental impact on the morale of players who had trained with the national team for several years, but were nevertheless excluded from the Olympic team.

3. When athletes go overseas to obtain better training conditions, it is difficult for their national coaches to monitor and control their training. For example, it was once common for Finnish runners to travel to sunnier climates (often the Caribbean) for winter training. However, when Arthur Lydiard started coaching the Finnish runners in the late 1960s, he insisted that they train in the Finnish winter so that they could maintain their preparation.

4. When athletes are selected on the basis of performances obtained while training overseas, their performance on the national team is not always comparable. In these instances, there are sometimes other athletes whose performances while training domestically suggest they would have been better selections. This has raised concerns about the fairness and adequacy of using overseas performances for selection to the national team. Thus, for example, New Zealand swimming selectors have required swimmers to qualify for selection in competitions held in New Zealand. Consequently, New Zealand swimmers at U.S. universities have had to travel home to qualify for the national team, even when their times in U.S. collegiate competitions were better than those of swimmers training in New Zealand.

Each country addresses this issue in its own way based on its experiences. Since international sport is dynamic in administration, ongoing evaluation of this procedure is warranted.

Coach Selection

The selection of coaches for national teams is never an easy task. Some countries try to limit the number of candidates by assuring minimum coaching competencies through certification programs. In other instances a national federation may have a coaching certification program. Regardless of coaching qualifications, three methods by which nations select national team coaches can be identified.

Special Assignment Coach

In this method, one or more coaches are named by the national federation to coach a team that has been selected for an international competition. The selected coaches are only with the national team for a short time, since their primary assignments are with club or school teams, rather than with the national team. The coaches and the team come together after selection to prepare for the competition. This method is common internationally, particularly in individual sports like cross-country or swimming. It may even lead to coaches working with athletes whom the coaches do not know. For example, the club coach of New Zealand's rhythmic gymnastics competitor at the 1988 Seoul Olympics was not selected as her Olympic coach. Instead, New Zealand gymnastics officials chose a coach from overseas for this competition.

Full Time Coach

One or more national coaches are appointed to oversee preparation of the national team throughout the period leading to the competition. In this instance, the national team is the coaches' primary (usually unique) assignment. For example, in the United States, two head coaches are selected by the United States Volleyball Association -- one for the men's team and one for the women's team. The head coaches then hire assistant team coaches. An effort is made to hire coaches for at least the quadrennium leading to the Olympic Games, although coaches may remain longer than that. Coaches are responsible for all preparation of the national teams.

Personal Coach

Coaches are selected on the basis of their athlete's performances. For example, any coach placing an athlete onto the U.S. Olympic gymnastic team becomes a coach of that athlete on that team.

It should be noted that there are also hybrids of these three types. For example, United States Swimming now retains a national coach, but selects other coaches for international teams on the basis of their athletes' performances at team trials.

Event Attendance

In the preceding section, competition selection for international teams was discussed. After the teams are chosen, the athletes can now focus externally on the upcoming international competition. In addition to the athletes, national team coaches and managers who have been working somewhat behind the scenes now take a more proactive role in order to prepare the athletes for the challenge. Because most national teams' coaches and managers have been athletes, or at least have experience with international caliber athletes, they are familiar with the very important task that lies ahead.

In general, the following outline indicates the steps from team selection to the athletes' returning home from the international event.

1. Team is selected for competition.
2. Athletes complete preliminary data about themselves.
3. Athletes either return home for training leading to the international competition, or athletes assemble for final practices before the competition.
4. Athletes and officials report to team assembly location for predeparture processing.
5. Team departs for either pre-event practice or competitions, or team travels directly to the international event.
6. Team registers at the event housing.
7. Team manager or coach reconfirms entries.
8. Competition occurs.
9. After competition, the team returns home, or some athletes, possibly with the team, participate at other competitions after the main international event. If there are additional competitions, the national federation continues to have responsibility for the athletes and staff until these people either return to their homes or agree to release themselves from their national federation's governance.

This chronology fairly represents an overview of the event attendance procedure no matter which national federation throughout the world is assembling its team for international competition.

Staff

Depending on the size of the traveling team and the sport involved, a team will also consist of administrators, coaches, managers, and sport medicine personnel. In total, this group is called a contingent. For multievent competitions such as the Goodwill Games, there is one person, the Chief of the Mission, who has the final authority for the entire group. Also with multisport competitions, the medical personnel may cover more than one team, especially if the teams do not compete simultaneously.

The duties of the contingent staff generally include

A. Chief of the Mission
   1. Highest administrative authority for the country at the competition.
   2. Represents the team/contingent at all ceremonies. Duties dictate that this person be familiar with protocol and adept at cultural events because of the importance of these factors with any international dealings.
   3. Coordinates all staff functions.
   4. Precedes over the resolution of problems that occur.
   5. Authors and edits the final mission report.

B. Head Coach
   1.   Acts as the chief of the mission, if there is none for a particular competition.
   2.   Works in coordination with the Head Manager during team selection, travel processing, and the return home after the competitions. The head coach and the head manager have specific duties respectively. Because neither can perform his or her duties well without the cooperation of the other, these people need to be in constant communication so as to present a unified program directed toward the athletes' success.
   3.   Develops the operational plan for the team prior to and during the major competition. Should there be pre-event competitions, the head coach sees that these events coordinate with the goal of having the athletes peak at the primary event.
   4.   Assigns and coordinates the duties and responsibilities of the assistant coaches.
   5.   Arranges for the medical personnel to be able to perform their duties.
   6.   Attends technical meetings at the event to include submitting or reconfirming team entries/rosters.
   7.   Attends to protocol as directed by the Chief of the Mission.
   8.   Submits application for record performance approval (e.g., a world record in the 400m hurdles).
   9.   Submits a report of the mission upon its completion.
   10. Aids with other duties as delegated by the Chief of the Mission.

C. Assistant Coaches
   1.   Assist the head coach as directed by the head coach.
   2.   Assist during team selection as directed by the head coach and/or head manager
   3.   If required, submit a report of the mission.

D. Head Managers
   1.   Usually lead the advance party to the competition site in order to arrange for meals, lodging, travel, entertainment, per diem money, medical care, and other items considered important to the teams' success.
   2.   Coordinate initial team processing during team selection. This processing includes medical examinations, passport and travel document needs, uniform and equipment sizing, and verifying team entry into the competition.
   3.   Develop the team travel itinerary with the head coach. (As stated, because athlete activity away from competition and practice often directly affects the athletes' athletic performance, the head manager *must* closely consult with the head coach when planning team functions and movements.)
   4.   Develop a team budget, authorize expenditures, and control team finances.
   5.   Delegate specific duties to the assistant managers.
   6.   Arrange for and supervise team assembly just prior to departure from the home country. This responsibility includes distribution of plane tickets, verification of the proper travel documents (and recording of each traveling party members' passport number and emergency information), uniform distribution, responsibility for luggage and equipment, including medical equipment and

legal drugs, arrangement of hotel transfers.

7. Upon arrival in a foreign country, see to immigration and customs needs, arrange for local transportation and luggage and equipment handling.

8. At the host village or housing, arrange for living accommodations and roommates, meals, practice facilities, and coordination between the Chief of the Mission, coaches, and medical staff.

9. Arrange for the delegation members' per diem allowance.

10. Submit a report of the mission upon completion of their duties.

11. Other duties as delegated by the Chief of the Mission.

E. Assistant Managers
   1. Assist the Head Manager as requested by the Head Manager.
   2. Assist in team selection arrangements.
   3. If required, submit a report of the mission.

F. Physician
   1. Arranges for the contingent's medical needs.
   2. Prepares and supervises the athletes' medical orientation, especially with respect to banned substances.
   3. Represents the team at the athletes' random drug tests.
   4. Coordinates with the Head Sport Medicine Trainer responsibilities of each sport medicine person with respect to covering team practices and rehabilitation sessions.
   5. Sees to the completion and submission of athlete or delegation injury/illness reports.
   6. Submits a report of the mission.

G. Sport Medicine Trainer
   1. Works in close coordination with the team physician on athlete injury prevention and rehabilitation needs.
   2. Assigns duties to the Assistant Sport Medicine Trainers.
   3. Advises and consults with the team physician concerning potential or actual medical problems or injuries.
   4. Supervises the team medical clinic, to include an accurate logging of treatments.
   5. Submits a report of the mission.

H. Assistant Sport Medicine Trainers
   1. Perform the duties as assigned by the Head Sport Medicine Trainer.
   2. Supervise the medical clinic when required,
   3. Advise the Head Sport Medicine Trainer about potential or actual medical problems or injuries.
   4. Submit a report of the mission.

Depending on the delegation size, complexity, and public attention generated by the event and sport(s) involved, some teams will travel with a press officer. This press officer's duties could include

1. Arranging for press releases to the local media prior to and during the event.
2. Being available to the media for information pertaining to team performances and medical conditions.
3. Notifying the media of athlete/team records being broken or other significant achievements as personal bests.
4. Obtaining and distributing, as needed, event results.
5. Arranging for athlete interviews and press conferences.
6. Submitting a report of the mission.

All of the aforementioned positions and responsibilities vary depending on the sport, size of the team or contingent, and length of the trip. In addition, the national federation, Olympic Committee, or sports ministry may have personnel whose duties duplicate or overlap these duties. In that case it is usually the responsibility of the full-time administrator to perform many of the duties of the head manager at the event. Usually this person has more intimate knowledge of the organizational details than does the volunteer manager. Olympic Committee and national federation position is discussed in greater detail in chapter 4 dealing with national federation duties and responsibilities.

Responsibilities of Athletes and Staff

A number of national federations such as USA Wrestling (1992), The Athletics Congress/USA (1988) (USA Track and Field), and United States Swimming (1990) have well-written, detailed and concise guides for the staffs and athletes to follow with respect to their duties and responsibilities for international travel.

This information is usually very detailed (e.g., how many pictures and their sizes to submit for passport and visa applications). U.S. Swimming even lists that "Form FS-192/ Optional Form 180" is to be completed when a death occurs overseas.

The following lists are topics that a national federation or national Olympic committee would include in a travel guide for international teams in order to aid in the smooth administration of the event.

<u>PRE-EVENT</u>

• Travel reservations
• Hotel reservations
• Menu selection
• Visa/Passport preparation
• Budget preparation
• Financial arrangements
• Medical/Release forms
• Staff selection
• Staff responsibility delineation
• Personal profile information
• Media guide preparation
• Uniforms and equipment distribution

- Personal packing information
- Medical supplies allocation
- Gifts for foreign distribution
- Foreign contacts and agreements, telephone and fax numbers that include embassies/ consulates/interest sections
- Information on countries to be visited including electrical voltage, food, recreation, and security
- Athlete eligibility status
- Competition rule books
- Practice sites, times, transportation, and equipment
- Administrative procedures (i.e., athletes' complaints)
- Foreign language interpreters if needed

DELEGATION ASSEMBLY SITE

- Complete arrangements from pre-event
- Check passport and visa documents
- Check transportation tickets
- Distribute uniforms and equipment
- Orient athletes and staff

DURING THE TRIP

- Complete previous arrangements, such as practices, medical needs, housing, transportation, competitions
- Keep accurate records of expenses and money disbursements
- Maintain flow of information among the athletes, coaches, managers, medical staff, public relations personnel, and Chief of the Mission
- Monitor drug testing procedures carefully
- Maintain competition results and record applications
- Complete accident records and insurance claims
- Check return travel arrangements
- Arrange for team photos
- Write thank-you notes
- Receive trip/event evaluations from delegation
- Handle special problems, such as serious injury of an athlete

POST-EVENT

- Submission of trip report by each staff member
- Submission to respective national federations, the national Olympic committee, and/or sport ministry
- Completion of financial report and return of unused funds
- Write thank you notes or letters to athletes, staff, and uniform and equipment suppliers

Cultural Awareness

All of the above are important to a successfully administered foreign trip. However, one aspect that cannot be fully appreciated in this listing is the need to educate the traveling party about cultural awareness. Depending on the person's point of reference, a cultural awakening may be needed in order to prepare each delegation member for the environment he or she is about to enter. Certainly the Chief of the Mission and head manager will be culturally aware as this is a prerequisite for these positions. However, it is not uncommon for an athlete to be unaware that, for example, touching the top of a Malaysian's head is very disrespectful or that warm soft drinks are the norm in Europe. Although no one can completely understand another region's culture, the more aware each delegation member is of the cultural idiosyncrasies of countries to be visited, the less likely the team member is to create a situation that person regrets and that will reflect poorly upon him or herself, the team, and indeed his or her country. During the opening ceremonies of the 1988 Seoul Olympic Games, the United States team broke its marching order and moved en masse, without order, around the track. In the process, the U.S. team engulfed smaller delegations. The U.S. team meant no disrespect or harm to anyone. However, that is the essential element of cultural awareness, to not create a cultural problem out of ignorance.

Real World Foreign Trip Experience

The previous sections stated procedures needed to organize attendance at an international event. Here are a few examples of actual situations that team officials and athletes have faced.

1. At the 1992 Barcelona Olympics, a United States swimmer's father died at the opening ceremonies. The athlete was unaware of this until early the next morning when the athlete's mother, coach, team manager, and USOC official could all be assembled in order to "break the news." In this case, the USOC, instead of U.S. Swimming, handled the arrangements for the body of athlete's father to return to the United States.
2. An American track and field team assembled in Los Angeles in order to depart for the Pan Pacific meeting in New Zealand. Unfortunately, not all the athletes could be fitted for uniforms in Los Angeles. The solution was to have the uniform supplier's representative in New Zealand meet the team and fit the remaining athletes there.
3. The United States Olympic track and field team was checking their equipment onto the plane in London's Heathrow Airport. When the airline counter attendant indicated that with the throwers' shots and disci, there was a luggage weight allowance problem, the U.S. manager explained to the attendant the team's needs and gave the attendant a USA Olympic Pin. No overweight duty was charged. (Team pins and collectibles have solved or prevented uncountable teams' logistic problems.)
4. A U.S. junior cross-country runner, while in Madrid for the World Cross Country Championships, could not sleep well because of the noise. The athlete proceeded to place chewing gum in his ears to lessen the noise. This tactic worked; however,

the next morning the sport medicine person had to take the athlete to the hospital in order to remove the dried gum.

5. During a long summer tour male and female teammates, who had an ongoing romantic relationship, had an argument. The women's team manager, sensing that the woman would not compete as well with this additional emotional burden while in Europe, sent flowers to the female athlete with a card indicating the flowers were from her male friend. The couple reconciled immediately, and both competed well.

6. Each part of the world has its popular sports. This can create a problem for the athlete, coaches, and managers when traveling. For example, Carl Lewis or swimmer Matt Biondi are famous in the United States. However, when they travel to Europe, where track and field and swimming are accorded greater acclaim, the logistics associated with housing, press conferences, and safety become a constant problem. A similar situation occurred with the very popular basketball Dream Team while preparing for the 1992 Olympics.

7. Luggage handling is a constant worry. One female athlete's luggage missed the flight from New York City to Moscow. The luggage was sent back to the athlete's home in Maine. The luggage, with the athlete already in Moscow, was routed back to New York City and then to Moscow. No one knows where the luggage went and the athlete, who was quite wide and thick through her upper body, had to wear men's clothing as none of the females' clothes would fit her.

8. There was a swimmer who had packed a suitcase of food in preparation for traveling to the 1988 Seoul Olympics. The athlete tested positive for a banned substance and did not make the trip. However, the food-packed suitcase traveled with the team. Although the food (energy bars and snacks) would not have contained a banned substance, the team managers wondered what should be done with the food, because it was too expensive to send back and the athletes would not touch it for fear of being tainted. The final decision was that the administrative staff ate the food.

9. At the Barcelona Olympics, the U.S. team had a problem with a young athlete who wanted to take part in the night life of the city. The athlete received written permission to stay out past curfew and her wish was granted. However, the team managers required the athlete to report to them when she returned to team housing. The next day the athlete failed to report as instructed, and she was sent back to the United States on the next airplane.

10. At the 1986 Asian Track and Field championships, all the countries' athletes were eating at the same venue. In order not to disrupt their preparation, the Japanese team leaders provided for the Japanese athletes to bring their own food to each meal, instead of eating the Indonesian prepared food.

11. Understanding cultural differences, even within a country, is important. In 1983, the Malaysian Track and Field championships were held at a naval base facility. All the athletes ate the same food, which was prepared in Malay style, spicy hot. Since the Malaysian-Indian and Malaysian-Chinese athletes typically do not eat spicy hot food, the team managers had to arrange, as well as possible, for the athletes to eat food prepared to their normal style.

All of these examples illustrate the need for adapting to specific needs for the athletes. Although careful planning can lessen or eliminate some problems, these examples indicate the need for well-qualified, experienced team personnel to handle whatever problem may arise.

Concluding Summary

The reason for sport is the athletes. Without the athletes, there is no need for administrators. This is a very important concept for the sport administrator to remember!

This chapter deals with selecting athletes for international competition and then servicing those athletes with the best possible coaches, managers, and administrators. The qualifications and duties of the non-athlete personnel are vital to the understanding of a successful international trip. The athletes spend years in preparation for their ultimate challenge; poorly selected or prepared support personnel can disrupt the athletes' preparation. This disruption can ruin the years of training.

It is important that support personnel understand the psychology of the elite, international athlete. Because of their superior athletic abilities and honed skills, these athletes become focused on their event. They want and deserve the coaches and administrators to handle the noncompetition details from travel to meals to housing. It is for this reason that support staff are usually skilled international team veterans who can handle the normal and the unexpected with equal ease in order to have the athletes perform at their peak.

Discussion, Analysis, Application, and Debate

Issues for Discussion

1. Discuss the pros and cons of the United States Gymnastic Federation's Olympic athlete selection process with respect to fairness to each competitor and placing the best team in the event. From what you know of other countries' sport governance systems, discuss the possibility of this method being used by these countries.
2. Based on the qualifying methods for swimmers to be selected for international teams that are presented in the text, present your feelings about each system and its fairness.
3. Considering Belgium's swimming teams' dichotomy by language/culture, do you think this could happen in Canada with English/French or the United States with English/Spanish or another country? Discuss.
4. Based upon the governmental and private sport governance systems, how would each system reconcile this problem: The Chief of the Mission requires all athletes to march in the event's opening ceremonies in order to show team unity, but the head coach does not want the athletes marching because the athletes must compete the next day.
5. The Greco-Roman world championships are being held in Sydney, Australia, next year. As the team's head manager, how and what would you prepare now for the event?

Matters for Analysis

1. The apparent fairness of athlete and coach selection is important when designing a selection policy. It goes beyond who is actually selected. There are two key issues: how athletes and coaches have been selected and whether or not there is an appeals procedure. For example, in some cases, athletes who are not selected for a team can challenge those who have been selected; if they beat those athletes, the challengers then replace them on the team. (This is what happened in 1984 with the United States coxless pairs: In a match race, two rowers who were not selected beat those who had been selected. They became the U.S. team to the Olympic Games.)

    What do you see as the relative pros and cons of keeping the selection process and/ or the selection criteria secret? What do you see as the relative pros and cons of allowing athletes or coaches to appeal a selection decision or to challenge a selected athlete or coach?

2. In a utopian world, qualifying for a national team would be "by the book" and with no problems. However, our world is not that way. How would you resolve the following situations:

    (a) A tie for second place in the 100m dash when only two athletes can qualify for an international event.
    (b) During the box-off qualifier, both boxers are knocked out by simultaneous punches.
    (c) With only two athletes qualifying, there is a tie in the 100m freestyle for second place between an athlete training domestically and one training in another country.

Application

Olympic hopefuls plan their training cycle to peak in the Olympic year. However, international and national federations want top performers at their world championships in non-Olympic years so that increased television ratings can generate greater television income. Select a sport and construct a 4-year schedule in order to maximize both media revenue and athlete performance assuming that the world championships are held on even years between the Olympics.

Ethical Debate

Being selected to a national team is a great honor. National team members are invited and expected to represent their countries in international competition. Because major international events do not always provide prize money or appearance fees, some athletes would rather attend a competition that pays them for their work. Should athletes represent their country in competition for no money when compensation is available at a competition conducted elsewhere at the same time?

References

Becker, D. (1994, December 15). Changes give U.S. women's hoops hope. *USA Today*. p. C1.

Becker, D. (1995, February 23). Pros weigh one-time offer to regain 'amateur' status. *USA Today*. p. C3.

Lawes, R. (1992, June 10). Versatility valuable commodity. *USA Today,* p. C9.

Lowenstein, R. (1992, July 27). The National Pastime, Passed over in Prime Time. *Wall Street Journal*, p. 9A.

Retton, M.L. (1992, June 15). *USA Today*, p. C10.

The Athletics Congress/USA. (1988). *Guide for team staff, 1988-1991*. Indianapolis: The Athletics Congress/USA

United States Baseball Federation. (1992). *Gold Medal Manual*. Trenton, New Jersey: United States Baseball Federation.

United States Gymnastics Federation. (n.d.) *The Business of Sport*. Indianapolis: United States Gymnastics Federation.

United States Figure Skating Association. (1994). *The 1995 Official USFSA Rulebook*. Colorado Springs: United States Figure Skating Association.

United States Swimming. (1990, January). *Olympic International Operations*. Colorado Springs: United States Swimming.

USA Wrestling. (1992). *Staff Guides for International*. Colorado Springs: USA Wrestling.

CHAPTER NINE ─────────

Sport for All

Overview

This chapter describes the structure of the international Sport for All movement, its objectives, and implications for sport managers. It shows that the movement seeks to promote mass participation in sport. Thus, Sport for All is concerned with developing a broad mass of active sportspersons, rather than elite competitors or sport spectators. Analysis of the German Sport for All program illustrates the potential of an integrated social marketing campaign to generate high levels of sport participation nationwide. The chapter concludes by describing four international organizations that work to serve the needs of special populations: the International Workers Sport Committee, the International Paralympic Committee, Special Olympics International, and the Federation of Gay Games.

Introduction

Since the Second World War, Olympic-style sport and professional sport have come to dominate international sport calendars and agendas. However, these forms of sport have focused primarily on elite performances and sport as entertainment. Over the past two decades, increasing international attention has been given to creation of infrastructures to promote mass participation in sport. The resulting movement is called "Sport for All" (Claeys, 1985). Although the movement has had relatively scant impact in North America (with the notable exception of Participaction in Canada), the goals of Sport for All have come to dominate sport policymaking in Europe and Australasia. The movement is also active in Latin America, Asia, and Africa. A time line of key events in the development of Sport for All is presented in Table 9-1.

Sport for All is avowedly participative. It seeks to involve all sectors of the population in physical activity throughout their life spans. It seeks to move people away from merely spectating to actually participating in sports activities at all levels (Donnelly, 1992). Sport for All distinguishes elite sports, in which competitive excellence is the goal, from participation for its own sake, for which the personal enjoyment and the physical benefits of sport are the goals. Sport for All distinguishes sport events that seek to entertain an audience, such as professional football matches or an Olympic Games, from sport programs designed to provide opportunities for everyone to participate. Although Sport for All often capitalizes on the interest in sport generated by elite competitors or popular sport entertainment, the goal of the Sport for All movement is to generate participation rather than excellence or audiences.

The advent of a significant international Sport for All movement bears profound implications for international sport management. Increased participation in sport can be

TABLE 9.1
Key Events In The Development Of Sport For All

1964 :   At the meetings of the International Council on Sport Science and Physical Education, European sports scholars and administrators coin the phrase "Sport for All" and agree to cooperate in development of Sport for All.

1966 :   The Council of Europe adopts Sport for All as the basis for European sports policy.

1968 :   Norway initiates its TRIMM campaign, which serves as an initial Sport for All model.

1969 :   Eight European nations participate in the first Trim and Fitness conference. The conference is repeated every 2 years. By 1989, 50 nations participate.

1975 :   At the Council of Europe conference in Brussels, sport ministers adopt the European Sport-for-All Charter, which specifies that (a) all citizens of Europe have the right to participate in sport, and (b) the right to participate is to be supported by public financial support, coordination of sports programs with government, development of facilities, and training of sport personnel.

1981 :   The International Association of National Organizations for Sport (IANOS) is formed to promote mass sport participation.

1984 :   The IOC enters into an agreement with the International Council of Sport Science and Physical Education to cooperate in the development of Sport for All.

1985 :   The IOC establishes a Sport for All Commission to assist NOCs in the development of Sport for All programs.

1986 :   The first International Sport for All Conference is held. It continues to be held every 2 years.

1988 :   The European Sport Conference establishes an information desk in Norway for international cooperation and information sharing about Sport for All. The UNESCO Sports Ministers' Conference adopts a resolution supporting Sport for All as its key international goal.

1990 :   Trim and Fitness International Sport for All (TAFISA) is formed to serve as an international clearinghouse and coordinating body for Sport for All.

expected to enlarge the market for sports equipment, sports programming, and sports facilities. Further, as Sport for All programs proliferate, there has been increased demand for international exchanges of expertise and program personnel. A recent survey of Sport for All programs in 97 countries found that almost two of every three were actively involved in international cooperation or bilateral exchanges (Skirstad, 1992).

Several organizations have been formed to promote international cooperation in Sport for All. Fourteen Latin American countries share cooperation in the Pan American Confederation of Sport for All. The Federation International Sport Pour Tous (headquartered in Belgium) has assisted projects in French-, Spanish-, and Arabic-speaking countries. Information sharing among nations of the Pacific is promoted by the Asian, Pacific, and Oceania Sport for All Association. The IOC maintains a Sport for All Commission to assist NOCs in the development of Sport for All programs. Trim and Fitness International Sport for All (TAFISA) serves as an international clearinghouse and coordinating body for Sport for All.

Countries vary in the ways that they implement their Sport for All programs. In her survey of national Sport for All programs, Skirstad (1992) found that 42% were administered by one or more government agencies or commissions, 19% were directly administered by national sports federations, 16% by a dedicated Sport for All organization, and only 8% by National Olympic Committees. The remaining 15% of Sport for All programs were administered by specialized sports institutes, associations, or councils.

Advocates of Sport for All argue that sport can serve as a potent weapon against the purported ravages of modern society. They argue that sport participation is not merely a want, it is a need (McIntosh, 1987). Two objectives are key: First, proponents of Sport for All seek to promote physical activity as a vital component of healthy lifestyles; second, proponents of Sport for All seek to encourage people to engage their world as active participants, and not merely as spectators. In fact, these objectives inspired the title of Australia's Sport for All campaign: "Life. Be in it." Thus, the movement is premised on the idea that appropriately implemented sports programs can promote the social and psychological health of participants.

Given these goals, it is not surprising that Sport for All programs are rarely concerned with the development of elite sport. Upon reflection, it might seem that mass participation in sport could serve to enlarge the pool of potentially elite athletes. However, Sport for All programs do not typically serve as a vehicle for promotion of elite sport. A 1989 survey of Sport for All programs in 57 nations found that only 8 (14%) use Sport for All to recruit potentially elite athletes into sport (Palm, 1991). Rather, as the movement's ideology would suggest, programs are aimed simply at expanding the volume of participation.

The German Sport for All program provides a useful illustration because it is unusually comprehensive and claims to be exceedingly effective. The German Sports Federation has documented a steady annual increase in sport participation from 18% of the population in 1960 to 69% in 1988 (Palm, 1991). An integrated social marketing campaign has provided the basis for the program's success. Palm (1991) outlines nine key elements:

1. Health problems associated with exercise deficit are stressed to government and citizens.
2. The economic benefits of sport development are identified and promoted.
3. New sports (e.g., cooperative games, foreign sports, and sports adapted for varied ages and abilities) are added to the sport system.
4. Many ways are created to socialize new participants into the sport system. The social elements of participation are stressed.
5. Sports clubs and volunteers are used extensively to recruit new members and to socialize them into regular participation.
6. Advertising emphasizes play and socialization, rather than competition.
7. Performance demands are leveled so that a wide range of skill levels is accommodated.
8. Inexpensive sports (e.g., jogging) are made widely available.
9. Programs and advertizing cater to a wide range of motivations for doing sport, such as exercising (e.g., basketball, swimming), obtaining new experiences (e.g., scuba, hiking), or self-development (e.g., body building).

Sport for All programs stress broad participation. Wherever possible, the programs work with organizations that reach out to populations that might otherwise be underserved. Four such organizations are described below: the International Workers Sport Committee, the International Paralympic Committee, Special Olympics International and the Federation of Gay Games. In point of fact, only the International Workers Sport Committee is strictly focused on promotion of participation. The other three organizations also promote large international competitions. However, as the following descriptions show, the international competitions provide an umbrella intended to encourage the participation of populations that might be underserved as a consequence of their special status. In this way, these international organizations help to promote the overall aims of the Sport for All movement--a fact noted by the IOC's own Sport for All Commission (Troeger, 1992).

The International Workers Sport Committee

In the late 19th century and early 20th century, the majority of sports organizations were exclusionist. Women, ethnic minorities, and/or laborers were not permitted to join. Similarly, early Olympic rules specified that "the following may not be considered as amateur sportsmen: workers or farm or day laborers" (quoted in Riordan, 1984, p. 98). In response to these restrictions, workers' organizations formulated their own sports movement. The workers' sport movement is significant because it was the first to stress mass participation in sport:

> Worker sport was to differ from bourgeois sport by being open to all workers--women as well as men, white as well as black. More than that: it was to provide a socialist alternative to ... competitive sport, to commercialism, chauvinism, and the obsession with stars and records...
> The founders of the workers' sports movement believed that sport could ... turn physical culture into a new international language capable of breaking down barriers. (Riordan, 1984, p. 99)

Workers' sports organizations began to form throughout Europe during the 1890s and early 1900s. In 1913, representatives from workers' sports organizations throughout Europe met at Ghent (Belgium) to establish the International Workers' Sports Movement. In 1920, it was renamed the International Association for Sport and Physical Culture. By the end of that decade, it served over four million workers and their families.

Throughout this period, the workers' sport movement was the dominant promoter of mass sport participation. In 1931, at the second Workers' Olympics in Vienna, over 100,000 worker-athletes from 26 countries competed. By contrast, although 37 nations were represented at the 1932 Los Angeles Olympics, only 1,408 athletes competed.

Although the movement struggled to survive the depression and the World War II, it was reconstituted in 1946 as the International Workers Sport Committee (IWSC). Headquartered in Brussels, Belgium, it seeks "to encourage the inclusion of sport in the life of all workers" (Deveen, 1992, p. 122). By the mid-1980s, it served over 2.2 million members in 14 countries.

There are two elements to IWSC strategy. The first is to promote Sport for All. Toward that end, the IWSC maintains a Sport for All department. Particular emphasis is placed on making sport participation affordable and on sponsoring sports programs and events in working class communities. The second strategy is to promote sport participation at the workplace. Member unions are encouraged to plan and implement sports activities.

The IWSC holds a congress of the membership once every 3 years. The congress elects an executive board by secret ballot. The executive board meets twice per year to oversee IWSC governance.

The IWSC coordinates its activities with other international sport organizations. It is recognized by the IOC as the organization to promote sport for workers. It is a member of the General Association of International Sports Federations and the International Council for Physical Education and the Science of Sport.

Despite continued post-war growth, the workers' sports movement has never approached its pre-war significance. Deveen (1992) attributes the organization's problems to inadequate finance, particularly its reticence to raise membership fees. Riordan (1984) argues that workers' sports organizations have lost some of their appeal as other (community, church, school, and private) sports organizations have come to admit women, ethnic minorities, and laborers. He also shows that many workers are unaware of the workers' sports movement because media coverage of workers' sport is typically confined to the workers' press, which, ironically, is read by only a small minority of workers.

As the 21st century approaches, the IWSC faces new challenges. It must do more to bring its programs to the attention of union members. It must locate new opportunities for funding its programs. It must find new ways to make sport relevant to workers, particularly those for whom the staggering poverty of urban centers in developing countries makes sport seem at best a luxury and at worst an imposition. If the IWSC meets these challenges, it will continue to play a significant role in the promotion of Sport for All.

The International Paralympic Committee

In 1948, Dr. Ludwig Guttman, a physician and German war exile in Britain, organized a sports competition between veterans from Holland and Britain. Primarily for wheelchair users, the Stoke Mandeville Games were the forerunner of the modern Paralympic Games. This low-key event held its opening ceremony on the same day as the opening ceremony of the Olympic Games held in London, thus beginning the parallel to the Olympic Games that would serve as a primary aim of the Paralympic Movement: to integrate disabled sport as far as possible into the Olympic Movement.

Toward this end, the Paralympics take place at the Olympic site immediately following the Olympic Games. With the exception of venue changes in 1968 and 1980, the Paralympics have been held in the Olympic city since the 1960 Games in Rome. The Rome Paralympics marked the inclusion of competition for disabled athletes not confined to a wheelchair, and featured 400 participants from 23 countries. By 1972, 1,400 athletes from 44 nations competed, including for the first time amputee and blind athletes. Growth and interest in the Paralympic Games have increased dramatically. The 1992 Games in Barcelona saw 4,000 athletes from 94 countries compete before 1.5 million spectators. Media interest has grown correspondingly, with over 1,000 journalists and 35 television stations covering events in 19 sports at the Games in Barcelona.

The Paralympics are intended to encourage individuals to take an active part in sport in order to increase their mobility and independence. Harald von Selzam, project director of the Berlin Paralympic bid, describes the challenge as "overcoming prejudices and accelerating the process of social integration" (unpublished bid materials, 1992). Similarly, Helmut Kohl, speaking as chancellor of the Federal Republic of Germany recognized the Paralympics as a way to "help to reduce prejudice, counter thoughtlessness and increase understanding on the part of the able bodied... They make us conscious of the fact that the integration of the disabled is a constant challenge... not only to the world of politics but to society as a whole" (unpublished bid materials, 1992).

The challenge of integration is echoed throughout the Paralympic ideology. The International Paralympic Committee (IPC) seeks to integrate disabled sport into the Olympic Movement, integrate the disabled into society through sport, and integrate athletes of various disabilities and nationalities through participation in the Paralympics and other sports opportunities. The IPC is the international umbrella organization for disabled sport and is responsible for the Paralympics. Similar to the IOC with its NOCs and IFs, the IPC works closely with national paralympic committees (NPCs) and Sports Assembly Executive Committees (SAECs) to develop disabled sport and disabled athletes.

Athletes from four sports federations compete in the Paralympics: (a) IBSA, blind and visually impaired; (b) CP-ISRA, cerebral palsy/mobility impaired; (c) ISMWSF, paraplegics; and (d) ISOD, amputees and those with other physical disabilities. In addition, competition in athletics and swimming is offered for athletes with intellectual disabilities. Athlete selection for the Paralympics is the responsibility of the National Paralympic Committee (NPC) in most countries. In countries where there is no NPC (for example, the United States), responsibility falls to the individual sports associations (e.g., National Handicapped Sports, Dwarf Athletic Association of America, etc.). Athletes are then classified for competition according to disability and severity.

The rapid growth in popularity and performance standards of the Paralympics has resulted in implementation of qualifying standards and a trend toward reducing the number of classes and competitions in the Paralympic program. These recent concerns suggest the success this movement has had in promoting sport for the disabled. Although the Paralympics themselves are an elite event, the Paralympic Movement remains committed to objectives embraced by the Sport for All movement. Paralympics and its affiliated sports federations encourage disabled individuals to actively engage their world through sport.

Special Olympics International

Founded in 1968 and headquartered in Washington, DC, Special Olympics International promotes programs of year-round training and competition in 23 sports for children and adults with mental retardation. Over 100 countries have accredited Special Olympics programs. More than 15,000 Special Olympics competitions are held each year throughout the world. The Special Olympics World Games are held every 2 years, alternating between winter and summer.

Participation in Special Olympics events and programs is open to all persons over the age of 8 years who have mental retardation. Participants are assigned to divisions commensurate with their ability. For participants with severe mental retardation or multiple disabilities, Special Olympics provides a specialized program called "The Motor Activities Training Program" (MATP). The MATP emphasizes training and participation, rather than competition.

Wherever possible, Special Olympics seeks to integrate athletes with mental retardation with athletes without mental retardation. The organization encourages (but does not require) its most able athletes to move from Special Olympics to school and community sport programs. The organization also offers a Unified Sports program. The Unified Sports program puts approximately equal numbers of athletes with and without mental retardation (but who are of comparable age and skill) onto the same team. Unified Sports teams compete against each other.

Special Olympics stresses the use of volunteers. Over 500,000 volunteers organize and administer Special Olympics programs worldwide. More than 140,000 of those volunteers are coaches. The organization runs extensive training programs for its volunteers. For example, Special Olympics has developed and tested training programs for each sport that it offers. Prospective coaches must attend a general training session covering mental retardation and Special Olympics guidelines. The prospective coach then attends a coaches' school where he or she is trained to coach a specific sport. Following successful completion of that training, the coach participates in a 10-hour practicum where he or she actually trains Special Olympics athletes. Only then is the volunteer eligible for certification as a Special Olympics coach.

Special Olympics programs contribute significantly to the international Sport for All movement. The organization's development of programs to integrate its special population of athletes with athletes from the general community is consistent with Sport for All's emphasis on inclusion over elitism. Similarly, Special Olympics' programs of volunteer recruitment and training provide useful models for the development of comparable volunteer efforts elsewhere in the Sport for All movement.

The Federation of Gay Games

In 1980, Tom Waddell, a San Francisco physician, proposed an international gay athletic event. In a subsequent interview, he explained his rationale this way:

> I want the [gay and lesbian] community to see what terrific self-esteem and self-worth they should have... We need to know about ourselves, and the Games are just a format for this... Ultimately, we have a lot to teach--about relationships and community support. And it all translates into an activity like the Games. (quoted in Coe, 1986, p. 13)

The first and second Gay Games were organized by San Francisco Arts and Athletics, and held in San Francisco in 1982 and 1986, respectively. Gay Games I drew 1,300 athletes from three countries. Gay Games II drew 3,500 athletes from 19 countries. Gay Games III, held in Vancouver, drew 7,400 athletes from 22 countries. Gay Games IV in New York drew over 10,000 athletes from over 25 countries.

In 1986, when Gay Games III was awarded to Vancouver, organizers agreed that a new, international organization would be required to govern the Games. In July, 1989, delegates from Canada, France, Holland, and the United States met in Seattle to form the Federation of Gay Games (FGG). The FGG is governed by an executive board of 43 gay men and women. The Federation's primary function is "to foster and augment the self respect of gay women and men throughout the world and to engender understanding from the non-gay world through the medium of non-competitive oriented cultural and athletic events promoted as 'The Gay Games'" (unpublished FGG mission statement, 1989).

The Gay Games seek to include all who wish to participate, regardless of age, race, ability, sex, or sexual orientation. Wherever possible, men and women compete together. Each sport is available to the physically challenged.

In order to promote the Games, the FGG has initiated an international outreach program to contact communities not yet participating in the Games. It has created an endowment fund to guarantee the long-term financial integrity of the Games. It also maintains a Gay Games Archives.

The Gay Games have had a measurable impact on the development of sport for gays and lesbians. The emphasis on sport as an expression of gay pride has served to promote sport participation in the gay community. For example, Pitts (1988-89) surveyed organizations providing sport to the American gay community. She found that all had been created after 1975, and that the rate of creation had increased from 3 per year prior to Gay Games I to 4.4 per year after Gay Games I.

Concluding Summary

The international Sport for All movement began in Europe in the 1960s and has since spread throughout the world. The movement asserts that participation in sport is a human right rooted in the need to live actively. The movement therefore seeks to promote participation in sport by persons of all ages and abilities. In order to further sport participation, international and regional Sport for All organizations have been created, and a network for information sharing has been established. Most nations with Sport for All programs report some international exchange of sports experts to foster sport development.

Sport organizations that target special populations have been created to reach out to persons who may be inadequately served by traditional sport organizations. The International Workers Sport Committee promotes sport participation at the workplace and sponsors sports programs and events in working class communities. The International Paralympic Committee promotes sport for persons who are blind, paraplegic, mobility impaired, or amputees. Special Olympics International develops sports programs for persons with mental retardation. The Federation of Gay Games promotes sport participation by members of the gay and lesbian community.

Disscussion, Analysis, Application, and Debate

Issues for Discussion

1. Proponents of Sport for All argue that sport helps to promote mental and physical health. Is that always true? How do you think sport programs should be designed to optimize their effect on mental and physical health?
2. How can the recommendations for sport diffusion (in chapter 4) be combined with Palm's suggestions for promoting Sport for All? What new strategies, tactics, or principles result?
3. What special problems or tactics might apply to development and promotion of Sport for All programs specifically targeted at members of labor unions? How might development of workers' Sport for All programs in the developing nations differ from development of workers' Sport for All programs in industrialized nations?
4. If a city is bidding to host the Olympic Games, what factors does the organizing committee need to consider when planning facilities in order to host the Paralympic Games immediately following the Olympic Games?
5. What special problems do you envision for coordinating a program to train volunteer coaches around the world, as Special Olympics does? How would you go about addressing those problems?
6. In what ways might the Gay Games help to promote gay pride? Assuming that one purpose of the Gay Games is to promote gay pride, what implications do you see for organizing and staging the Gay Games?

Matters for Analysis

1. As Sport for All programs succeed in elevating sport participation, there will be an increased demand for sporting goods. This suggests that the profit impact of sporting goods will improve as the Sport for All movement becomes more successful.
   If you were a sporting goods manufacturer, would this be a sufficient reason for you to invest in the Sport for All movement? If not, why not? If so, why and how should you invest?

2. Consider again the matter of linking sporting goods manufacturers to development and promotion of Sport for All. Does the fact that sporting goods manufacturers are stakeholders suggest that proponents of Sport for All should seek to involve sporting goods organizations in Sport for All campaigns? If not, why not? If so, why and how?

Application

Using the ideas suggested by Palm for fostering Sport for All, design a Sport for All program and promotional campaign for your community.

Ethical Debate

Sport for All was developed and is propounded by people who like sport. Most surveys find that a substantial percentage of the population does not enjoy sport. Yet, Sport for All programs seek to persuade people to participate in sport.

Is this coercive? If so, how? If not, how could it become coercive? What are the implications for formulating and administering Sport for All campaigns?

References

Claeys, U. (1985). Evolution of the concept of sport and the participation nonparticipation phenomenon. *Sociology of Sport Journal, 2,* 233-239.

Coe, R.M. (1986). *A sense of pride: The story of Gay Games II.* San Francisco: Pride Publications.

Deveen, M. (1992). Aims and progress of sport for all in the context of the International Labor Movement. *Proceedings of the 31th session of the International Olympic Academy* (pp. 117-125). Lausanne: IOC.

Donnelly, P. (1992, July). *Between a rock and a hard place: The impact of elite sport ideologies on the development of Sport for All.* Paper presented at the Olympic Scientific Congress, Malaga, Spain.

McIntosh, P. (1987). *Sport in society* (rev. ed.). London: West London Press.

Palm, J. (1991). *Sport for all: Approaches from Utopia to reality.* Schorndorf: Verlag Karl Hofmann.

Pitts, B.G. (1988-89). Beyond the bars: The development of leisure activity management in the lesbian and gay population in America. *Leisure Information Quarterly, 15*(3), 4-7.

Riordan, J. (1984). The workers' Olympics. In A. Tomlinson & G. Whannel (Eds.), *Five ring circus* (pp. 98-112). London: Pluto Press.

Skirstad, B. (1992, July). *The situation of Sport for All around the world*. Paper presented at the Olympic Scientific Congress, Malaga, Spain.

Troeger, W. (1992). Sport for all: Aims and expected influence on the Olympic Movement. *Proceedings of the 31st Session of the International Olympic Academy* (pp. 72-77). Lausanne: IOC.

CHAPTER TEN

POLITICS AND BOYCOTTS

Overview

This chapter explores international sport as a political tool. The first section examines political uses of sport to build national prestige, to compare ideologies, to bolster national self-esteem, to initiate diplomatic relations, and to provide intelligence cover. The following section examines ways in which international sports events become venues for promoting causes or venting grievances. In a discussion of managerial implications, sport managers working internationally are encouraged to develop skills in political analysis and diplomacy.

The chapter concludes with a discussion of the most common form of political expression in sport: the boycott. Two types of boycotts are examined: boycotts as political sanctions and boycotts of events.

Introduction

Throughout popular media and public debate one commonly hears the contention that sport has nothing to do with politics (Lund, 1963). The assertion of sport's independence from politics is heard throughout the world of sport. It is most clearly represented in the folklore and rules of the Olympic Movement. One Olympic athlete, dismayed by the politics he witnessed at the 1968 Olympics in Mexico City, wrote, "No matter how much we may disagree with any nation or sympathize with any people, the Olympics must not be used as an instrument of politics" (Schollander & Savage, 1971, p. 192). Indeed, the ideal of sport's separation from politics is illustrated in the *Olympic Charter* by requiring that NOCs be independent of governments (Rule 32): "Governments or other public authorities shall not designate any members of an NOC" (International Olympic Committee, 1993, p. 50). Bylaw 9.4 of that same rule amplifies the point by requiring that NOC funding "be accomplished ... in such a manner that the dignity and independence of the NOC are not harmed" (p. 54). Yet, as preceding chapters show, the tasks of international sport governance are inevitably tasks requiring political acumen. The visibility of sport performances and their seemingly clear outcomes have rendered them ideal for political uses. The sport manager who works most competently in international settings will be sensitive to the political impact and applications of sport. Let's examine sport as a political tool.

Sport As Politics

During the era of the Cold War, sport served as a proxy for ideological combat; the systems of capitalism and communism were being tested on the playing field, on the track, and in the pool. The matter generated substantial diplomatic concern. For example, after East German (GDR) athletes had finished second to Soviet athletes at the 1976 Olympic Games in Montreal, the U.S. embassy in Berlin cabled the following analysis to the Department of State in Washington and to seven other U.S. establishments in Europe and North America (see Chalip, 1987 for a discussion):

> The GDR media pulled out all the stops on their coverage of the 21st Montreal Olympic Summer Games beginning several weeks before they opened in mid-July. The excellent performance of the GDR team, second only to the USSR, provided grist for the GDR propaganda mill, which emphasized the following themes in its coverage:
>
> (A) Socialist athletes did better than capitalist ones. In citing that socialist athletes obtained 56.5% of the medals awarded, the GDR coverage implies that Olympic competition proves in yet another way that socialist societies are superior to capitalist ones. In reflecting on GDR successes during the closing ceremony at Montreal one GDR TV commentator could not refrain from concluding that the GDR second place was proof that the GDR is a "healthy" society and added that the world and "North America" would now be impelled to investigate why this was so and their own citizens were "so sick."
>
> (B) GDR victories are a cause for East German patriotism. The GDR media here and the announcers from Montreal could not conceal their elation at GDR victories, and found occasion to play down with faint praise American and other Western winners. GDR TV coverage, incidently, was quite full, particularly because the GDR bought extra (and expensive) satellite transmission time. Such time was used to full advantage in portraying the competitions in which East German athletes participated.
>
> It is evident from random conversations with East Germans that they felt an identity with the successes of GDR athletes in Montreal. (quoted in Chalip, 1987, p. 560)

Two years before those Games, then Vice President Gerald Ford (1974) wrote:

> Do we realize how important it is to compete successfully with other nations? ... I don't know of a better advertisement ... than a healthy athletic representation... With communications what they are, a sports triumph can be as uplifting to a nation's spirit as, well, a battlefield victory. (p. 17)

These examples are instructive because the use of international sport to build national prestige or compare ideologies has never been limited to Cold War confrontations. As long as athletes and teams are representatives of their nations, sports contests convey political meaning. Chalip (1987) documents the political impact of smaller-scale sports encounters, such as Indian competitions with Pakistan and New Zealand rivalries with

Australia. He also shows how relatively successful sports performances have been used by developing nations to bolster national self-esteem. For example, one Fijian commentator commented about the performances of Fijian yachtsmen, "[Our team's] results ... showed that although young in experience, Fiji is not the least of ... nations" (quoted in Chalip, 1987, p. 556).

Ironically, the claim that sport is independent from politics has enhanced its value as a political tool. Sport has seemed an innocuous vehicle by which to further political ends. President Richard Nixon's uses of table tennis to initiate diplomatic relations with the People's Republic of China are often cited as a prototypical example. At the beginning of the 1970s, President Nixon facilitated a series of exhibition contests in China by the U.S. Table Tennis Team. At the time, the United States had no diplomatic relations with the government in Beijing. President Nixon followed the table tennis exhibitions by visiting the Chinese mainland in 1973 to pursue establishment of normal diplomatic relations.

Sport's uses as a political tool have not been limited to "Ping Pong diplomacy." For example, Cuba's diplomatic strategies have included athlete exchanges and sports assistance programs to developing countries. These exchanges have enhanced Cuba's relations with developing nations and have often come as part of a package that included military support for nations fearing counterrevolutionary activity (Slack & Whitson, 1988). Canada established a "sport desk" within the Department of External Affairs in 1972 to further the use of sport as an instrument of foreign policy. Canada has used sport to express diplomatic protest, generate propaganda, and promote trade, tourism, and investment (Franks, Hawes, & Macintosh, 1988). The Republic of Korea took advantage of hosting the 1988 Olympic Games to enhance the country's international image and to obtain new diplomatic and trade relations (Ricquart, 1988).

Sport's asserted independence from politics has also made it an ideal intelligence cover. Former CIA operative Philip Agee (1975) provides detailed descriptions of his use of sport as a cover while gathering intelligence in Latin America. For example, during the 1968 Olympics in Mexico City, Agee was assigned as a "cultural attache" to cover his real assignment, which was to collect information about leftist organizations in Mexico. Agee also describes encounters with intelligence agents from other countries engaged in similar work. Peter Ueberroth (1985), who headed the Los Angeles Olympic Organizing Committee, notes that "the FBI ... assumed whomever the Soviets chose as an [Olympic] attache would be KGB [Soviet intelligence]" (p. 189). MacAloon (1992) quotes an unnamed CIA officer who found covers during travels as an athlete, coach, and sports official to be an ideal means by which to mask his primary assignment, which was to provide counterinsurgency training to the soldiers and police of developing countries: "[Most people] would rarely think to suspect something so innocent as our happy little sport" (p. 119).

Nevertheless, international sports events can obtain the kind of international attention that disenfranchised political groups seek. The very popularity of international sport can render international events vulnerable to attack. For example, during the 1972 Olympic Games in Munich, eight Palestinians invaded the rooms in the Olympic Village that housed Israeli athletes and coaches. Two Israelis were killed, and nine athletes and coaches were taken hostage. The Palestinians demanded that 200 prisoners in Israeli jails be released in exchange for the hostages. In the end, the nine Israeli hostages and eight Palestinians were killed. The Palestinian attack had nothing to do with sport or the Olympic Movement. Rather, the Palestinians chose the Olympics as a venue in order to obtain the intensity of attention to their cause that they felt unable to obtain elsewhere. As one analyst wrote: "The Olympic Games had once again become the staging ground ... for a particular political cause. The Munich massacre vividly underscored the unique simultaneity of the Olympics as actor and stage, participant and arena" (Espy, 1979, p. 158).

The value of sports events "as actor and stage" can be more subtle than in the case of the Palestinian attack on the Israeli team. Sport can become a venue for venting political frustrations. The "Keith Walker affair" during the 1988 Olympics in Seoul provides a useful illustration. During the Olympic boxing competition, a Korean boxer attacked the referee, Keith Walker, who was a New Zealander. Initial press reports in Korea identified Keith Walker as a New Zealander and accused him of biased (anti-Korean) refereeing. The New Zealand embassy estimated that it received over 50 irate phone calls within the first day. Yet within a few days, Korean ire was transferred from New Zealand to the United States. U.S. television coverage of the Olympics had been broadcast within Korea over AFKN (American Forces Korea Network). Within days of the incident, the Korean press ceased to mention the New Zealand connection, but complained instead about the extensive and (to Koreans) insulting coverage of the event on U.S. television:

> Mediation of the Keith Walker affair by a colonializing American network made possible the transformation of anti-New Zealand sentiment into anti-American sentiment. The portrayal of the episode on U.S. television came to represent for Koreans much of what seems unacceptable about their relations with the United States. As the incident became another indicator of Koreans' long-standing frustrations with felt American hegemony, the incident's New Zealand connection became unimportant. (Chalip, 1990, p. 432)

There are significant lessons in the foregoing examples for sport managers who work internationally. The power of sport to generate large audiences, international exchanges, and salient political meanings has had the effect of placing international sport squarely within the realm of international politics (cf. Houlihan, 1994; Pound, 1994). In order to administer sport internationally, the manager must develop the skills of political analysis and diplomacy. Prior to international events or exchanges, the manager must appraise potential impacts of multinational confrontations, media attention, and cross-national exchanges. These appraisals form the basis for proactive planning to fortify potentially beneficial outcomes and blunt potentially detrimental impacts. During the event or exchange, the manager must monitor occurrences in order to exploit useful effects and minimize the damage caused by adverse incidents.

Boycotts

Perhaps the most common form of political expression in sport is the boycott. The lengthy and controversial history of boycotts in international sport warrants particular attention to them here. If the past is any guide, sport managers working internationally are likely to face a boycott or a threatened boycott at some time during their careers.

It is useful to distinguish two forms of boycott: (a) boycotts implemented as sanctions against a particular country and (b) boycotts implemented against a particular event. Boycotts of the first type are relatively long-term, and are intended to coerce the target country to alter one or more policies. The most celebrated example of this type of boycott is the campaign against sports contacts with South Africa, which continued into the 1990s when that country moved from White minority government to Black majority government. Boycotts of the second type are expressions of protest and are relatively short-term insomuch as they are targeted at a single event. The most familiar examples are the many boycotts of the Olympic Games.

It is not the purpose of this text to provide detailed histories of all sport boycotts. Rather, key examples of each type are described to illustrate the implications for the management of international sport.

Boycotts as Political Sanctions:
The Campaign Against South Africa

Through a series of acts and decrees over several decades, South Africa institutionalized the separation of the races. Among the more than 200 key pieces of legislation were provisions for segregated education (in 1893), prohibitions on mixed marriages (in 1949), and requirements that there be separate public amenities for Whites, Blacks, and "coloureds" (in 1953). One observer characterized the situation this way: "Everything in South Africa's white dominated societal paradigm seems to be documented, controlled, and regulated ... by those in supreme power in an atmosphere that might be characterized best as ... Whites Only" (Krotee, 1988, p. 126).

This institutionalized racism, known as "apartheid," came under increasingly vehement international attack and has been condemned in hundreds of international declarations, resolutions, and agreements (Nafziger, 1988, pp. 108-116). Sport rapidly became a key battleground for those seeking to compel South Africa to discontinue its policies of racial separation. Although apartheid in general (and not merely in sport) was commonly the target, it was the application of apartheid to sport that provided the key legitimation for extending the battle against apartheid into sport:

> Whenever black sportsmen and women sought membership in the so-called establishment (white) sports bodies, their applications were repeatedly refused on the grounds that "government policy" prohibited the mixing of races on the sports field. Frustrated by the blocking procedures of the Whites, black sports organisations and individuals appealed to international and Commonwealth associations for help. (Ramsamy, 1991, p. 539)

The moral claim of those seeking to isolate South African sport was bolstered by the official and implicit ideologies of sport. Fundamental Principle 6 of the *Olympic Charter* specifies that, "The goal of the Olympic Movement is ... sport practised without discrimination of any kind..." (International Olympic Committee, 1993, p. 11) Kidd (1988) argues that this official ideology is bolstered by implicit ideologies that also stress equal opportunities for and treatment of athletes:

> Athletes are expected to accept the same conditions, obey the same rules, and treat competitors as co-players without whom the pleasure of the contest could not be obtained. The presiding officials, or referees, are expected to treat all players the same... It did not take much of leap ... to extend [these understandings] in the form of a prohibition against discrimination [in] sports of all kinds and at all levels. (p. 650)

Antagonists of apartheid were thus able to enlist the ideologies of sport to legitimize boycotts of South African sport. As the years went by, the campaign against South African sport was increasingly effective (Kidd, 1991). In 1956, the IF governing table tennis expelled white South Africa from membership, becoming the first IF to do so. In 1963, the South African Olympic Committee (SANOC) was suspended by the IOC. In 1970, it was expelled. In 1988, the IOC established a Commission on Apartheid and Olympism to further the isolation of South African sport. On the Commission's recommendation, the IOC ruled that athletes who had competed in South Africa would be ineligible for participation in the Olympic Games. It also encouraged IFs to expel South Africa from membership. In 1989, the International Cricket Conference banned players who competed in South Africa from international competition. During the 1970s and 1980s, governments throughout the world established restrictions on entry of South African athletes and officials, and discouraged their own athletes and national federations from engaging in sport with South Africa. During the same period, South African athletes and teams were commonly greeted by vigorous protests whenever they appeared in international competition. By the 1990s, the boycott of South African sport had been extended into professional sports. The World Boxing Council imposed sanctions on promoters, managers, and boxers who had ties to South Africa. The Association of Tennis Professionals deleted events in South Africa from the Grand Prix tour.

The effort to eliminate apartheid, particularly in sport, enjoyed some measure of success. The National and Olympic Sports Congress (NSC) has emerged as a grassroots movement to develop non-racial sport (Rees, 1992). Although not officially launched until July 1989, it began as a body created by the African National Congress in 1988 to bring black independent sports bodies together with nonracial sports bodies. In 1990, the Association of National Olympic Committees in Africa (ANOCA) gave its support to the newly formed National Olympic Committee of South Africa (NOCSA), which was supported by the NSC. The framework was thus in place to establish nonracial sport governance in South Africa and to bring South African sport back into the Olympic Movement.

The campaign against apartheid sport in South Africa demonstrates that political protests in sport can be effectively implemented when they are arguably consistent with the dominant ideologies of international sport governance. Those protests can have profound impacts on the management of sport programs and events. Such pivotal elements as site selection, program participation, and event security are likely to be affected.

Boycotts of Events: Spurning the Olympic Games

The Olympic Games have been plagued by boycotts throughout most of their modern history (Guttmann, 1992). Between 1976 and 1984, the Olympic Games suffered three massive boycotts: by African nations in 1976, by the United States and its allies in 1980, and by the Warsaw Pact nations (except Romania) in 1984. In 1976, African nations used their boycott to protest New Zealand's continued sports contacts with South Africa. In 1980, the United States led a boycott of the summer Olympic Games in Moscow to protest the Soviet Union's invasion of Afghanistan. In 1984, all Warsaw Pact nations (except Romania) boycotted the summer Olympic Games in Los Angeles. Although that boycott was widely assumed to be in retaliation for the U.S.-led boycott in 1980, the Soviet Union officially protested protocol violations of the *Olympic Charter* by the U.S. State Department (see Ueberroth, 1985 for a discussion). In 1988, Cuba, Madagascar, Nicaragua, and North Korea boycotted the 1988 summer Olympic Games in Seoul to protest South Korean foreign policy.

Although different issues have been at stake during each boycott, lessons for the management of international sport have been relatively consistent. For purposes of illustration, two boycotts are contrasted here in detail: (a) the boycott of the 1976 Olympics in Montreal by African nations and (b) the boycott of the 1988 Olympics in Seoul by four nations. The first case illustrates ways in which an international sports event can become vulnerable to distant political affairs and the actions of non-Olympic sports. It suggests potential pitfalls when event organizers fail to incorporate proactive political strategies into event administration. The second case illustrates the diplomatic complexities of international event management. It suggests the value of a proactive political strategy. Taken together, the contrast between these two cases highlights the difference that a political strategy can make.

The Montreal Olympics

In June 1976, New Zealand's national rugby team, the All Blacks, toured South Africa despite vigorous protests from the Supreme Council for Sport in Africa (SCSA), which was helping to lead the fight against apartheid sport. When the New Zealand Rugby Football Union and the New Zealand government confirmed their support of the tour, the SCSA demanded that New Zealand be ejected from the Montreal Olympics. The IOC refused on the grounds that New Zealand's NOC had done nothing to violate the *Olympic Charter*. Indeed, rugby was not an Olympic sport. In response, the SCSA called for a boycott of the Montreal Olympics. Approximately 30 African and sympathetic developing nations consequently refused to participate in the Games (Wheeler, 1987).

It would seem that organizers of the Montreal Olympics were unwitting victims of a political dispute over which they had no control. After all, the disputants were not Canadian, and the sport in question was not an Olympic sport. Yet, throughout the period leading to the All Blacks' South African tour and the SCSA's call for an Olympic boycott, there were pivotal moments during which a more politically proactive strategy might have prevented escalation of the dispute into a boycott. Although one can never be certain that the boycott could have been prevented, it is instructive to revisit events leading to the All Blacks' South African tour and the SCSA's call for a boycott of the Montreal Olympics.

In point of fact, the All Blacks' tour of South Africa was vigorously opposed by many New Zealanders. Organizations like Citizens for Racial Equality (CARE) and Halt All Racist Tours (HART) had worked for years to end all sports contacts between New Zealand and South Africa. Even after the tour proceeded, there was sufficient domestic opposition that the New Zealand government and the New Zealand Olympic and Commonwealth Games Association (NZOCGA) could have convincingly expressed some regret over the tour. Indeed, there was substantial anti-tour sentiment throughout New Zealand in 1976. A national mobilization against the tour drew an estimated 15,000 protestors. The three largest churches in New Zealand (the Anglican, the Catholic, and the Presbyterian) produced anti-tour statements. A June poll by the *Auckland Star*, one of New Zealand's largest newspapers, found that over half the population did not support the tour.

It is useful to remember that New Zealand was not the only nation at the time whose athletes and non-Olympic NFs were continuing sports contacts with South Africa. International matches in tennis, golf, and lawn bowling continued to welcome South Africans and continued to be scheduled in South Africa. British cricket players continued to play extensively in South Africa. What made the All Blacks' tour so different and so reprehensible to the SCSA was the fact that it had overt support from the New Zealand government. As we shall see, this difference provided a key but unexploited point of leverage.

During the early 1970s the Labour Party was in power in New Zealand. Norman Kirk, New Zealand's prime minister, had worked hard to build strong relations with African nations, particularly those in the Commonwealth. When the New Zealand Rugby Football Union scheduled a visit by the Springboks, South Africa's national rugby team, the Labour government denied visas to the South African players.

However, New Zealand's economy had suffered a series of blows during the early 1970s. The international recession had substantially reduced the nation's trade. The oil embargo of 1973 had placed considerable inflationary pressure on New Zealand's economy. Britain's entry into the European Common Market eliminated in one stroke New Zealand's largest foreign market. The nation's economic ills eroded support for Labour, causing the National Party to come to power in the elections of 1975.

Unlike the Labour Party, the National Party gave explicit support to sports contacts with South Africa. At the farewell to the All Blacks as they left for their South African tour, Ken Comber, the government's Under-Secretary for Sport, said, "The All Blacks leave for their South African tour with the blessing and goodwill ... of the New Zealand government" (quoted in Wheeler, 1987, p. 44). It was the government support more than the tour itself that so infuriated the SCSA. As Abraham Ordia, president of the SCSA put it: "The timing of the All Black tour of South Africa is a slap in the face for African nations. It is deliberate. It has government support. You say you don't agree with apartheid but you are playing with it" (quoted in Wheeler, 1987, p. 44).

In order to provide a forum for the SCSA to express its views to the New Zealand public, Ordia was invited in early June, 1976 (weeks before the opening ceremonies of the Montreal Olympics) to discuss the SCSA's position on New Zealand television. The government was invited to send a spokesperson to the broadcast, and Ordia took advantage of his New Zealand visit to request a meeting with government officials. However, the New Zealand government refused to participate in the broadcast and also refused Ordia's request for a meeting. New Zealand's Prime Minister, Robert Muldoon, said:

> There is no way that we are going to alter our policy. Nor is the government going to meet with Mr. Ordia. His is not a diplomat or a member of a government. He is some sport of sports administrator.
> (quoted in Wheeler, 1987, p. 57)

Insulted by Muldoon's rebuff, Ordia cancelled the remainder of his visit, and returned to Africa. Yet, he left the door open for the New Zealand government to save face and also prevent an African Olympic boycott. He said: "It may not be prepared to stop the tour, but at least the New Zealand government should disassociate itself from it... That would be enough" (quoted in Wheeler, 1987, p. 58).

The government refused, and the NZOCGA also refrained from expressing any disapproval of the tour. The SCSA implemented the boycott it had threatened.

Throughout the period before the boycott, the SCSA made it clear that the issue was not the All Blacks' South African tour per se, but was New Zealand government support for the tour. Had the New Zealand government hedged its support of the tour (or at the very least remained silent), or had government officials allowed Ordia a sympathetic hearing, the outcome for the Montreal Olympics could well have been different.

There were several domestic and international avenues for Montreal's Olympic organizers (through the Canadian government) to bring diplomatic pressure to bear on New Zealand's government to drop its public support of the tour. New Zealand's difficult economic situation rendered it particularly sensitive to pressures from potential trading partners. Its membership in the Commonwealth provided well-established venues for diplomatic initiatives. In other words, there were significant economic and political levers by which the New Zealand government could have been encouraged to withhold official support from the All Black's South African tour. Those means were never fully exploited by the Olympic organizers.

The story of the boycott of the 1976 Olympics is one of missed political opportunities. The political stakes and the political stakeholders were readily identifiable. There were ready economic and diplomatic channels via which to implement tactics to reduce the boycott's political legitimacy. The story of the 1976 Olympic boycott illustrates the potential value of incorporating politically sensitive and proactive procedures into event planning and administration. As we shall see, this contrasts with the effective use of political tactics by the Seoul Olympic organizers.

The Seoul Olympics

Of 167 NOCs in 1988, only 7 did not participate in the Seoul Olympics: Albania, Cuba, Ethiopia, Madagascar, Nicaragua, North Korea, and the Seychelles. North Korea, an implacable foe of South Korea, had called for a boycott of the Seoul Olympics by socialist nations (Ricquart, 1988). However, only Cuba and Madagascar boycotted in solidarity with North Korea. Albania had never attended an Olympic Games. Nicaragua boycotted to protest the South Korean government's role in providing funds to arm the Contra guerrillas, who were trying to overthrow Nicaragua's Sandinista government. As one Nicaraguan official put it, "How could we go to Korea's Olympics when they were paying for the Americans to kill our people?" (quoted in MacAloon & Kang, 1990, p. 122). Reasons for the absence of Ethiopian and Seychelles delegations were never made clear, although their absences were widely attributed to economic rather than political concerns.

The almost-complete attendance at the Seoul Olympics was a tribute to the effective political planning and maneuvering of the Korean organizers. When the Games were awarded to Seoul in 1981, many commentators felt that the Games' prospects were bleak. South Korea had no diplomatic relations with 30 member nations of the IOC. Of even deeper concern, South Korea was still technically at war with North Korea, which was allied with both the Soviet Union and China. After the 1984 Olympics in Los Angeles, 11 communist nations expressed official "unease" over the choice of Seoul as host of the 1988 Olympics. In 1985, North Korea demanded the right to co-host the Olympics, and called for a boycott if it was not allowed the right to co-host.

South Korean politicians and Olympic organizers initially reacted negatively to North Korean demands and threats. However, the South Koreans quickly realized that by entering into negotiations with the North, they would demonstrate good will to the international community. They also "began to realize that the north had made a major tactical blunder-following through [with co-hosting] would force [North Korea to] open" (Ricquart, 1988, p. 34).

Consequently, the South Korean Olympic organizers accepted an IOC invitation to negotiate with North Korea to co-host the Games. Delegations from the two countries' NOCs met in October 1985, January 1986, and July 1987. It was eventually agreed that North Korea would host table tennis, archery, women's volleyball, the first segment of the 100 km. cycling road race, and some preliminary rounds of soccer. However, the agreement was promptly overruled by the North Korean government, which asserted its desire to host at least a full third of Olympic events.

As a result of South Korea's seeming good faith in negotiations, the participation of China, the Soviet Union, and Eastern European nations was secured. As one European diplomat said:

> No one in Seoul really believed that negotiations with the north would get anywhere, but in an attempt to ... secure the East-bloc participation everybody desired, South Korea entered into negotiations with [North Korea]. As things turned out, the co-hosting talks secured the full participation of the East-bloc. Seoul ... censored any criticism of [IOC] diplomacy... [In contrast] North Korea's actions have not lent credibility to its cause, and have embarrassed friend and foe alike. (Ricquart, 1988, pp. 47, 50)

South Korean Olympic organizers now had the political upper hand and did not let the matter drop. They worked through Mario Vasquez Rana, chairman of the Association of National Olympic Committees (ANOC) to put further pressure on North Korea and to bring Cuba into the Games (Park, 1990, pp. 62-65; Pound, 1994). Despite the resulting diplomatic exchanges North Korea remained intransigent. North Korea's consequent political isolation from its communist allies was intensified at a meeting of East European

Deputy Ministers of Sport on June 10, 1988, when a resolution was adopted urging North Korea to participate in the Seoul Olympics.

In addition to their efforts to isolate North Korea politically, South Korean Olympic organizers worked proactively to encourage all NOCs to attend the Games. During 1987 and 1988, 321 delegates from 53 countries were hosted in Seoul. These included delegates from 11 countries that had diplomatic relations with North Korea but not South Korea. During this time, delegations from the Soviet Union visited Seoul six times, from East Germany five times, and from Hungary and Poland three times each (Park, 1990, p. 60).

The Soviets were particularly concerned about their team's security. On June 24, 1987, two officials of the Seoul Olympic Organizing Committee (SLOOC) met with Soviet Deputy Sports Minister Gavrilin at a secret meeting in Tokyo to discuss SLOOC provisions for the Soviet team. One month later, Soviet NOC officials visited Seoul for further discussions. During follow-up meetings with Soviet sports officials at the end of December 1987, SLOOC completed a joint agreement with the Soviet NOC. The president of SLOOC described the agreement this way:

> The document was in fact a list of agreements concerning licenses and conveniences to be offered by the Korean government when the Soviet team participated in the Seoul Olympics. The agreement allowed the Soviet Union to designate persons to handle consular affairs, which marked a turning point in improving the relationship between the two nations, which had had no diplomatic ties till then. The agreements also prompted other socialist countries to consolidate their decision to come to Seoul. (Park, 1990, pp. 60-61)

In addition to their extensive political maneuvering, SLOOC officials developed other initiatives to entice participation in the Seoul Olympics. No Olympic organizing committee has been more attuned than the Koreans to the international political significance of the Olympic ceremonies (MacAloon & Kang, 1990). SLOOC planners departed from past Olympic practice by implementing plans to include performers from throughout the world in portions of the opening ceremonies other than the parade of nations. In order to celebrate the torch relay and symbolize the Olympic theme, "The world to Seoul and Seoul to the world," SLOOC officials invited folk dance groups from around the world to Seoul. Twelve nations responded favorably and sent teams that performed throughout the relay and during the opening ceremonies (Chalip, 1990). In addition, SLOOC planners worked with the International Parachuting Federation to create an international team of skydivers to perform during the opening ceremonies. The plan brought together skydivers from 22 countries, including representatives from the Eastern-bloc (Park, 1990, pp. 21-24). Although the matter was not discussed publicly, the plan had particular symbolic significance diplomatically because it brought representatives of elite Korean and (formerly hostile) Eastern-bloc military units together in joint peaceful purpose for the first time. It had the added effect of creating pro-SLOOC stakeholders in countries that might otherwise boycott.

The political acumen of SLOOC organizers is instructive. Despite many predictions that the Seoul Olympics could only fail, the organizers worked reactively and proactively to forestall any boycott. They responded quickly and decisively to political threats, thus blunting opposition to their Games. They identified key stakeholders and worked tirelessly to address their concerns, thereby turning distrust into support. They broadened participation in the event's ceremonies, thus creating added incentives for nations to attend.

Concluding Summary

International sport and international politics are inextricably intertwined. Indeed, as we have seen, assertions to the contrary merely serve to mask sport's political significance, thus intensifying, rather than reducing, its political value. As one activist put it:

> Moral and political views cannot be divorced from sport because sport
> does not occur in a vacuum but is an integral part of life. Thus the cry to
> "keep politics out of sport" is based upon a romantic caricature of the
> real nature of sport: it is tantamount to saying "keep life out of sport."
> (quoted in Hargreaves, 1982, p. 233)

Sport managers who work internationally must, therefore, develop some measure of political acumen and diplomatic skill. The effective manager will assess political risks, analyze stakeholder interests, and appreciate the ideological bases of emerging controversies. As events are planned, the manager must gauge the potential impacts of multinational confrontations, international media attention, and cross-national exchanges. As events are staged, the manager must monitor political occurrences.

Boycotts have been a particularly common form of international political expression in sport. Two types of boycotts can be identified: (a) boycotts implemented as sanctions against a particular country and (b) boycotts implemented against a particular event. The former type is typically known in advance of the event and can be accommodated when planning site selection, program participation, and event security. The latter type is typically threatened or implemented as the event becomes imminent. In order to minimize the prospects for a boycott, event managers should be sensitive to stakeholder interests and should work proactively to provide inducements and address stakeholder concerns.

Disscussion, Analysis, Application, and Debate

Issues for Discussion

1. What political monitoring and/or analysis procedures would you recommend for the organizers of international sports events? For managers or promoters of international sports exchanges? Why?
2. How does a boycott as a political sanction differ from a boycott of a specific event?
3. With the advantage of hindsight, what would you suggest that the organizers of the Montreal Olympics should have done to reduce the likelihood of a boycott? What lessons from the Seoul Olympic organizers might have been applied by the Montreal organizers?

Matter for Analysis

Sport is obviously intertwined with politics; yet international sport organizations continue to assert the independence of sport from politics. What (and whose) purposes seem to be served by that assertion? How?

Application

Develop a manual of political monitoring and analysis procedures to be used in the administration of international sports events and exchanges. Specify the kinds of data to be watched and the ways those data might be analyzed. Suggest specific strategies that might be useful to exploit a political opportunity and to blunt political threats.

Ethical Debate

Some argue that sport is so intrinsically tied to politics that it is naive to believe that it could ever be free from political actions like boycotts. Others contend that athletes bear the unfair burden for political uses of sport, especially boycotts.

What ethical constraints, if any, should there be on political uses of sport? Why? How realistic do these seem?

References

Agee, P. (1975). *Inside the company: CIA diary*. New York: Stonehill.

Chalip, L. (1987). Multiple narratives, multiple hierarchies: Selective attention, varied interpretations, and the structure of the Olympic program. In S-P. Kang, J. MacAloon, & R. DaMatta (Eds.), *The Olympics and cultural exchange* (pp. 539-576). Seoul: Hanyang University Institute for Ethnological Studies.

Chalip, L. (1990). The politics of Olympic theatre: New Zealand and Korean cross-national relations. In B-I. Koh (Ed.), *Toward one world beyond all barriers* (Vol. 1, pp. 408-433). Seoul: Poong Nam.

Espy, R. (1979). *The politics of the Olympic Games*. Berkeley, CA: University of California Press.

Ford, G.R. (1974, July 8). In defense of the competitive urge. *Sports Illustrated*, pp. 14-18.

Franks, C.E.S., Hawes, M., & Macintosh, D. (1988). Sport and Canadian diplomacy. *International Journal*, *43*, 665-682.

Guttmann, A. (1992). *The Olympics: A history of the modern Games*. Champaign, IL: University of Illinois Press.

Hargreaves, J. (1982). *Sport, culture and ideology*. London: Routledge and Kegan Paul.

Houlihan, B. (1994). *Sport and international politics*. New York: Harvester Wheatsheaf.

International Olympic Committee (1993). *Olympic charter*. Lausanne:International Olympic Committee.

Kidd, B. (1988). The campaign against sport in South Africa. *International Journal*, *43*, 643-664.

Kidd, B. (1991). From quarantine to cure: The new phase of the struggle against apartheid sport. *Sociology of Sport Journal*, *8*, 33-46.

Krotee, M.L. (1988). Apartheid and sport: South Africa revisited. *Sociology of Sport Journal*, *5*, 125-135.

Lund, S.A. (1963). Sports and politics. *Quest*, *1*, 33-36.

MacAloon, J.J. (1992). The ethnographic imperative in comparative Olympic research. *Sociology of Sport Journal*, *9*, 104-130.

MacAloon, J.J., & Kang, S-P. (1990). Uri Nara: Korean nationalism, the Seoul Olympics, and contemporary anthropology. In B-I. Koh (Ed.), *Toward one world beyond all barriers* (Vol. 1, pp. 117-139). Seoul: Poong Nam.

Nafziger, J.A.R. (1988). *International sports law*. Dobbs Ferry, NY: Transnational Publishers.

Park, S-J. (1990). *The stories of Seoul Olympics*. Seoul: Chosun-Ilbo.

Pound, R.W. (1994). *Five rings over Korea*. Boston: Little Brown.

Ramsamy, S. (1991). Apartheid and Olympism: On the abolishment of institutionalized discrimination in international sport. In F. Landry, M. Landry, & M. Yerles (Eds.), *Sport ... The third millennium* (pp. 537-546). Sainte-Foy, Quebec: Les Presses de l'Universite Laval.

Rees, C.R. (1992, February). *The NOSC and the non-racial sports movement: Towards post-apartheid sport in South Africa*. Paper presented at the International Symposium for Olympic Research, London, Ontario.

Ricquart, V.J. (1988). *The games within the Games*. Seoul: Hantong Books.

Schollander, D., & Savage, D. (1971). *Deep water*. New York: Crown.

Slack, T., & Whitson, D. (1988). The place of sport in Cuba's foreign relations. *International Journal, 43*, 596-617.

Ueberroth, P. (1985). *Made in America*. New York: Fawcett Crest.

Wheeler, G.L. (1987). *New Zealand and the Olympic boycott 1970-1976*. Unpublished master's thesis, University of Maryland, College Park.

CHAPTER ELEVEN

PROFESSIONAL SPORTS

Overview

This chapter presents the internationalization of professional sports. Although modern professional sport has been international since Canadian ice hockey moved into the United States, its emergence globally is a recent phenomenon. The global expansion of the NBA, MLB, NFL, and NHL are examined through the need to proactively and retroactively address marketing their product to new populations. Other professional sport organizations are examined, but to a lesser extent, in order to further illustrate the extent to which various sports move across country borders.

Introduction

The bulk of this book deals with what have traditionally been considered amateur sports. Many of these sports are associated with the Olympic movement. However, there is a group, professional sports, that is beginning to operate more internationally.

As has been stated previously, much of sport management deals with generating sufficient revenue to cover the expenses incurred. Because professional sport is a product that must have mass appeal in order to succeed financially, it is obvious that attracting a multinational audience could be advantageous to professional sports that traditionally were contested within a country.

The purpose of this chapter is to examine professional sports with respect to their international involvement and plans in this area. The leagues presented will include Major League Baseball (MLB), the National Hockey League (NHL), the National Football League (NFL), and the National Basketball Association (NBA), as well as others.

Considerations for International Expansion

With the extension of companies worldwide, management is examining its options in order to move the product or service across country borders. Punnett and Ricks (1992) in *International Business* delineate the reasons why organizations move across borders. They classify these as reactive reasons and proactive reasons. Reactive reasons mean that there is a perceived threat to the organization that must be answered. The proactive reasons relate to management's seeing an opportunity that the organization can seize in order to grow.

With respect to reactive reasons, two justifiably relate to professional sport -- international customers and international competition. With the telecommunications explosion of the last quarter century, more and more people are seeing, hearing, and reading of sport. As the mass media grow, especially in developing nations, electronic programming needs and print space require filling. Sport fills this need and has helped to create customers. Other factors -- merchandise marketing, the Olympic movement, and better management -- are involved but communications development enhances all the factors.

The second reactive reason is international competition. Soccer has established itself as the world sport. However, some professional sports have realized that as soccer and other sports grow, progressive organizations will seize the opportunity to take their professional sport to new levels in new markets. This was particularly evident after the United States' National Basketball Association players participated in the 1992 Barcelona Olympics. The massive media coverage accorded to the already- well-known gold medal-winning "Dream Team" created intense interest from Major League Baseball and the National Hockey League. Both of these leagues are examining how they can allow their players to participate in the Olympic media blitz.

Proactive reasons for looking internationally are numerous. First, and most importantly, are new markets. These new markets open opportunities for live broadcasts, taped contest presentations, merchandise sales, and an increased number of franchises. All of this leads to increased revenues.

Second, moving to another country allows an organization to exploit its strengths. An example of this is the NBA's using its superior basketball product to market its merchandise to aspiring players and to the growing number of fans worldwide. The National Football League took its marketing experience and skills to Europe in forming the World Football League.

Third, the movement to other countries creates greater resources. Major League Baseball (MLB) has long attracted talent from Central America. However, with baseball's growth within the Olympic movement, MLB is also becoming more active internationally. This should create more opportunities for baseball players the world over to compete for MLB rosters, and in turn, MLB can market to these countries. For example, the Los Angeles Dodgers baseball team signed Chan Ho Park from South Korea and Hideo Nomo of Japan, both providing not only excellent playing skills but also the dimension of major media and merchandice markets in Asia for the Dodgers and MLB (Beaton, 1995a). Additionally, the Atlanta Braves signed an agreement with the Mexico City Tigers that will allow the Braves to have an inside track for scouting Mexican baseball players (Beaton, 1995b). With Atlanta known worldwide as the home of the 1996 Olympic Games, any non-American athlete on an Atlanta team is going to be well known in his home country and thus generate merchandising opportunities for that ball club and league.

Fourth, with greater international involvement comes greater power and prestige. Most people do not have the opportunity to travel far from their country. As a result those who do travel internationally are perceived positively.

David Stern, Commissioner of the National Basketball Association, has had to travel extensively to Europe because of the NBA's involvement with marketing, licensing, and the Olympics. No doubt there are many who see Stern as more powerful because he works in the global community, not just the United States.

Last, a good defense is a good offense. This statement indicates that in order to protect one's market, at times it is good business to take one's product into the other person's ballpark. This may be a motivating factor in professional sports in the next decade. With the growth of the marketing of sport as entertainment, there is a question of the depth and breadth of that market. In order for revenue increases to continue, there will be pressure to protect the home market and to expand into others. With soccer continuing to grow in popularity with America's youth, one would expect football and baseball to react in a manner that increases their popularity outside North America. In fact this is occurring with the World League of American Football's move into Europe, with Major League Baseball's greater work with the International Baseball Association, and with the Canadian Football League's expansion into the United States.

All of these factors taken together are evaluated when considering international involvement of professional sports. It is important to remember that professional sports are businesses; without covering expenses, there is no organization. As such, a careful evaluation needs undertaken to see if moving across borders will improve profits.

Also important to remember is that these considerations are interrelated. A league will have reactive and proactive reasons working simultaneously in order to dictate its business moves.

International Expansion

Should a professional sport organization decide to move into the international arena, it must be prepared to face some difficult times. Among the aspects it must consider are

1. Can it adapt to a new culture?
2. Are the fans ready for this sport on a professional basis?
3. Will the fans support a new sport, possibly to the detriment of current sports?
4. Will the local companies be willing to purchase advertising to support a new professional sport/team?
5. Can staffing needs for players, coaches, and administrative staff be met?
6. Will the league be able to financially support this new venture?
7. What are the risks, especially working with multiple countries' laws?

Management must carefully evaluate each of these in order to fully understand the move and its consequences. Certainly the NFL studied the concept of the World League of American Football before initiating the WFL coincidentally in the United States and in Europe. Although the initial thrust of the WFL was successful in Europe, the American side could not survive. With some revision, a WFL within Europe may succeed. However, one factor needs additional attention: Can the WFL survive in Europe with primarily North American players?

In 1994 both Major League Baseball and the National Hockey League had part of their seasons cancelled because of player-owner disputes. The ramifications this may have on the internationalization of these sports is unclear. However, what has become quite evident is that sport marketers are now more careful of the structure of their marketing programs, including international marketing (Horovitz, 1994). In addition, the labor problems have emphasized the need for franchise agreements specifically stating which country's laws handle legal issues, for example, labor disputes (Scripps Howard, 1995) and visa rules (Beaton, 1995c).

National Basketball Association (NBA)

In 1987 *Sports Inc.* (Gloede and Smith Muniz) published an article entitled the "NBA Goes Global." The article stated, "The NBA would `peak' within five years. To keep the sport growing, Stern decided to go overseas, patterning his strategy after the largest U.S. consumer products companies. As their domestic markets matured, they turned to global markets" (pp. 29-30). In doing so the NBA has reacted to the global need to fill video programming and proactively created new markets.

The NBA playoffs are broadcast to well over 100 countries; many of these broadcasts are live programming (Weir, 1993). In Europe, there is a great deal of discussion about the growth of basketball's popularity, especially after the 1992 United States Olympic team included such well known players as Michael Jordan, Magic Johnson and Larry Bird, which resulted in the NBA's European income doubling in the year following the Dream Team's success (Kasten, 1994).

To examine why professional basketball has achieved such international success, Weir (1993) points to these reasons. First, basketball has long been an international sport. Working through the FIBA, basketball's international federation, and the national federations in each country, basketball has ongoing organizations in place promoting the game. Second, although soccer has great strength in Europe with the men, basketball is played by both men and women there, and it is becoming more popular. Third, playing basketball far surpasses baseball and American football in ease of play. Fourth, "basketball lets its (sic) stars shine brighter" (p. A2) by having them in play close to the audience much more often than most other sports do. Last, people just enjoy the spectacle of basketball's slam dunk and slick passing more than they enjoy other sports.

This popularity has not been lost on the marketers of basketball merchandise. Many of the same companies that advertise on NBA telecasts in the United States also sell products and promote the sport worldwide: Nike, Converse, Coca-Cola, Gatorade, Schick, and Reebok. In fact, one of the early NBA methods to move overseas was linking with the International Basketball Federation and McDonald's, the fast food chain, to sponsor an international tournament with an NBA team and teams from three other counties. McDonald's world omnipresence and customer demographics have fit very well with this tournament since its inception in 1987 (Gloede & Smith Muniz, 1987). The McDonald's Championship has been so successful that Stern had considered expanding it from four teams to six or eight (Zucker, 1992, August 7). Eventually, the event moved to six teams in 1993. In addition, in order to move the McDonald's Championships closer to a world championships for clubs, the NBA and FIBA invite teams from outside Europe and North America, with the NBA champion as a participant (N. Anderson, personal communication, February 24, 1995).

So the NBA is a U.S. product that sells overseas. Will the core product move successfully across the U.S. border? Probably. An NBA franchise was awarded to Toronto and to Vancouver, Canada. In addition, with the growing popularity of professional basketball, it is probable that a pan-European league will evolve as well as multinational professional leagues in other parts of the world. These ideas are dependent upon the profit potential within and between each global region.

Major League Baseball (MLB)

To those not fully aware that Major League Baseball is not just an American product, two events in 1992 served as a wake-up call. First, the Seattle Mariners were bought by a group led by Hiroshi Yamauchi of Nintendo Co. Ltd. of Japan. This was the first time that "America's pastime" was bought at the Major League level by a non-North American. However, Japanese investors did already have part ownership in minor league teams in Birmingham, Alabama, and Salinas and Visalia in the California League ("Japanese Have Stakes," 1992).

Second, the Toronto Blue Jays won MLB's World Series, the first non-U.S. team to do so. With Toronto's success came speculation of the possibility of MLB's expanding outside the United States and Canada. Neuharth (1992) considers Tokyo, Havana (post Castro) and Hong Kong as good candidates. Klein (1992) mentions Mexico City, Seoul, Taipei, and Manila. With these cities alone, should MLB want to expand globally, there is the possibility of five cities in Asia that would make the move more feasible since travel time and jet lag would be less of a factor for teams crossing the Pacific Ocean on a road trip. Presently, it is difficult enough for the Atlanta Braves to travel to America's west coast and perform well without expecting athletes to perform at their normal level with the jet lag encountered during a swing through Asia.

Without disregarding Asia, Latin America, or the rest of the world, it appears that MLB's greatest profit potential in the near term lies in Europe. From $300,000 US in 1989 to $85-$100 million US in 1993 from licensed merchandise sales, Europe has become a very important region for MLB (Norton, 1993).

MLB's vehicle through which to capture part of Europe's sports, as well as those of the rest of the world, is Major League Baseball International Partners (MLBIP), consisting of MLB, the General Electric unit of the National Broadcasting Corporation, and Pascoe Nally, Inc., a British marketing company. This partnership that is MLBIP is proactive in implementing four strategies:

1. Providing an ever-increasing variety of television products that include regular season games, the All-Star Game, League Championship Series, the World Series, This Week in Baseball, Baseball '93..., and instructional programs;
2. Increasing consumer awareness of MLB products through worldwide licensing agreements to create, promote, and sell a greater variety of products;
3. Promoting the play of baseball worldwide through creation of youth leagues, adult seminars, instructional material distribution, umpire clinics, and U.S. college players' work in foreign countries; and

4.   Creating sponsorship relationships to enhance the game and increase television exposure. Special events developed include MLB All-Star Team Tour of Japan, European pre-season games, Legends of Baseball European and Pacific Rim tours, baseball conferences, Mexican exhibition games and Minor League All-Star Tour of Europe and the Pacific Rim (Major League Baseball International informational brochure, no date).

MLB also has gained a new partner in its global development -- USA Baseball, America's national federation for amateur baseball, which is a member of the International Baseball Federation, baseball's international federation. By working with USA Baseball, MLB gains access to the established baseball market in each country, as the NBA has done in basketball. In addition, with baseball as a new Olympic medal sport, instant access is gained into new markets as countries seek to develop the Olympic sports.

National Football League (NFL)

Since television began broadcasting North American professional football (not soccer), it has grown to be possibly the most popular sport in the United States. Certainly in terms of media coverage, no other sport has the regional and national presence of football. However, in terms of a global approach, the NFL was later than the NBA and MLB in formally organizing to address the international market.

With respect to the world's knowing and viewing American football, the NFL started going overseas in 1983 when former Minnesota Vikings General Manager Mike Lynn took his team to London. The Super Bowl has been regularly broadcast to many countries, often with the viewing countries' own announcers. The American Bowl playing in London's Wembley Stadium started in 1986 when the Chicago Bears beat the Dallas Cowboys. However, not until October 1991 was NFL International created by the team owners (National Football League, 1992a). This initiative was meant to be the NFL's "strategic plan to respond to the exploding interest throughout the world in American football" (p.1). The five strategic areas addressed by NFL International were

1.   The World League of American Football
2.   The American Bowl Series of international games
3.   Sponsorship and licensing
4.   Grassroots and Amateur football development
5.   Television.

1. The World League of American Football started in 1991 with teams from the United States and Montreal, London, Barcelona, and Frankfurt. The league had little success in the U.S. television market as many people considered it a minor league for the NFL. However, in Europe the crowds and attention generated were good. The league was then suspended for the 1993 season but reemerged in 1995 with an all-European format. Teams from Amsterdam, Dusseldorf, and Edinburgh joined holdovers Barcelona, Frankfurt, and London in competition for World Bowl Championship. Additionally, in order to continue to promote its licensed products and television packages to the large

European market, this NFL presence is wise.

2. The American Bowl series places NFL teams in pre-season games. In addition to Europe, Japan has also hosted NFL football. These games draw large crowds and were the precursor to the World League. It is doubtful that the league would have been as successful as it was in Europe had the public's taste not been whetted by the American Bowl series.

3. With the NFL's greater international awareness and popularity have come greater opportunities for sponsorships and licensing. Coke, Kodak, and Delta have been worldwide sponsors contributing in the areas of television, educational programs, and the sponsoring of amateur leagues.

The growth of licensed sales has been good. In Japan the NFL expected to grow from 35 stores in 1992 to over 100 in 1994. As with other American professional leagues, merchandise sales in Europe have mushroomed as the league presence has increased. Times have certainly changed since 1980 when NFL merchandise could be bought in Germany, but the teams' names and colors were not coordinated; for instance, a Dallas Cowboys shirt was printed in the black and gold of their rival, the Pittsburgh Steelers, two of the dominant teams of that time.

4. The NFL considers grassroots growth of amateur teams to be very important. In 1991 with over 75,000 Europeans playing on approximately 650 teams in 15 European countries, the need for the NFL to contribute through education programs appeared great. (Japan and Australia have also developed teams.) This educational assistance and organizational promotion are evident with the NFL/Wilson World Partnership Clinics in Europe, including having NFL Hall of Famer Mel Blount conduct youth clinics in Seville, Spain, and having NFL offices in London and Frankfurt (National Football League, 1992b).

If the NFL can assist these teams and leagues to prosper, here will be a continuing market for NFL merchandise and television products. Also helping these sales will be non-North American players earning roster positions in the NFL as has happened in MLB, the NBA, and the NHL.

5. NFL games are seen in over 150 countries on a weekly basis with 174 countries receiving the 1995 Super Bowl in 13 languages. Japan broadcasts more than 150 games a year, and Great Britain broadcasts games on a same-day basis. The NFL looks to expand the sales of its television rights worldwide in the hopes that NFL football will grow in popularity in a similar manner that football did in the United States when television presented the game in the 1960s (P. Avitante, personal communication, February 25, 1995).

As with baseball and ice hockey, football will require more public education overseas in order to create a lasting demand for its product. A factor in American football is that unlike baseball, basketball and ice hockey, it is not an Olympic medal sport. Thus, football receives neither the worldwide publicity through the Olympic movement nor the governmental promotion that the ministries of sport provide indigenous and Olympic sports. A look at the NFL International initiative shows both reactive and proactive reasoning. By increasing its commitment, the NFL was reacting to the demand that had been building for years. There was a ready market. Proactively, increasing the market for its products added great incentive. As with other professional sports and leagues, merchandising their products requires marketing and promotion. The NFL is addressing these areas in a positive way.

National Hockey League (NHL)

The National Hockey League has been an international league since 1924 with the inclusion of the Boston Bruins and the New York Americans into the previously Canadian league (Quirk & Fort, 1991). However, in today's world Canada and the United States cooperate so closely in professional sports that to think of the NHL, MLB, NBA, or the Canadian Football League as being international is a bit misleading. However, what cannot be dismissed is that all international sports do deal with laws and regulations from more than one country. Thus, the NHL was the pioneer in this field.

The irony of the NHL's position is that, with the exception of the United States-Canada connection, the NHL has fallen behind the other major professional North American leagues with respect to globalizing. The NHL has not created a separate program or office to deal with marketing its product outside North America. There have been tours of Europe since 1958, players in the Olympics, and occasionally special competitions like the Canada Cup, but no follow-up to date. However, this will be changing.

In 1993, the NHL hired Gary Bettman as its new commissioner. Bettman came to the NHL from the NBA. It is reasonable to assume that the recent promotional successes that the NBA has enjoyed were certainly of interest to the NHL team presidents when selecting their new commissioner. In fact Bettman indicated that a McDonald's-type tournament sponsored by the International Ice Hockey Federation (IIHF) would be appealing. However, he saw no NHL franchises in Europe soon, even though there is keen hockey interest in England, Sweden, Finland, Russia, the Czech Republic, and the Slovakia ("What the Commissioner Said," 1993). It is thought that the NHL needs to strengthen its North American market before it could expand overseas (Mansur, 1994). Additionally, with the Walt Disney Company owning the Anaheim Mighty Ducks, Disney's creative expertise and global positive reputation can help the NHL's marketing and public relations program.

During the 1994 Winter Olympics in Lillehammer, Bettman met with IOC and IIHF officials in order to seek a way in which National Hockey League players could play in the 1998 Winter Olympics in Nagano (Allen, 1994). The major hurdle was releasing the NHL players from their professional teams in order to have them play for their countries for up to 2 weeks. Although this might have been a problem prior to 1992, the success of the United States basketball Dream Team in creating worldwide public awareness has created a situation in which those associated with the NHL believe the benefits of Olympic participation outweigh the costs.

An interesting proactive approach is being tried by the Pittsburgh Penquins and the Anaheim Mighty Ducks. In 1994 these teams came to an agreement to have Russia's Central Red Army team be a minor league affiliate. This shows a unique and possibly highly effective method to tap into a recognized source of fine hockey talent (Shuster, 1994). In addition the Moscow Penquins, as the team is now known, logo is being sold on merchandise in the United States (Lilley, 1994).

Others

MLB, the NBA, the NHL, and the NFL are the professional sports many people envision as moving more internationally. However, there are other professional sports that have made their presence felt internationally. Those presented here are Professional Golf Association Tour, Canadian Football League, World Basketball League, and Association of Tennis Professionals. There are others, but these organizations should give the reader a fuller understanding of what is happening in professional sports.

PGA TOUR

The PGA TOUR operates over 100 golf events on three tours, many of which it co-sponsors. There are also tours held in Australia, Europe, Japan, South Africa, and Asia. The golfers participating on these tours, no matter their country of origin, must meet eligibility criteria for each respective tour organization.

PGA TOUR in the United States is proactively addressing the international scene through three methods. First, television packages of PGA TOUR events are sold throughout the world to over 80 countries through various methods such as agencies or directly to the networks. Japan is the largest market with over 40 events being broadcast either live or on tape-delay.

Second, PGA TOUR provides through licensed distributors soft goods with its logo, such as shirts, hats and, golf gloves. Creating this brand identity is an area that PGA TOUR feels has good potential, although there are limitations due to confusion with other golf organizations.

Third, the PGA TOUR owns and operates golf courses named Tournament Players Clubs. The courses are in United States, Japan, Thailand, and China with efforts being made to expand into Europe, South America, and Southeast Asia. PGA TOUR oversees these courses in order to maintain top quality golf facilities (M. Bodney, personal communication, January 27, 1995).

It is seen that PGA TOUR is assisting the tremendous growth of golf throughout the world. As golf grows the PGA TOUR will continue to expand its services for golfers the world over.

World Basketball League (WBL)

The World Basketball League began in 1988. It started with teams from the United States and Canada. The league's unique aspect was having players whose maximum height was 6' 5" (1.96m). The other unique feature of the WBL was that it scheduled games with national teams visiting the United States -- teams from the USSR, Israel, Spain, Belgium, Finland, Holland, Greece, and Yugoslavia (World Basketball League, 1991). The league planned to expand into a European Division. Ultimately, a North American-European Divisions Championship would be held.

The WBL was innovative in having professional competitions internationally. However, the league went bankrupt in 1992, and with it some of those ideas. Whether the NBA or other professional sport organizations gathered some ideas from the WBL remains to be seen.

Canadian Football League (CFL)

The Canadian Football League was formed in 1958. Its players have been primarily Canadian with a limited number coming from the United States. However, in 1993 that changed, with the addition of the Sacramento (California) Gold Miners to the CFL. Since 1993, additional United States franchises have been awarded. Therefore, the CFL now is an international league -- albeit, as was previously stated, the Canada-USA connection in professional sports has been well established.

As with all professional sports, economics was the motivating factor to expand into the United States. The CFL was struggling financially and league officials saw a need to increase revenue. With Sacramento's entry came a US$3 million expansion fee, an opening into a mid-level, non-NFL league city, and a renewed fan interest in the competition because of the natural rivalry between the United States and Canada. Sacramento's owner, Fred Anderson, saw the CFL franchise as a revenue generator by using a football stadium left empty by the cancellation of the World Football League (Hoffer, 1993).

An interesting ramification of the CFL's international expansion has been a CFL rule waiver due to U.S. law. Normally, on the 37 player roster, 20 athletes must be Canadian born. However, because this would be illegal discrimination against United States' worker-players, this rule has been waived in the United States. The change has resulted in all four U.S. teams having no Canadians in 1994 (K. Smedley, personal communication, January, 30, 1995).

Whether international expansion by the CFL will materially change the League's financial fortunes remains to be seen. However, the Canadian Football League exemplifies how professional sports are reaching into new markets when opportunity in their existing market seems limited.

Association of Tennis Professionals (ATP)

The Association of Tennis Professionals is as far reaching as any professional sport organization. In 1993, the ATP, with IBM's sponsorship, administered 87 tournaments in 34 countries including Qatar, Dubai, Indonesia, Malaysia, and China as well as throughout Europe and North America. The ATP's headquarters are in Ponte Vedre Beach, Florida, but they have offices in Monte Carlo, Monaco, and Sydney.

Interestingly though for professional sport, the ATP is a nonprofit organization. Therefore, its duty is to "redistribute" revenue through reduction in tournament fees and prize money to the players.

Among the duties of the ATP are player rankings, rule enforcement, training of full-time supervisors and chair umpires, media services, and administration of their charities program (ATP Tour, personal communication, August 31, 1993).

Concluding Summary

Professional sports have been active internationally from the early 1900s when a Seattle team played for the then Canadian Stanley Cup in ice hockey. However, it has only been comparatively recently that professional sports gained notoriety with their international development. The main reason for this is marketing related to television and merchandise sales. The booming world of technology has taken broadcast sports to virtually every corner of the globe. Where there is an audience, there is a market. Professional sports seek to address these viewers with the best athletes in the world. Merchandisers seek to use the sports to provide the fans with items they recognize through sport. For that reason, professional sport administrators are truly high quality administrators dealing in the international sport world. Whether proactively or reactively addressing their international movements, all the professional sports are earning for their product the revenue generated from world markets.

Discussion, Analysis, Application, and Debate

Issues for Discussion

1. If you were the National Hockey League commissioner, how would you expand the NHL's presence outside North America considering the questions delineated in this chapter?
2. From what you know of the Chinese government, speculate on whether professional sport's movement into Bejing would assist or hurt China's Sport for All program.
3. In 1993 the Canadian Football League expanded into the United States by awarding a team to Sacramento. Discuss what may have been the proactive and reactive reasons for this expansion.
4. If you were the marketing director for the NBA, would you market NBA basketball in Europe by showcasing American or European players? Present a rationale for both methods.

Matters for Analysis

1. Considering the differences between individual and team professional sports, what differences would occur between expanding a golf tour overseas and expanding a baseball league across country borders?
2. Assume you are the business consultant to a wealthy Middle Eastern prince. The prince would like to expand team handball, a popular sport in the region, into a professional league throughout western Asia. Present your considerations and recommendation for this plan.

Applications

Do a stakeholder analysis for the NFL owners creating three divisions: North America, Europe, Asia.

Ethical Debate

When any new product or service enters the marketplace, there is always the threat that it will draw resources and interest from the existing status quo. This is particularly true of professional sports that will have a large cash flow. Therefore, should professional team sports from primarily Western cultures consider franchises in Asia, in Africa, in South America? Consider each seperately, weighing the possible long-term advantages and disadvantages to the geographical region.

References

Allen, K. (1994, February 18). NHL's Bettman won't let go of dream. *USA Today*, p. E11.

Beaton, R. (1995a , February 14). Japanese star signs with L.A. *USA Today*, p. C3.

Beaton, R. (1995b, February 17). Braves strike unique Mexican deal. *USA Today*, p. C12.

Beaton, R. (1995c, January 12). Visa rules could sideline top foreign prospects. *USA Today*, p. C3.

Gloede, B. and Smith Muniz, C.L. (1987, November 16). NBA does global. *Sports Inc.*, pp. 29-30.

Hoffer, H. (1993, July 12). South of the border. *Sports Illustrated*, pp. 38-41.

Horovitz, B. (1994, October 31). Jittery sponsors scramble for solid 'alternatives'. *USA Today*, p. C7.

Japanese have stakes elsewhere. *USA Today*, (1992, June 10). p. C7.

Kasten, S. (1994, October). *New markets for the sports industry.* Presented at the International Conference on Sports Management, Atlanta.

Klein, F.C. (1992, October 23). The International Pastime? *The Wall Street Journal*, p. A12.

Lilley, J. (1994, January 10). Russian revolution. *Sports Illustrated*, p. 56-61.

Major League Baseball International (no date). Informational brochure.

Mansur, B. (1994, October). Keynote address. Presented at the International Conference on World Sport Management, Atlanta.

National Football League (1992a, March 30). Press release.

National Football League (1992b, October 27). Press release.

Neuharth, A. (1992, October 16). Next: Letting world in on World Series. *USA Today*, p. A9.

Norton, E. (1993, June 11). Baseball hopes to be big hit in Europe. *The Wall Street Journal*, p. B1.

Punnett, B.J., & Ricks, D.A. (1992). *International Business*.   Boston: PWS-Kent.

Quirk, J., & Fort, R.D. (1992). *Pay dirt - The business of professional team sports*. Princeton, NJ: Princeton University Press.

Scripps Howard (1995, February 10). Kansas City, Ontario? *Alliance (Ohio) Review*, p. 6.

Shuster, R. (1994, July 1). Commentary. *USA Today*. p. D3.

Weir, T. (1993, June 18-20). Basketball's appeal is international. *USA Today*. pp. A1-A2.

What the commissioner said. *USA Today*, (1993, September 29). p. C12.

World Basketball League (1991). Press release.

Zucker, J. (Executive Producer) (1992, August 7). *The Today Show*, NY: National Broadcasting Company.

CHAPTER TWELVE

THE FUTURE OF SPORT GOVERNANCE IN THE GLOBAL COMMUNITY

Overview

This chapter focuses on future trends and their implications for international sport governance. Building on the work of futurists, eleven trends are discussed: (a) a boom in the global economy, (b) increased interest in the arts, (c) the development of "free-market socialism," (d) cultural nationalism, (e) the privatization of welfare, (f) the increasing importance of the Pacific Rim, (g) increasing numbers of women in leadership, (h) rapid advancement of applied biological sciences, (i) religious revival, (j) increased individualism, and (k) sport for participation versus sport as spectator entertainment.

Introduction

The preceding chapters show that international sport has become a significant feature of the international economic, political, and social landscape. International sport affects and is, in turn, affected by the vast changes that have swept our globe in the latter half of the 20th century. We have argued that the international sport manager must think as an administrator, a diplomat, and an anthropologist. The international sport manager must also think as a futurist.

Trend analysis has emerged as a substantial management tool in its own right (e.g., Celente & Milton, 1990; Heath & Nelson, 1986; Merriam & Makower, 1988). Indeed, projections about the future have generated an industry of their own. For example, in their popular book, *Megatrends 2000*, Naisbitt and Aburdene (1990) project 10 trends that they claim will shape our world in the 21st century: a boom in the global economy, increased interest in the arts, the development of "free-market socialism," cultural nationalism, the privatization of welfare, the increasing importance of the Pacific Rim, increasing numbers of women in leadership, rapid advancement of applied biological sciences, religious revival, and increased individualism. It is interesting to speculate about the potential impact of these trends on international sport.

A Boom in the Global Economy

Naisbitt and Aburdene (1990) contend that the rapid development of telecommunications is one of the factors driving development of the global economy. Information is being shared more quickly and more cheaply than ever before. Teleconferencing and global computer networking are making it possible to share information rapidly and without regard to distance.

The development of information sharing has already found its way into sport. International computer-based interest groups share information daily about many elements of sport, such as sport psychology, sport sociology, sport management, and leisure behavior, to name but a few. The number of interest groups sharing information about sport and its elements continues to grow.

The potentials of teleconferencing make it possible to teach classes and, sometimes, to coach athletes at a distance. Whereas the training of coaches, athletes, officials, and administrators once required them to go to the experts (or the experts to come to them), it is now possible to provide seminars internationally without requiring any participant to travel to a single site to attend.

These new technologies make it possible for innovative sport practices to travel the globe at rates never before possible. The gap in knowledge between countries with sport research traditions and those where sport research is not yet developed is likely to shrink (cf., Rogers, 1983). The diffusion of sport knowledge will accelerate.

Increased Interest in the Arts

Naisbitt and Aburdene (1990) claim that "the arts will replace sports as society's dominant leisure activity" (p. 84). They assert that artistic events, like ballet and opera, and venues of art, such as museums, will replace sports events and programs as preferred sources of entertainment. Thus, they contend that sport will find itself "in an increasingly competitive battle for people's leisure time and dollars" (p. 84). As a consequence, they argue that "corporate sponsorship of sports will plateau, while arts sponsorship continues to grow" (p. 91).

If Naisbitt and Aburdene are correct, then sport organizations face new marketing challenges in the years ahead. Programs of family-based marketing designed to socialize children into sport participation and sport spectating are likely to become increasingly important for sport organizations (cf., Guber & Berry, 1993). Similarly, sports events and organizations may find it beneficial to link themselves to art, much as the Olympic Games have done by including the Olympic Arts Festival as one of the activities that surrounds the Olympic Games or as the United States Sports Academy has done with its sport art gallery and presentation of the Sport Artist of the Year.

The Development of "Free-Market Socialism"

The command-driven economies of the Soviet Union and its allies are being transformed into market-driven economies. We have already seen the profound impact this change has had on sport. The massive state-sponsored infrastructures for developing athletes that once characterized sport programs throughout the Warsaw Pact nations (Riordan, 1981) have been substantially dismantled. One impact has been to increase the numbers of athletes from formerly communist countries who now seek to compete in professional leagues throughout the world. Although the professional leagues in many countries continue to restrict the number of foreign players who can be included on team rosters, the trend for athletes to seek professional opportunities around the globe is likely to accelerate, adding new pressures to review restrictive rules of eligibility.

Cultural Nationalism

International sport teams become representatives of their place of origin. In most international competitions (e.g., regional tournaments, world championships, the Olympic Games), athletes and teams represent their country. Occasionally, however, they may represent local-level communities, as when professional soccer teams compete internationally.

Events of the 1980s and 1990s have begun to alter the international political landscape, suggesting the potential for new levels of team representation (cf., Hall, 1992). For example, formation of the European Community is furthering the social and economic integration of Western Europe. As old national allegiances diminish, older ethnic allegiances obtain new significance. Regional (e.g., Catalonia in Spain), linguistic (e.g., Flemish speakers in Belgium), and cultural (e.g., the Basques of Spain) identities become increasingly salient. Meanwhile, in Eastern Europe and Central Asia, formerly multi-ethnic nations have fragmented into separate nations dominated by single ethnic groups.

In some instances, national team representations are synonymous with regional, linguistic, or cultural identifications. However, in other cases, they are not. In those cases, there may be substantial interest in obtaining opportunities for international representation as an ethnic (rather than strictly national) group. For example, in the United States, over 500 Indian tribes have come together to press for independent recognition by the IOC (Drape, 1993). The objective is to have Native Americans compete together on an Indian team, rather than as representatives of the United States. Indian athletes in Canada have also been invited to join. The National Congress of American Indians and the International Indian Treaty Council have endorsed the concept of an independent international sport identity for Native Americans. They lobby the IOC, the USOC, and the IFs through the United Now Indian Olympic Nation (UNION), an intertribal organization founded to promote international recognition of Native American teams.

As new multinational alliances like the European Community emerge, the significance of old national identities will be reduced. At the same time, local, regional, linguistic, and cultural identifications obtain increased significance. When this is the case, opportunities for international teams to represent entities other than nations may enhance the interest of athletes and spectators. It may prove effective to develop events wherein teams represent cities, provinces, or self-defined ethnic groups.

The Privatization of Welfare

Naisbitt and Aburdene (1990) argue that governments will gradually shift the burden of public services to private organizations. To the degree that their projection can be generalized to sport, it suggests that public expenditures for sport services will decrease, and private organizations will be delegated responsibility for developing sport. This, in turn, will create opportunities for new business ventures supplying sport services that were once provided by governments.

The Increasing Importance of the Pacific Rim

The growing economies of countries on the Pacific Rim, particularly Japan, Singapore, Taiwan, and the Republic of Korea combine with the massive economic potentials of China to make Asian markets particularly significant. The development of these economies bears three important implications for international sport. First, nations of the Pacific Rim will have increasing potential as markets for sporting goods and services. Second, manufacturers of sporting goods and providers of sport services will face increasing competition from manufacturers and providers from Pacific Rim nations. Third, as the economies of these countries expand, so will the tourist travel of their citizens. As resorts and tourist destinations compete for the tourist dollars from the Pacific Rim, they will need to cater to the sport preferences of Asian travelers (cf., Inskeep, 1991). For example, Australia and New Zealand are already developing new resorts catering to Japanese travelers' fondness for golf.

Increasing Numbers of Women in Leadership

Naisbitt and Aburdene (1990) note that "women have reached a critical mass in virtually all the white-collar professions, especially in business" (p. 223). They go on to observe that "women are already leading their own businesses, which they are now starting at twice the rate of men" (p. 226). Thus, they contend that ability rather than gender will increasingly dictate who moves into management.

If this is true, international sport organizations seem to be behind the trend. For example, by the mid-1990s, fewer than 10% of IOC members were women. Perhaps one reason women are starting businesses at twice the rate of men is that they find more opportunity when self-employed than when dependent on the whims of male executives for advancement. If this is the case, one suspects that entrepreneurship may become the preferred route for women into the management of international sport enterprises.

Rapid Advancement of Applied Biological Sciences

It is no longer possible for athletes to reach international calibre by training casually. Today's international athlete is supported by an array of science and scientists, technology and technicians (see Hoberman, 1992, for a discussion). Physiologists monitor training loads and develop new techniques to enhance adaptations to training. Biomechanists evaluate technique and recommend improvements. Psychologists teach mental rehearsal, goal planning, and arousal control. Engineers design better equipment and more efficient tools of measurement. Pharmacists invent ergogenic aids.

In the days of the Cold War, there were endless rumors about the secret sport science of Eastern Europe, particularly East Germany. Stories were told about specialized equipment and technologically sophisticated training centers. Although many of the rumors turned out to be exaggerated, there was some truth to them. In fact, many of the techniques the communists were claimed to use were actually in use in the West. By the late 1970s

Olympic Training Centers were being developed in the United States. By the early 1980s, the blood lactate of many American endurance athletes was tested during their training sessions. The use of biomechanical analyses of athlete performances has increased steadily in recent years, particularly as photo-analytic techniques have become computerized. Indeed, for the past three decades, the development of new equipment for training and competition has continued to accelerate.

These equipment developments are costly. Training centers can cost millions of dollars to establish. State-of-the-art equipment can cost hundreds of thousands of dollars. The experts required to use that equipment can also be expensive. In order to mount its programs, the United States Olympic Committee budget for the 1993-1996 quadrennium exceeds $480 million. That is not the total expenditure. Each NF has an additional budget for development of its sport and its athletes. Club and school teams also have their budgets. Although the requisite data are not available to determine the total expenditure on athlete development in the United States, it is clear that the annual figure is in the hundreds of millions of dollars.

The costs do not end there. Equipment also increases expenses. Sleds, luges, rowing shells, and even shoes are becoming increasingly sophisticated. Other sports, like sailing, are even more expensive; it costs millions of dollars to field a challenge in the Americas Cup.

Winning and, sometimes, even competing require technological capability. That, in turn, requires investment--often substantial investment. The requisite investments are beyond the capability of most developing nations. Consequently, the gap in sports capacity between developed and developing nations is widening. The gap threatens to diminish in the long-term the interest that international sports events can engender in developing nations. Thus, even though information transfer is becoming more rapid with the "boom in the global economy," the limiting factor in the use of this knowledge may be in its application through new equipment.

The gap is ironic, since sport has often been a tool of nation building. Wright (1978) describes the use of sport as a tool for creating a sense of nationhood in Nigeria. McHenry (1980) reports uses of sport as a tool of national development in Tanzania. MacAloon (1984) indicates that Puerto Rico (a U.S. territory) asserts its own national identity through its international sports teams.

International sport obtains its utility as a tool of nation building, in part, because sports provide a symbol of group cohesion and unity against an outside group (e.g., Frankenberg, 1957; James, 1963). Recent research shows that the value of group membership is enhanced as sports fans "bask in the reflected glory" of athletes or teams with whom they share a common identity (Cialdini et al., 1976; Cialdini & Richardson, 1980; Reeves & Tesser, 1985).

However, as we noted in chapter 8, athletes of developing nations who have international potential must frequently relocate to developed countries in order to obtain state-of-the-art training and competition. Indeed, Olympic Solidarity's scholarship program is an explicit recognition of this necessity. Nevertheless, athletes who train overseas become "expatriate nationals." Their value as symbols of national unity is diluted (cf., Chalip, 1987; MacAloon, 1984).

The problem is compounded by the expenses of fielding international teams that, in the end, are not competitive. At world championships and the Olympic Games, the majority of nations attending win no medals. As the athletes who represent those nations come to represent the technological capacity of the developed nations within which they train (rather than the unity of their own national group), their value as representatives of their home nation may be diminished.

The argument here is relatively simple: The increasing significance of technology in international sport is widening the gap between what developed and developing nations can achieve. The gap threatens to reduce the level of interest those countries may have in developing sport nationally or fielding teams internationally. International sports events and international sports markets will fail to attain their fullest potential.

If managers seek to develop international sport fully, one obvious implication of the analysis here is that more must be done to enhance the capacities of developing nations to meet the technological challenges of modern sport. However, research suggests three additional strategies: (a) increased stress on non-Olympic sports and regional competitions, (b) further development of ceremonies, and (c) location of ways in which outcomes can be non-zero-sum.

Religious Revival

Naisbitt and Aburdene (1990) argue that people are increasingly seeking spiritual fulfillment. Some seek it by identifying with fundamentalist religions; others by defining their own "New Age" spirituality. Religious sentiments have found their way into international sport in three significant ways:

1. Organizations like the Fellowship of Christian Athletes provide an institutional basis for athletes to link their sports practices to their religious beliefs (Morton & Burger, 1981). At international events, like an Olympic Games, organizations of religious athletes often sponsor religious services. These are often planned in the tradition of revivalist meetings. Planners of international sports events may find it increasingly necessary to make allowances for such meetings.
2. Evangelical groups plan and execute campaigns of evangelism at international sports events. For example, the expenditures of international evangelical groups at the 1994 Soccer World Cup were estimated as over U.S.$1 million (Tapia, 1994). Preparation for international sports events increasingly requires managers to locate ways to minimize the disruptions crowds of spectators experience as they negotiate their way around the many evangelists who are proselytizing outside the event's entrances and exits.
3. Because religion is often synonymous with culture, an international events manager must continue to monitor and provide for the athletes' ethnic needs, such as dietary habits and prayer requirements.

Increased Individualism

Naisbitt and Aburdene (1990) argue that there is "new respect for the individual as the foundation of society and the basic unit of change" (p. 298). They contend that individual achievements will be increasingly rewarded, and entrepreneurial activities will increasingly dominate the political and economic landscape. If they are correct, we can expect new international sports ventures designed and created by visionary entrepreneurs, such as Ted Turner's Goodwill Games or an international boccie tournament in Canton, Ohio.

However, the opportunities for entrepreneurial activity are driven in no small way by the trends and countertrends in international sport. Thus, following Naisbitt and Aburdene's example, it is useful to conclude by describing a key trend in international sport, and noting its implications for sport governance in the global community.

Sport-for-Participation versus Sport-as-Spectator-Entertainment

International sport has become big business. As audiences have grown, so has the interest of sponsors (MacAloon, 1993; Whannel, 1993). However, sponsors are more concerned to obtain large audiences for sports events than to obtain high levels of mass participation in sport (Sleight, 1989). Sponsors are particularly interested in elite competitions that can draw large numbers of spectators; and as technology has driven up the cost of training and competing at elite levels, sponsorship dollars have become increasingly important to national sport organizations.

It would seem that a broad base of participation might be a useful way to obtain a pool of talent from which to develop elite competitors. However, the focus on elite sport has typically drawn dollars and administrative energies away from development of local-level opportunities to participate (Chalip, 1991). In North America, rates of sport participation have often declined as elite sport has thrived (Donnelly, 1992). Resources and expertise flow upwards--from participant-oriented programs to elite programs, rather than the other way around. Mass participation is sacrificed to prepare elites to compete. Consequently, where sport-for-all programs have been successful, they have been administered independently from programs designed to generate elite competitors (Palm, 1991).

The emphasis on entertainment over participation has begun to threaten the very existence of sports that do not play well on television. Noting the impending reduction or elimination of wrestling, darts, snooker, and lawn bowling from British television, Tomlinson (1992) observed that broadcasters "were complying with the demands of advertisers for higher income, bigger spending and younger audiences" (p. 193). Some sports have had to fight for their very existence. For example, modern pentathlon has had difficulty interesting sponsors, and there has been speculation that the sport will die. The sport's lengthy competitions in fencing, shooting, equestrian events, running, and swimming have not attracted television audiences, and modern pentathlon officials have had to lobby hard to retain the sport's place on the Olympic program. In order to survive, modern pentathlon has altered its structure of competition in a desperate attempt to attract spectators and, thereby, sponsors. Competitions are no longer held over several days, and placings are not calculated strictly on the basis of accumulated points. Instead, competitions are head-to-head and are completed in a single day.

National and international sport administrators are charged with the task of fostering interest and participation in the sport they govern. That requirement is explicit in the *Olympic Charter* and the charters of virtually every IF. Yet, one of the more difficult challenges facing sport administrators today is the task of balancing the needs of participation-oriented sport programs with the requirements of elite, entertainment-oriented sport. The steady increase in the use of professional athletes on national teams merely serves to complicate the problem. Perhaps, as Palm (1991) suggests, participation-oriented programs should be administered separately from programs seeking to serve or develop elite competitors. However, as long as sport-as-entertainment attracts the lion's share of sponsorship dollars, participation-oriented sport programs will languish in their shadow.

If participation-oriented sport is to thrive, managers must locate sources of funding comparable to those obtained by entertainment-oriented programs. A great deal of the political agenda for Sport for All has been driven by arguments advancing sport as a tool of national health care (Rondoyannis, 1992). However, with a few European exceptions, those arguments have been insufficient to generate substantial funding for participation-oriented sport (Donnelly, 1992).

The economic benefits of participation-oriented sport programs have been inadequately specified by sport advocates. Two sources of economic benefit are documentable. First, sport facilities and programs can improve the quality of life in a city or region, thereby helping to attract investment and industry (cf., Kotler, Haider, & Rein, 1993). Second, opportunities to participate in sport can attract tourists and tourist dollars. For example, Belgian data show that the demand for sport participation by tourists rose over 1,300% between 1967 and 1989 (De Knop, 1992), making sport tourism one of the fastest growing industries in the world today. It is projected that one of every four travelers now seeks some form of sport participation during the vacation experience. That translates to worldwide revenues of over $66 billion (cf., Kurtzman & Zauhar, 1991). By documenting and promoting economic benefits like these, sport managers can go a long way toward fostering both public and private investment in sport programs.

Concluding Remarks

Throughout this text, we have emphasized sport's connections to politics, culture, and the economy. Old fables about "the universal language of sport" or "sport's independence from politics" have proven to be useful rhetorical strategies for promoting sport across otherwise hostile borders. Nevertheless, sport managers must recognize those rhetorical strategies for what they are: assertions of a pragmatic fiction. International sport managers must not be lulled by those fables into false notions of sport's universality or autonomy. Managers who believe such fables risk being ambushed by international events and trends.

The monitoring of trends and the consequent development of strategies to blunt threats and capitalize on opportunities are well-established tools of management (Celente & Milton, 1990; Heath & Nelson, 1986; Merriam & Makower, 1988). As the foregoing analysis illustrates, they can be profitably applied to management of sport internationally. Each of the trends examined above has already had a demonstrable impact on sport governance in the global community. However, that examination exhausts neither the range nor the ramifications of contemporary trends. For example, global environmental concerns are already finding manifestation in local and national sport management (Cachay, 1993; Eichberg, 1993). Similarly, as recent developments in computer technology, like virtual reality (Rheingold, 1991), are applied to sport, the gap between the sporting capabilities of developed and developing nations will widen.

Trends are rarely inherently good or bad. They can offer as many opportunities as threats (Littlejohn, 1986). The management challenge is to identify emerging trends and probe their possibilities.

References

Cachay, K. (1993). Sports and environment: Sports for everyone--room for everyone? *International Review for the Sociology of Sport, 28,* 311-323.

Celente, G., & Milton, T. (1990). *Trend tracking: The system to profit from today's trends.* New York: John Wiley & Sons.

Chalip, L. (1987). Multiple narratives, multiple hierarchies: Selective attention, varied interpretations, and the structure of the Olympic program. In S-P. Kang, J.J. MacAloon, & R. DaMatta (Eds.), *The Olympics and cultural exchange* (pp. 539-576). Seoul: Hanyang University Institute for Ethnological Studies.

Chalip, L. (1991). Sport and the state: The case of the United States. In F. Landry, M. Landry & M. Yerles (Eds.), *Sport: The third millennium* (pp. 243-250). Sainte-Foy, Quebec: Les Presses de l'Universite Laval.

Cialdini, R.B., Borden, R.J., Thorne, A., Walker, M.R., Freeman, S., & Sloan, L.R. (1976). Basking in reflected glory: Three (football) field studies. *Journal of Personality and Social Psychology, 34,* 366-375.

Cialdini, R.B., & Richardson, K.D. (1980). Two indirect tactics of image management: Basking and blasting. *Journal of Personality and Social Psychology, 39,* 366-375.

De Knop, P. (1992, July). *New trends in sports tourism.* Paper presented at the Olympic Scientific Congress, Malaga, Spain.

Donnelly, P. (1992, July). *Between a rock and a hard place: The impact of elite sport ideologies on the development of sport for all.* Paper presented at the Olympic Scientific Congress, Malaga, Spain.

Drape, J. (1993, March 14). Native Americans seek niche in Olympics. *Atlanta Journal/Atlanta Constitution,* p. F6.

Eichberg, H. (1993). New spatial configurations of sport? Experiences from Danish alternative planning. *International Review for the Sociology of Sport, 28,* 245-264.

Frankenberg, R. (1957). *Village on the border: A study of religion, politics and football in a North Wales community*. London: Cohen & West.

Guber, S.S., & Berry, J. (1993). *Marketing to and through kids*. New York: McGraw-Hill.

Hall, L. (1992). *Latecomer's guide to the new Europe*. New York: American Management Association.

Heath, R.L., & Nelson, R.A. (1986). *Issues management: Corporate public policymaking in an information society*. Newbury Park, CA: Sage.

Hoberman, J. (1992). *Mortal engines: The science of performance and the dehumanization of sport*. New York: Free Press.

Inskeep, E. (1991). *Tourism planning: An integrated and sustainable development approach*. New York: Van Nostrand Reinhold.

James, C.L.R. (1963). *Beyond a boundary*. New York: Pantheon.

Kotler, P., Haider, D.H., & Rein, I. (1993). *Marketing places: Attracting investment, industry, and tourism to cities, states, and nations*. New York: Free Press.

Kurtzman, J., & Zauhar, J. (1991, June). *The emerging profession: Tourism sport manangement*. Paper presented at the Annual Meetings of the North American Society for Sport Management, Ottawa, Ontario.

Littlejohn, S.E. (1986). Competition and cooperation: New trends in corporate public issue identification and resolution. *California Management Review, 29*, 109-123.

MacAloon, J.J. (1984). La Pitada Olimpica: Puerto Rico, international sport, and the constitution of politics. In E.M. Bruner (Ed.), *Text, play, and story: The construction and reconstruction of self and society* (pp. 315-355). Washington, DC: American Anthropological Association.

MacAloon, J.J. (1993). Sponsorship policy and Olympic ideology: Towards a new discourse. *Proceedings of the 32nd session of the International Olympic Academy* (pp. 62-76). Lausanne: IOC.

McHenry, D.E. (1980). The uses of sports in policy implementation: The case of Tanzania. *Journal of Modern African Studies, 18*, 237-256.

Merriam, J.E., & Makower, J. (1988). *Trend watching: How the media create trends and how to be the first to uncover them.* New York: AMACOM.

Morton, C., & Burger, R. (1981). *The courage to believe.* Englewood Cliffs: Prentice Hall.

Naisbitt, J., & Aburdene, P. (1990). *Megatrends 2000.* New York: William Morrow.

Palm, J. (1991). *Sport for all: Approaches from Utopia to reality.* Schorndorf: Verlag Karl Hofmann.

Reeves, R.A., & Tesser, A. (1985). Self-evaluation. maintenance in sports team rivalries. *Bulletin of the Psychonomic Society, 23,* 329-331.

Rheingold, H. (1991). *Virtual reality.* New York: Summit Books.

Riordan, J. (Ed.) (1981). *Sport under communism* (2nd ed.). London: C. Hurst & Co.

Rogers, E.M. (1983). *Diffusion of innovations.* New York: Free Press.

Rondoyannis, G. (1992). Sport for all and health. *Proceedings of the 31st session of the International Olympic Academy* (pp. 126-144). Lausanne: IOC.

Sleight, S. (1989). *Sponsorship: What it is and how to use it.* London: McGraw-Hill.

Tapia, A. (1994, July 23). Churches hit goal in World Cup effort. *Washington Post,* pp. B7-B8.

Tomlinson, A. (1992). Shifting patterns of working class leisure: The case of knur-and-spell. *Sociology of Sport Journal, 9,* 192-206.

Whannel, G. (1993). Profiting by the presence of ideals: Sponsorship and Olympism. *Proceedings of the 32nd session of the International Olympic Academy* (pp.85-93). Lausanne: IOC.

Wright, S. (1978). Nigeria: The politics of sport. *Round Table, 272,* 362-367.

REGIONAL MULTISPORT COMPETITIONS

The following list includes some of the regional associations recognized by the International Olympic Committee and regional competitions each regional association recognizes. In addition several prominent multinational multisport games are included.

Olympic Council of Asia (OCA)

The OCA sanctions competitions between its members. The biggest of the events is the Asian Games. However, there are, in total, seven regional games sanctioned by the OCA:

1. Asian Games
2. Southeast Asian Games
3. South Asia Federation Games
4. East Asian Games
5. Pan Arab Games
6. Gulf Cooperation Council Games
7. Islamic Women's Games.

Some of these games will be presented here.

Asian Games

The first Asian Games were held in New Delhi, India, in 1952. These Games are of a format closely related to the Games of the Olympiad, being celebrated every fourth year on the even years between the Summer Olympics. There have been 12 Asian Games with the last in Hiroshima, Japan in 1994. Bangkok, Thailand, will host in 1998.

A city must bid for the Asian Games by answering a series of 13 questions. These questions are generally similar to the Themes of the IOC. One major difference, however, is the OCA has only two mandatory sports, athletics (track and field) and swimming. Also as with the Olympics, a cultural event is required.

Because the Asian Games are a regional competition the OCA is very specific in Article 56 of its Constitution and Rules on eligibility. Obviously, they want only Asian citizens to participate but this article also is to establish which country a competitor may represent.

The sport program for the Asian Games must include at least six sports other than athletics and swimming. The sports must be practiced by at least six countries with a minimum of four entering. The host proposes the sports to be included (see Table A1). Subject to Bureau approval two demonstration sports are also permitted.

TABLE A1
Sports Eligible For The Asian Games

1.	Archery	16.	Judo
2.	Badminton	17.	Kabaddi
3.	Baseball	18.	Rowing
4.	Basketball	19.	Sepak takraw
5.	Body-building	20.	Shooting
6.	Boxing	21.	Squash
7.	Canoeing	22.	Table tennis
8.	Cycling	23.	Taekwondo
9.	Equestrian	24.	Tennis
10.	Fencing	25.	Ten-pin bowling
11.	Football	26.	Volleyball
12.	Golf	27.	Weightlifting
13.	Gymnastics	28.	Wrestling
14.	Handball	29.	Yachting
15.	Hockey (Field)		

The number of entries to the Asian Games is fixed by the Council but cannot exceed two per event for athletics and swimming and one for the other individual events. For team events, there is one team per member country with the number of athletes per team as prescribed by the respective IF.

The Winter Asian Games are held every 4 years beginning from 1986. Only two sports must be contested from the following list in Table A2. At least two OCA member countries must be included in the program (Olympic Council of Asia, 1991).

TABLE A2
Sports Eligible For The Winter Asian Games

1. Biathlon
2. Bobsleigh
3. Ice hockey
4. Luge
5. Skating
6. Skiing

Southeast Asian Games

The SEA Games (Southeast Asian Games) were first hosted by Thailand in 1959. At that time they were called the South East Asian Peninsular Games (SEAP Games). The SEAP Games were created to help develop the athletes from this region and to improve relations among the countries.

In 1975, only Thailand, Burma, Malaysia, and Singapore competed in the SEAP Games. Because of the few countries participating, Negara Brunei Darussalam, Indonesia, and the Philippines were invited to join. With these three countries, the SEAP Games became the SEA Games.

The SEA Games are held biennially between the Olympic Games and the Asian Games: the Philippines in 1991, Singapore in 1993, and Thailand in 1995. The current members of the SEA Games Federation are included in Table A3. The host country rotation is alphabetical from the English spelling of each country. If the designated country cannot host the next Games, the honor falls to the next country in the order (Southeast Asian Games Federation, n.d.).

TABLE A3
SEA Games Countries

1. Negara Brunei Darussalam
2. Cambodia
3. Indonesia
4. Laos
5. Malaysia
6. Myanmar
7. Philippines
8. Thailand
9. Vietnam

The Southeast Asian Games Federation Council is responsible for the SEA Games. This Council is responsible

- to promote development of those physical and moral qualities which are the basis of sport;
- to educate young people through sport in a spirit of better understanding between each other andfriendship thereby helping to build a better and more peaceful world;
- to spread the Olympic principles throughout Southeast Asia thereby creating goodwill in the region; and
- to bring together athletes of Southeast Asia in biennial sport festival. (Southeast Asian Games Federation, 1993, p.3.)

The ultimate authority for the SEA Games is with the Council of the Southeast Asia Games Federation. The Council's work is facilitated by an Executive Committee composed of the Council's President, Honorary Secretary, and one member from each country. The rules under which the Games are held are very similar to the Olympic Games and Asian Games with respect to doping, gender, and athlete eligibility.

The host organizing committee, subject to Executive Committee approval, selects the sports to be contestedat each SEA Games. The required sports are track and field and swimming, to include diving and water polo. These are Category I sports. A minimum of 14 Category II sports must be contested (Table A4). Category III may have a maximum of eight sports contested (Table A5).

TABLE A4
SEA Games Sports Category II

1.	Archery	11.	Hockey
2.	Badminton	12.	Judo
3.	Basketball	13.	Sepak takraw
4.	Bowling (ten pin)	14.	Shooting
5.	Boxing	15.	Table tennis
6.	Cycling	16.	Tennis
7.	Fencing	17.	Volleyball
8.	Football (Soccer)	18.	Weightlifting
9.	Golf	19.	Yachting
10.	Gymnastics		

TABLE A5
SEA Games Sports Category III

1.	Baseball	11.	Silat olahraga
2.	Billiards and snooker	12.	Softball
3.	Bodybuilding	13.	Soft tennis
4.	Canoeing	14.	Squash
5.	Equestrian sports	15.	Taekwondo
6.	Handball	16.	Traditional boat races
7.	Karate-do	17.	Water skiing
8.	Modern pentathlon	18.	Wrestling
9.	Rowing	19.	Wushu
10.	Rugby football		

The host organization determines the maximum number of sports to be contested. However, for a sport to be included at the SEA Games, at least four countries must indicate that they will participate. This is important because the regional nature of some of the sports (i.e., sepak takraw) means that not all countries will have interested athletes or coaching to prepare for every proposed event. In addition, the cost to transport, house, food, and clothe a contingent can be enormous. Many of the SEA Games Federation countries are developing nations that have scarce resources.

As is the case with regional events, the host will work closely with the respective IFs to assure that the facilities and officials are of the highest quality.

East Asian Games

The first East Asian Games were held in Shanghai, China in 1993. The countries that participated were China, Democratic Peoples Republic of Korea (North Korea), Hong Kong, Japan, Macau, Mongolia, South Korea, and Taiwan. These same countries have indicated that they will participants in future East Asian Games, including Pusan, South Korea in 1995 (M. Ahmad, personal communication, February 18, 1995).

The grouping of these countries should prove to create another power block in the OCA. With Japan and South Korea having hosted the Olympics, sport expertise is recognized. What is possible is that these countries, which have been known recently for their economic strength, will seek greater influence in the OCA and the Olympic Movement (Huba, no date).

Islamic Women's Games

The first Islamic Women's Games were held in Tehran, Iran, in 1993. This event was held over 7 days with 10 countries competing. The countries represented a cross-section of the Islamic world from Syria, Pakistan, Iran, and Malaysia to the former Soviet republics of Turkmenistan and Tadjikistan. It is hoped that these Games will held every 4 years.

This event is significant because it provides a multi-sports competition for women who might normally not have the opportunity. In addition, this event can produce Olympic athletes in shooting, skiing, and equestrian sports as these events can be contested in public without violating the Islamic women's dress code (Brooks, 1993).

Association of Oceania National Olympic Committees

Three regional games are held within the ONOC:

1. South Pacific Games
2. South Pacific Mini Games
3. Micronesian Games

Interestingly, neither Australia nor New Zealand participates in these Games as their athletic standard is considered far above those of the other island nations.

South Pacific Games

South Pacific Games, the Olympics of the South Pacific, were first held in 1963 with Fiji hosting. The last Games were hosted by Papua New Guinea from 7 to 21 September, 1991, with 1923 athletes participating from 16 countries (Table A6). According to the ONOC *Annual Report and Statement of Accounts* (1992), the most popular sports were athletics (track and field), basketball, boxing, lawn bowls, golf, lawn tennis, soccer, volleyball, weightlifting, cricket, netball, and softball.

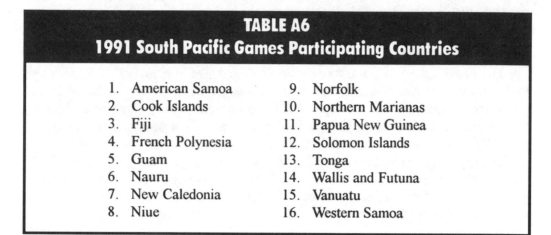

TABLE A6
1991 South Pacific Games Participating Countries

1. American Samoa	9. Norfolk
2. Cook Islands	10. Northern Marianas
3. Fiji	11. Papua New Guinea
4. French Polynesia	12. Solomon Islands
5. Guam	13. Tonga
6. Nauru	14. Wallis and Futuna
7. New Caledonia	15. Vanuatu
8. Niue	16. Western Samoa

South Pacific Mini Games

This competition began in 1981 as a means for the smaller South Pacific nations to host an international multi-event competition. The most recent Games were scheduled to be held at Pota Vila, Vanuatu, in August, 1993 (Association of Oceania National Olympic Committees, 1993).

Micronesian Games

These Games date to 1969. Saipan hosted them again at their revival in 1990. Due to their success in 1990, the Micronesian Games was held again in 1994 in Guam (Association of Oceania National Olympic Committees, 1993). In 1998, the Republic of Palau will be the host (B.J. Wightman, personal communication, February 13, 1995).

European Olympic Committees (EOC)

There are two regional multisport events with EOC's authority: the Mediterranean Games and the Games of the Small European States.

Mediterranean Games

Mediterranean Games cannot be strictly under the authority of EOC as some of the participating countries are in Asia and Africa, as well as Europe (Table A7).

TABLE A7
Countries Winning Medals In The 11th Mediterranean Games
Athens, Greece

1. Italy	8. Egypt
2. France	9. Morocco
3. Turkey	10. Syria
4. Spain	11. Cyprus
5. Yugoslavia	12. Lebanon
6. Algeria	13. Tunisia
7. Greece	14. Albania

The Games include 18 countries participating in 26 sports over a 15-day period. The events include world popular sports, such as track and field, swimming, gymnastics, and soccer as well as world developing sports, such as judo, fencing, table tennis, yachting, cycling, and water polo.

In 1991, Greece hosted the Mediterranean Games. The Greek success was used to show the world that Greece does have the infrastructure needed to host a major international, multisport event. This information is significant because it helped to answer one criticism Greece received during its bid to host the 1996 Games of the Olympiad. Additionally, Greece used the Mediterranean Games in an effort to promote sport participation and excellence in "minor" sports. This same justification is common when a country hosts an international multisport event (Association of the European National Olympic Committees, 1991a).

Israel may join EOC (Huba, 1994). Although located in west Asia, Israel has long been associated with the European nations. In addition, because the nations geographically near Israel have philosophical and religious differences with Israel, Israel's full acceptance into the Asian community is still way in the future. Therefore, Israel may join this competition as a "European" nation someday.

Games of the Small European States

The Games of the Small European States are confined to those EOC members with populations of fewer than one million people. This event has been contested every other year beginning in 1985 in San Marino. Other hosts have been Monaco, Nicosia, and Andorra. In 1993, Malta hosted the event, with Luxembourg scheduled for 1995. (Association of European National Olympic Committees, 1992). The remaining three nations of these Games are Iceland, Liechtenstein, and Cyprus. The events contested in Andorra in 1991, where 1,300 athletes competed, were track and field, swimming, judo, cycling, tennis, shooting, basketball and volleyball.

Events of the magnitude of these Games rarely are noticed outside of Europe. However, for the countries involved and for the ideals of Olympism, the event is significant. It shows that the country's size is not the most important issue; it is the participation that counts. In addition, the host uses the event to enhance its own facilities and event management reputation -- both legacies remaining after similar larger events like the Olympics, Asian Games, etc. (Association of the European National Olympic Committees, 1991b).

Pan American Sports Organization

Pan American Games

The Pan American Games, sometimes called the Pan Am Games, are held every 4 years. The summer version started in 1951, and the Winter Games began in 1990. Because of the Winter Olympic Games being changed to 1994, the Winter Pan Am Games were held in 1993. Entry into the Games is based on the rules of the IOC.

Eighty percent of the Pan Am Games sports must be on the program of the next Olympic Games. The Summer Pan Am Games sports, minimum 20, are selected by the PASO General Assembly 3 years before the event. At that time, the next Olympic sport program should be complete. Sports that are important to the Americas with respect to development (e.g., baseball) will be given preference.

The Pan Am Games, similar to the Olympics, require that a cultural program about the Americas be held during the contest. In addition, congresses dealing with sport and sports medicine are also planned in conjunction with the Games (Pan American Sports Organization, 1989).

Central American and Caribbean Sports Games

The Central American and Caribbean Sports Organization (CACSO) was formed to develop sport in its region. CACSO is a subregional organization formed within the area of PASO. CACSO countries are included in Table A8.

TABLE A8
Central American and Caribbean Sports Organization Countries

Antigua, Netherlands Antilles, Aruba, Bahamas, Barbados, Belize, Bermuda, Colombia, Costa Rica, Cuba, El Salvador, Grenada, Guatemala, Guyana, Haiti, Honduras, Cayman Islands, U.S. Virgin Islands, British Virgin Islands, Jamaica, Mexico, Nicaragua, Panama, Puerto Rico, Dominican Republic, St, Vincent and the Grenadines, Surinam, Trinidad & Tobago, Venezuela (Central American and Caribbean Sports Organization, 1988).

CACSO's (1988a) *Statutes* read similarly to those of PASO, which could be expected because CACSO's NOCs also are members of PASO. The major difference is that CACSO allocated two votes to those countries that have hosted its Games, whereas the other countries get one vote. CACSO appears to have no direct link to PASO through its *Statutes* (1988a) or its *General Regulations of the Central American and Caribbean*

Sports Games (1988b). However, through numerous references, CACSO refers to the IOC *Charter* as being the source for rules and regulations interpretation.

The Central American and Caribbean Sports Games were first held in Mexico City in 1926. The next most Games were held in Puerto Rico in 1993. The Games would normally have been held in 1994, but the Puerto Rico request to PASO to hold them in November 1993 was accepted. The Games do not exceed 15 days in duration. The event program includes 15 to 18 sports from the list on Table A9.

TABLE A9
Central American And Caribbean Sports Games
Event Possibilities

1. Athletics	14. Judo
2. Archery	15. Modern pentathlon
3. Basketball	16. Rowing
4. Baseball	17. Shooting
5. Boxing	18. Softball
6. Canoeing	19. Swimming (all disciplines)
7. Cycling	20. Table tennis
8. Equestrian sports	21. Tennis
9. Fencing	22. Volleyball
10. Football (Soccer)	23. Weightlifting
11. Gymnastics	24. Wrestling
12. Handball	25. Yachting
13. Hockey	

For the Central American and Caribbean Games, two competitors from each country or territory are permitted for individual events for those events which the IF permits more than one competitor per event. One team may represent each country or territory in team events.

CACSO's event organization is quite explicit for a subregional event. For example, CACSO's *General Regulations* (1988b) go into great detail on eligibility for sport competition, just as the Asian Games do. CACSO's rule states that, "If a competitor has represented a country in Olympic, Continental or Regional Games or in World or Continental Championships recognized by the respective International Federation Concerned,he cannot represent another country in the Central Americanand Caribbean" (p.3). However, exceptions to this rule are provided. This is an example of regional or subregional event rules that are handled by individual NOCs for other contests.

CACSO shows unique detail in its organization Games, by requiring the host organization to "Submit various typical menus in conformity with the eating habits of the different regions" (Central American and Caribbean Sports Organization, 1988b, p.7). This explicitness is implied by other event guidelines but rarely stated. This regulation, additionally, shows that appreciation of cultural differences even within a subregion of the Olympic world.

Another example of CACSO organizational detail is its Flame. To start the CACSO Games, the Central American and Caribbean Flame is lit. The Flame, by regulation, starts from the "Cerro de la Estrella" in Mexico City. This is interesting because it pays tribute to the Games' birthplace, as per Greece and the Olympics, whereas CACSO's permanent offices are in Caracas, Venezuela (Central American and Caribbean Sports Organization, 1988b).

Association of National Olympic Committee of Africa

All-African Games

The Association of National Olympic Committees of Africa (ANOCA) sponsors the All-African Games, such as that held in September 1995 in Harare, Zimbabwe.

The All-African Games was first conceived by Pierre de Coubertin in 1920 after a discussion with the only African IOC member, Angelo Bolanaki of Egypt. After further planning and preparation the first All-African Games were scheduled for Algiers in 1965. However, the games were never held due to lack of financial support and an agreed upon definition of African residency (Omo-Osagie, no date).

A games of Africa actually began small. First there were games sponsored by dual meets sponsored by the British. Then the French had the Inter-African Games in The Central African Republic in 1959. These games were between French-speaking African countries. In 1960 came the Community Games in Madagascar. At these games sixteen African countries and France participated. In 1963 the Friendship Games were held in Senegal with a number of non-French colonial countries participating among the 24 countries. Finally, the first All-Africa Games were held in Brazzaville, Republic of Congo in July, 1965. It is interesting to note that neither France nor any colonialists participated in the first All-African Games. It truly was a games for Africans (Omo-Osagie, no date).

The All-African Games are to be held every four years, if possible. The competition rules are those of the international federations and athletes must "possess the nationality of the country they are representing, either by birth or by legal naturalization" (pp. 88-89). For a sport to be contested at least 10 countries must participate (Ono-Osagie, no date).

Today, the ANOCA, the Supreme Council for Sport in Africa, and the African Sports Confederation, work in close cooperation to plan the All-African Games (Association of National Olympic Committees of Africa, 1989).

Other Multisport Competitions

World University Games

The World University Games, sometimes called the Universiade, are contested every other year. Participants must meet the following qualifications:

1. The athlete must represent the country of which they are a citizen.
2. The athlete must be at least 17 years old and less than 28 years old on January 1 of the competition year.
3. The athlete must be a full-time university/college student or a student who graduated the year before the competition.
4. Exceptions to these rules can be made for nations with fewer than two million people or 5,000 university/college students (International Federation for University Sport, 1993).

The World University Games had its birth in 1910 when the International World Student Games were held in Rome, Italy. In 1924 the International Confederation of Students (CIE) was formed in Warsaw, Poland. The CIE continued regular competitions until World War II.

After World War II, the Communist-bloc nations formed the International Union of Students, and the International Federation for University Sport (FISU) was created by many Western European countries. In 1957, these two groups were merged under FISU and the combined competitions began in turn in 1959 with 45 countries participating.

The World University Games now have a summer and a winter event. The summer competition has 10 mandatory sports (Table A10).

TABLE A10
World University Games Mandatory Sports

1. Athletics	6. Soccer
2. Basketball	7. Swimming
3. Diving	8. Tennis
4. Fencing	9. Volleyball
5. Gymnastics	10. Water Polo

The organizing committee may add up to three additional sports. These additions have included baseball, canoe-kayak, hockey, judo, rhythmic gymnastics, rowing, and wrestling.

The summer Universiade is the second largest gathering of athletes after the Olympics. In 1987 Zagreb, Yugoslavia, hosted 3,905 athletes from 121 nations; and in 1991 Sheffield, England, had 3,346 athletes from 101 nations. Buffalo, New York, hosted the 1993 Universiade, with 1995 in Fuknoka, Japan, 1997 in Sicily and 1999 in Palma de Mallorca, Spain.

The Winter Universiade was first hosted in Chamonix, France, in 1960. These contests are also held every 2 years, with 1993 being in Zakopane, Poland, and 1995 in Jaca, Spain.

For the Winter Universiade six sports are mandatory (Table A11).

TABLE A11
Winter Universiade Mandatory Sports

1. Alpine skiing
2. Cross-Country skiing
3. Figure skating
4. Ice hockey
5. Short track speedskating
6. Ski jumping

One optional sport is available to the host (International Federation for University Sport, 1993).

Goodwill Games

The Goodwill Games started in 1986. They were conceived by Ted Turner, founder of the Turner Broadcasting System. Turner's rationale and motivation stemmed from the cold war political tensions between the Soviet Union and the United States. The United States had led a boycott of the 1980 Moscow Olympic Games and the Soviet Union led a boycott of the 1984 Los Angeles Olympic Games. Turner wanted to create a competition where the best athletes in the world would compete without politically motivated boycotts, hence the name Goodwill Games. Additionally, an arts festival is held as a part of this event.

Alternately being held in the Soviet Union and the United States in the mid-year between the summer Olympics, originally, the Goodwill Games were to be primarily a USSR-USA contest, although 79 countries were represented in 1986. However, after the first Goodwill Games in Moscow in 1986, the competition format changed. The second Goodwill Games, held in Seattle, Washington, included the best U.S. and Soviet athletes/team. In addition, however, the top six ranked athletes/teams from around the world were invited in each event. This new format guaranteed outstanding competitions.

With the dissolution of the Soviet Union, there was some question of the fate of this event. However, the Goodwill Games did continue with St. Petersburg hosting the event in 1994, and New York City doing the honors in 1998. As of the printing of this book, there is a possibility that the venue for the 2002 games will be changed from Russia.

The interesting aspect of the Goodwill Games is that its structure is unique. These Games do not have an obvious core to hold them together as the Maccabiah Games for Jews, the Commonwealth Games for members of the British Commonwealth, or the SEA Games for countries of Southeast Asia. These Games started as a "goodwill" gesture to promote peace. Although the Soviet-USA tensions have lessened, the Goodwill Games continue. This event has the support of the international federations and the NOCs as a quality world-class event. Beside the camaraderie of the athletes and teams, the individual NFs and NOCs use the Goodwill Games to evaluate their programs in a mid Olympic year.

Whether the Goodwill Games continue appears to be in the hands of the television viewers. These Games have lost millions of dollars since their inception. However, if the management of Turner Broadcasting Company continues to feel it is important, the Goodwill Games will continue.

Maccabiah Games

The Maccabiah World Union sponsors the Maccabiah Games for Jewish people worldwide. The Games, which began in 1932, are held every 4 years in Israel. The purpose of the Maccabiah Games is to raise the "Jewish identity, fashioned by a commitment to physical and spiritual strength" (Maccabi World Union, no date).

At the 13th World Maccabiah Games in 1989, 4,000 athletes from 43 nations competed in 30 sports. At the 1993 Games, 56 countries with 5,300 athletes participated (U.S. Committee Sports for Israel, 1993). These numbers make the Maccabiah Games one of the largest international competitions.

With this large gathering there are four unique aspects relative to this major multisport events:

1. Master's, junior's, and disabled competitions are included with the open categories.
2. The same country --Israel-- hosts each Maccabiah Games.
3. Some unique events have been or will be contested -- chess, lawn bowls, clay pigeon shooting, bridge.
4. Athletes are housed by event instead of by country.

In addition to the World Maccabiah Games, the Maccabiah World Union sponsors regional competitions. The events presently contested include the European Maccabi Games, Pan American Maccabi Games, North American Maccabi Youth Games, and others in Australia, South Africa, and Colombia (Maccabi World Union, no date).

Commonwealth Games

The Commonwealth Games (CG) were originally the British Empire Games. They also have been known as the British Empire and Commonwealth Games and the British Commonwealth Games. The CG were first held in 1930 in Hamilton, Ontario, Canada, primarily due to the motivating force of Canadian Bobby Robinson. These first Games were attended by 11 countries and territories. The 1994 CG in Victoria, British Columbia, Canada will hosted 66 countries from five continents.

The Commonwealth Games, held every 2 years between the Summer Olympics are awarded to a member federation by the Commonwealth Games Federation (CGF). The CGF's patron and president are HM Queen Elizabeth II and HRH Prince Philip, Duke of Edinburgh, respectively. However, the federation is administered by its chairman. Six vice presidents representing Africa, America, Asia, Caribbean, Europe, and Oceania represent their geographical areas.

There are only three committees in the CGF: Finance, Sports Programme, and

Advisory. As would be expected, the Finance Committee handles the monetary aspects of the federation, and the Sports Programme committee handles requests for sport event program and related matters. The advisory Committee considers factors relating to the Commonwealth Games in order to make recommendations to the CGF General Assembly and officers (Commonwealth Games Federation, 1987).

These committees provide information to the ultimate CG authority, the General Assembly, for attention. Each member federation has one vote in the General Assembly.

The present CGF procedure allows for not more than 10 sports to be chosen from the list in Table A12 (Commonwealth Games Federation, 1991). Additionally, demonstration sports are permitted; for example, Kuala Lumpur will exhibit netball in 1998. The unique aspect of these eligible sports is that, by mandate, all CG sports must be individual, no team sports are allowed for medals (Commonwealth Games Federation, 1991).

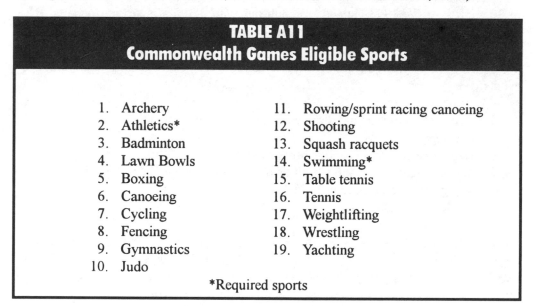

TABLE A11
Commonwealth Games Eligible Sports

1. Archery	11. Rowing/sprint racing canoeing
2. Athletics*	12. Shooting
3. Badminton	13. Squash racquets
4. Lawn Bowls	14. Swimming*
5. Boxing	15. Table tennis
6. Canoeing	16. Tennis
7. Cycling	17. Weightlifting
8. Fencing	18. Wrestling
9. Gymnastics	19. Yachting
10. Judo	

*Required sports

As previously noted, the Commonwealth Games Federation is composed of six regions: Africa, America, Asia, Caribbean, Europe and Oceania. The countries of each region are listed in Table A13. When viewing this listing, one cannot help but be in wonder of the pervasiveness that the British Empire once had.

The CG is organized and administered in a manner that is common for major international multisport events. However, there are three unique and interesting aspects of these Games. First is the reimbursement of delegation traveling expenses. The Commonwealth Games Federation (1991) Constitution dictates what percentage of the expense the organizing committee will return, ranging from 25% of expenses for delegations from 1-10 members to 5% for over 100 members.

The second unique feature is the Queen's Relay. It is now common to have a torch relay run from some point to the opening ceremonies venue. However, the CG uses a baton to carry the Queen's message, or address, if she is to be present at the opening.

Last are the "official receptions" and "limited receptions." CG mandates that the host organizing committee maintain a list of receptions, official or otherwise. This is done in order to limit the overlap of social functions that are part of international gatherings.

TABLE A13
Regional Area Commonwealth Games Federation Members

Africa	America	Asia	Caribbean
Botswana	Belize	Bangladesh	Antigua
The Gambia	Bermuda	Brunei	Bahamas
Ghana	Canada	Hong Kong	Barbados
Kenya	Falkland Islands	India	British Virgin
Lesotho	Guyana	Malaysia	Islands
Malawi	St. Helena	Maldives	Cayman Islands
Mauritius		Pakistan	Dominica
Namibia••	**Europe**	Singapore	Grenada
Nigeria	England	Sri Lanka	Jamaica
Seychelles	Cyprus		Montserrat
Sierra Leone	Gibraltar	**Oceania**	St. Kitts
Swaziland	Guernsey	Australia	St. Lucia
Tanzania	Isle of Man	Cook Islands	St. Vincent
Uganda	Jersey	Fiji•	Trinidad and Tobago
Zambia	Malta	Nauru	Turks and Caicos
Zimbabwe	N Ireland	New Zealand	Islands
	Scotland	Papua/New Guinea	
		Norfolk Islands	
		Tonga	
		Tuvalu	
		Vanuatu	
		Western Samoa	

•Affiliation in suspension
••Application pending
(Commonwealth Games Federation, 1991).

World Cup of Soccer

The World Cup of soccer is the most watched sports event in the world. Over 1.5 billion people watched the 1990 World Cup final on television.

The World Cup grew out of the Olympic soccer tournament. After seeing that the Olympic Games were producing the soccer champion, FIFA, soccer's international federation, started the World Cup. Uruguay hosted and won the first World Cup in 1930.

The World Cup finals are now contested every 4 years. The pursuit of the cup actually begins 2 years prior to the championship tournament with the qualifying rounds contested in six worldwide regions. Over the 2 year period leading to the 1994 final tournament over 500 qualifying games were played by 141 nations (World Cup USA 1994, nd).

An interesting aspect of the World Cup is the qualifying for the final tournament. Each region is allocated a number of qualifying teams depending on the recognized strength of that region's soccer performance. For the 1998 World Cup the 32 qualifying teams include CONCACAF (North and Central America and the Caribbean) - 3, Oceania - possibility of one, Asia - 3 with the possibility of a fourth in a play-off with Oceania, Africa - 5, South America - 5, and Europe - 15. For the World Cup, FIFA automatically includes the immediate past champion, Brazil in 1994, and the host, France for 1998 (Nance, 1994).

References

Association of the European National Olympic Committees (1991a, November). Athens The 11th Mediterranean Games. *Sport Europe*. pp. 19-21.

Association of the European National Olympic Committees (1991b, November). Andorra IV Games of the Small European States. *Sport Europe*. pp. 37-39.

Association of European National Olympic Committees (1992). *Statutes*. Rome: Association of European National Olympic Committees.

Association of National Olympic Committees of Africa (1989). *Constitution*. Yaounde, Cameroon: Association of National Olympic Committees of Africa.

Association of Oceania National Olympic Committees (1992). *Annual Report and Statement of Accounts*. Wellington, New Zealand: Association of Oceania National Olympic Committees.

Association of Oceania National Olympic Committees (1993). *Yearbook 1991/1992*. Wellington, New Zealand: Association of Oceania National Olympic Committees.

Brooks, G. (1993, February 25). Iran games bar men so Muslim women can dress for sport. *The Wall Street Journal*. pp. A1, A6.

Central American and Caribbean Sports Organization (1988a). *Statutes*. Mexico City: Central American and Caribbean Sports Organization.

Central American and Caribbean Sports Organization (1988b). *General Regulations of the Central American and Caribbean Sports Organization*. Mexico City: Central American and Caribbean Sports Organization.

Commonwealth Games Federation (1987). *The Commonwealth Games Federation and the Commonwealth Games*. London: Commonwealth Games Federation.

Commonwealth Games Federation (1991). *Constitution of the Commonwealth Games Federation*. London: Commonwealth Games Federation.

Huba, K.H. (no date). *Sport Intern*.

Huba, K.H. (1994, September 30). *Sport Intern*. p. 2.

International Federation for University Sport (1993). *Factbook*. Rome: International Federation for University Sport.

Maccabi World Union (no date). *A sound mind in as sound body - A history of Maccabi*. Tel Aviv: Maccabi World Union.

Nance, R. (1994, October 28). Africa gains most from World Cup expansion. *USA Today*. p. C9.

Olympic Council of Asia (1991). *Rules and Regulations*. Eastbourne, U.K.: Olympic Council of Asia.

Omo-Osagie, A.I. (no date). *African unity through sports*. Benin City, Nigeria: Ambik Press.

Pan American Sports Organization (1989). *Statutes*. Mexico City: Pan American Sports Organization.

Southeast Asian Games Federation (1993). *Statutes and Rules*. Singapore: Singapore National Olympic Council.

Southeast Asian Games Federation (n.d.). *History of the SEA Games*. Singapore: Singapore National Olympic Council.

U.S. Committee Sports for Israel (1993, Fall). *14th Maccabiah Games*. Philadelphia: U.S. Committee Sports for Israel.

World Cup USA 1994 (no date). *Making soccer history*. NY: World Cup USA 1994, Inc.

APPENDIX B

DIRECTORIES OF INTERNATIONAL AND NATIONAL ORGANIZATIONS

Cylkowski, C.J. (1988). *Developing a career in sport*. Ithaca, NY: Movement Publications Inc.

Cylkowski, C.J. (1992). *Developing a lifelong contract in the sports marketplace*. Little Canada, MN: Athletic Achievements.

Daniels, P.K., & Schwartz, C.A. (Eds.). (1994). *Encyclopedia of associations*. Detroit: Gale Research, Inc. (Dialog File 114).

Kobak, E. *The sports address bible*. Morgantown, WV: Fitness Information Technology, Inc.

Lipsey, R.A. (Ed.). (1994). *Sports market place 1994*. Princeton, NJ: sportsguide.

Moss, A. (Ed.). (1995). *The sports summit sports directory*. Bethesda, MD: E.J. Krause & Associates, Inc.

SUBJECT INDEX

AUTHOR INDEX